Peace and the politics of memory

Manchester University Press

New Approaches to Conflict Analysis

Series editors: Peter Lawler (School of Social Sciences, University of Manchester – United Kingdom) and Emmanuel-Pierre Guittet (Centre for Conflict, Liberty and Security, CCLS, Paris – France)

Until recently, the study of conflict and conflict resolution remained comparatively immune to broad developments in social and political theory. When the changing nature and locus of large-scale conflict in the post-Cold War era is also taken into account, the case for a reconsideration of the fundamentals of conflict analysis and conflict resolution becomes all the more stark.

New Approaches to Conflict Analysis promotes the development of new theoretical insights and their application to concrete cases of large-scale conflict, broadly defined. The series intends not to ignore established approaches to conflict analysis and conflict resolution, but to contribute to the reconstruction of the field through a dialogue between orthodoxy and its contemporary critics. Equally, the series reflects the contemporary porosity of intellectual borderlines rather than simply perpetuating rigid boundaries around the study of conflict and peace. *New Approaches to Conflict Analysis* seeks to uphold the normative commitment of the field's founders yet also recognises that the moral impulse to research is properly part of its subject matter. To these ends, the series is comprised of the highest quality work of scholars drawn from throughout the international academic community, and from a wide range of disciplines within the social sciences.

To buy or to find out more about the books currently available in this series, please go to: https://manchesteruniversitypress.co.uk/series/new-approaches-to-conflict-analysis/

Peace and the politics of memory

Johanna Mannergren, Annika Björkdahl, Susanne Buckley-Zistel, Stefanie Kappler and Timothy Williams

Manchester University Press

Published by Manchester University Press
Oxford Road, Manchester, M13 9PL

www.manchesteruniversitypress.co.uk

British Library Cataloguing-in-Publication Data
A catalogue record for this book is available from the British Library

ISBN 978 1 5261 7831 2 hardback

First published 2024

Typeset by Newgen Publishing UK

To our children

Ben
Ella
Erik
Maya
Miles
Miranda
Sophie
Theo

Contents

Figures

Acknowledgements

Writing a book is a journey that cannot be accomplished alone. The co-authoring of this book has taken us on a truly collective journey, bringing not only academic insights but also lifelong friendships. We learned and laughed together, discussed and debated, explored and engaged, talked and travelled. Many precious memories will prevail.

We want to acknowledge the many individuals and institutions that have supported this journey and contributed in various ways to the research.

First and foremost, we would like to express our heartfelt gratitude to all the students, scholars and practitioners who have dedicated their lives to the study and pursuit of just peace. Your insights, expertise and commitment have inspired and guided the ideas presented in this book.

Furthermore, we are deeply indebted to all the persons in Cyprus, Bosnia and Herzegovina, Cambodia, Rwanda and South Africa who over the years have been willing to share their experiences, stories and perspectives of living in the aftermath of war and violence. Thank you for enriching the narrative and deepening our understanding of the complexities of peace and the politics of memory.

An earnest thanks for research support in South Africa goes to Damian Samuels, Steven Kuo, Lisa Linossi, Ruth Murambadoro and Chenai Matshaka. In Cyprus we would extend our deepest thanks to our colleagues Professors Yannis Papadakis, Maria Hadjipavlou, Costas Constantinou, Rebecca Bryant, Mete Hatay and Ahmet Sözen and to the persons that shared their insights into Cyprus' stalled peace process in interviews and conversations. For invaluable input during the research process in Bosnia and Herzegovina, we thank Danijela Dugandžić, Lejla Somun and Dženita Pašić. In Cambodia, our deepest thanks go to Kum Somaly, Tann Boravin, Keo Duong, Chhay Visoth and the staff at Tuol Sleng, Chhang Youk and the staff at DC-Cam, Soy Kimsan and the staff at CSHL, Jan Reinermann, Steffen Siegle, Theresa de Langis, Helen Jarvis, Ali Al-Nasani and Robert Cutler. In Rwanda, our thanks go to various individuals and organisations whose anonymity we have decided to keep.

We would like to extend our gratitude to the funders of this research Riksbankens Jubileumsfond (RJ) and The Swedish Research Council who have generously supported our work. Their resources have provided the necessary foundation for the research and writing process.

We would also like to acknowledge the support and encouragement of our academic institutions: Durham University, Lund University, Center for Conflict Studies at Philipps University Marburg, The Swedish Institute of International Affairs (UI), Södertörn University and University of the Bundeswehr Munich. Our sincere appreciation goes to our colleagues and friends who have provided insightful feedback and engaged in stimulating discussions throughout the development of this book. Your enthusiasm and critical thinking have been instrumental in shaping the final product. In particular, we are grateful to Aniela Jesse, Yaas Bahmani and Gunda Menrad for their research assistance.

We also thank the editorial team at Manchester University Press for their professionalism and expertise in bringing this book to fruition. Their guidance and meticulous attention to detail have been invaluable in the publication process.

Finally, we would like to express our deepest gratitude to our families for being there for us with love and encouragement. Their support has been the cornerstone of this joint journey.

Johanna Mannergren
Annika Björkdahl
Susanne Buckley-Zistel
Stefanie Kappler
Timothy Williams

Introduction

In societies transitioning from conflict to peace, the violent past lingers on into the present. The commemoration of violent events, whether they occurred in a context of war, genocide, apartheid, colonialism or other forms of repression, is a conflictual, messy and multi-layered undertaking. The process of mourning the victims is often not just a matter for surviving relatives but is also a societal undertaking. Monuments may be erected to the victims of violence as well as to those who fought in the name of freedom, perhaps, or for the nation. Other monuments may be dismantled. Rituals and ceremonies are organised and museums built to mark the memories, while a whole range of agents engage in constructing and critiquing collective memory, based on their particular interpretations of the past: curators, politicians, grassroots activists, victim associations, international donors, artists. They recount stories in thunderous voices or quiet whispers, bringing people closer together or separating them even further. Mnemonic rituals and practices are instigated, drawing people to take part in events that may build bridges between former enemies or tear them down. Apologies are announced by heads of state – consoling to some, infuriating to others – while commemorations at memorial sites and museums, or impromptu gatherings in the streets, may bring people together or alternatively provoke them into resentful abstention. These reckonings with a difficult past may have the capacity to heal, yet also to hurt. Societies tend to remember the glory and sufferings of certain groups while deliberately forgetting shameful acts and the sufferings of other groups. Survivors may have to fight hard to achieve recognition.

Such is the nature of memory politics in societies emerging from conflict. Of course, there are many gradations between a process that brings about healing and a process that deepens divisions. The tension-laden relationships between former parties to a violent conflict are constantly renegotiated in the present, challenged or confirmed. Animosity may be maintained or there may be a movement towards a less antagonistic relationship, and even a just peace.

In a sense then, memory politics is about both change and continuity. Societies make efforts to break with a violent past, yet recognise that social cleavages and political divisions persist. It is therefore not surprising that peace research as well as transitional justice research are paying increasing attention to memory politics. It seems clear that how the past is remembered – and forgotten – influences the quality of the peace in the present. But how exactly? Are there ways to remember that are not harmful, that may even be conducive to peace? Ways that recognise the sufferings of the other without furthering divisions, that let multiple voices speak and point towards a different future? That trickle down through mundane, ordinary acts of remembering that are tolerant, inclusive, kind and empathetic rather than divisive, aggressive, hostile and hurtful? Such hopes are central to transitions from conflict to peace, yet it is not an easy task to fulfil them. It is difficult to grasp the shifting and multi-layered ways that memories are entangled in societies affected by conflict.

So far, there have been few attempts to trace systematically the connections between memory and peace. This book takes on this challenge and addresses the issue of how the politics of memory affects the quality of peace in societies transitioning from violent conflict. We propose a novel analytical framework and an approach that enables thick comparison through empirically grounded studies of salient topics. In so doing we are able to draw conclusions about the ways in which memory politics can be conducive to a just peace. We find that a type of memory politics that enables memories to be entangled in ways that allow for plurality, inclusivity and dignity is conducive to a just peace. In contrast, if memories are entangled in a way that is divisive and unacknowledged, any peace that results will be shallow.

We draw on empirical investigations carried out in five diverse settings that in many ways have become emblematic of contemporary struggles to build peace on a divisive past. Cyprus, Bosnia and Herzegovina, Rwanda, South Africa and Cambodia have painful histories of violence, repression, war, atrocities and genocide that deeply affect their present situation. While culturally, socially and politically diverse, they all struggle with a contentious past that is productive of politics and power in the present. We view these societies as conflict affected: there are no on-going, direct hostilities, but the continuities of violence are very much present, as the line between past and present is volatile and contention can flare up in a moment, with an instant activation of difficult memories. Recently in Bosnia and Herzegovina there were heated protests against murals glorifying convicted war criminals. With survivors demanding justice, recognition and compensation for the violence of the war, the memorialisation of perpetrators was becoming a 'second wound'. In South Africa, likewise, there have been a number of demonstrations against statues of historically contested figures, linking the more recent phenomenon of apartheid to its deep roots in colonialism and slavery. #RhodesMustFall protests originated at the University of Cape Town in 2015, before the more global Black Lives Matter movement led to various statues of Christopher Columbus being taken down. Such statues function as icons of memory and become sites around which questions of social peace and justice are discussed. Thus, their fall, despite its apparent ephemerality, represents more than a fleeting moment.

In Rwanda, in contrast, public commemorations of the genocide of 1994 are recurring events that tend to be initiated from above. The dominant discourse of reconciliation and social cohesion post-genocide is a government narrative that plays a central role in present-day politics. It is manifested in yearly remembrance practices which people are expected to participate in en masse, with little leeway for protesting or abstaining. Likewise, reckonings with the Cambodian genocide, the commemoration of those who died in the killing fields of the Khmer Rouge, is a public and ritualistic undertaking that centres on educating the next generation. At the same time, the practice of displaying human skulls and bones, as forceful reminders of the terrible past, brings fresh pain to those still living. Even in Cyprus, where the conflict is often described as frozen, the embers of the past may flare up, opening up opportunities to destabilise the bifurcal memory politics of the two opposing nationalist struggles on the island, as civil society initiatives seek to break silences and call for material restitution as well as reconciliation.

All in all, these cases cast light on the ways in which the past is connected to the present and the strong impact that politics of remembrance can have on social, political and economic configurations. Tensions around markers of the past can be found in all the societies as they attempt to reconfigure their relationship with the past. Indeed, mnemonic processes, whether in the form of tearing down monuments or putting them up, re-enacting historical events or silencing some victims' appeals for recognition, are part and parcel of peace processes at both the everyday level and the formal level of politics.

Mnemonic formations and entangled memories: the argument in brief

The book seeks to make an original contribution to seminal debates in both Peace and Conflict Studies and Memory Studies. The two fields have closely shared interests yet tend to remain in parallel intellectual realms. The insights of previous research have often remained restricted to individual case studies on the politics of memory and there has been no sustained attempt to draw conclusions the relationship between the politics of memory and the building of peace. Moreover, we have noticed that most case studies focus on one particular aspect of memory politics, such as sites (memorials or museums, for instance), while others focus on historical narratives (such as speeches or stories), yet others on agents (for example, victim groups), and finally some on events, such as peace walks or national days of mourning (see Feindt et al., 2014). In response, this book develops an analytical framework with four conceptual entry points – sites, agents, narratives and events – and their mutual interactions making up the SANE framework. This framework enables an investigation across cases in order to understand how and why memory politics may contribute either to a just peace or to the perpetuation of conflict.

Key to this endeavour are mnemonic formations. As thematic clusters around certain particularly salient issues or phenomena in a society, they bring memory and politics together. We suggest that in order to study the impact of politics of memory on the quality of peace, mnemonic formations provide a useful starting point. Mnemonic formations are societally salient topics regarding some facet of a conflict affected society's memoryscape. Importantly, while such formations may appear stable, they are in fact restless; they emerge and fade, congeal and fracture over time. Any analysis can thus only provide a snapshot in time. In our study, mnemonic formations are considered to be diagnostic sites from which we can draw wider conclusions on how memory politics impacts the quality of peace. In Cyprus, we investigate the lasting impact of competing nationalisms that divide the small island; in South Africa, we look at the legacy of colonialism in the shadow of apartheid remembrance; in Cambodia, we consider the productive power of the dead and the spirits that remain behind following the violence of the Khmer Rouge; in Bosnia and Herzegovina, we study the often contradictory commemoration practices around the siege of Sarajevo, showing the power of the memories of ordinary people who lived through the siege; and in Rwanda we zoom in on the memory politics around the contested role of the international community in the genocide.

By focusing our investigations on mnemonic formations rather than on more general memory politics, it becomes possible to home in on the entangled weave of memories. We draw out how memory is entangled around these salient topics and how different memories conflict, co-exist or connect with each other, and how this affects the quality of peace. The mnemonic formations are read through the SANE framework, which will be introduced in depth in the next chapter. In essence, we approach the relevant mnemonic formations from four different conceptual entry points: sites, agents, narratives and events. We focus on memory *sites* that often entail an abundance of material artefacts with affective consequences. At the same time, we stress the role of *agents*, with their various agendas in memory politics, in shaping these narratives and these sites. This provides a more nuanced understanding of agency that moves beyond the obvious political agents and their hegemonic narratives. We also take into consideration the role that *narratives* play in memory politics and recognise that these narratives are always emplaced: they are stories of what happened in certain places. We moreover acknowledge that the past is not only narrated through stories and discourses but is also performed through practices that agents engage in. Thus, our fourth component concerns *events*, defined as temporally circumscribed manifestations and practices of memory politics. It is this interaction of sites, agents, narratives and events that constitutes our analytical inroad for studying mnemonic formations, allowing us to understand the underlying dynamics within the politics of memory in transitions from war and violence to peace.

Consider, for instance, the worn Monopoly board displayed in the War Childhood Museum in Sarajevo. Responding to the question 'What was a war childhood to you?' residents have handed in their treasured objects. They are the most ordinary things that form part of many childhoods – a game of Monopoly, a diary, a swing – each presented with a personal story told by its owner. In our analysis of the siege in Chapter 3, we note how the Monopoly board and its affective power brings forth what it was like to hide in a cellar during long hours as a child. The museum site is one node in the conflicted mnemonic formation of the siege, which is read in juxtaposition with the elite narrative constructions of ethno-nationalist, military heroism that ignore the civilian resistance and resilience against war. These are just two of the nodes in the mnemonic formation that the analysis brings forth, enabling us to tease out whether memories of the siege are entangled in ways that are conducive to peace or not. Likewise, in the analysis of South Africa's legacy of colonialism, the colonial nostalgia expressed at the exclusive Rand Club – a symbol of past imperial glory and resource wealth – stands in stark contrast to the painful narratives about the colonial migrant-labour system that made this wealth possible, as told by the community-led Lwandle Migrant Museum. While the museum as well as other initiatives point to increasingly successful demands for recognition, the privately run Rand Club is testimony to the strong influence of private agents seeking to maintain their privileges, which also comes with a certain disregard for the dignity of the victims of colonialism.

As these examples illustrate, the mnemonic formations selected for analysis are diverse. Yet the analytical framework makes it possible to compare them with each other and generate some broad conclusions regarding the relationship between memory and peace. In this effort, we address the lack of detailed yet systematic investigations into this relationship, advancing and placing in dialogue two bodies of literature: on the one hand, bringing a comparative perspective to Memory Studies, which has been dominated by qualitative, single case studies; on the other hand, enriching the large body of quantitative and qualitative research on peace with a perspective that integrates memory politics.

This approach recognises that memory is expressed in various ways based on diverse and, at times, conflicting interpretations of the past. It has been key to understanding how multi-layered memories interlink to form 'entanglements' resulting from asymmetries, multiple perspectives and cross-references in memory practices (Feindt et al., 2014: 35). Conceptualising memories as entangled is a way of understanding different views of the past and their mutual interactions (Delanty, 2017; Heuman, 2014). For Conrad (2003: 86), the concept of 'entangled memories' relates to the production of memories as a means to cast light on 'complex impulses in the present'. These complex impulses are instrumental in the constitution of peace in a conflict-affected society and we draw out findings pertaining to how the entanglement of memory affects the quality of peace.

In brief, the argument in this book thus runs as follows: in societies transitioning from violence there is a large variety of often diverse and at times conflicting interpretations of the past that come together and become apparent in certain mnemonic formations. Mnemonic formations can be unpacked and studied through the conceptual entry points of sites, agents, narratives and events, allowing one to analyse how memories are entangled in various ways. The way memory becomes entangled is illustrative of the quality of peace. The empirical analysis will demonstrate that if memory is entangled in a certain way – plural, inclusive and dignified – we can observe a just peace. However, if memory is entangled in a way that is divisive and without acknowledgement, peace remains shallow.

The politics of memory

Memory and peace processes are intimately connected, yet so far only limited attention has been paid to how they interrelate. This is surprising since understanding memory politics as an integral part of the (re)constitution of society has been a key topic since the early days of studies of collective and political memory (Halbwachs, 1992: 47; Renan, 2018).

To explore this interrelation we situate ourselves in an approach to Memory Studies that analyses collective memory and the political power of memory, asking 'who wants whom to remember what, and why' (Confino cited in Maurantonio, 2017: 219). From this perspective, power lies at the core of memory politics, with agents vying for the power to define the past so as to legitimise their position in the present and to influence the future peace.

Crucially, though, we are wary of the use of the term 'collective memory' as introduced by Maurice Halbwachs (1992), which stresses the cohesive and reproductive force of memory as something rather static and fixed (Rufer, 2012). In contrast to Halbwachs, we do not understand collective memory as a fairly cohesive memory 'of' a group because groups are rarely coherent organisms. They change and constantly negotiate who is part of this collective and who is not. We therefore agree that '[h]ow memories are reintegrated and what new narratives we form, as individuals and a society, are crucial in terms of our identity and our relationship to others and the world around us' (Wielenga, 2012: 5; see also Buckley-Zistel, 2006c; Strömbom, 2017). A case in point is Jelena Subotic's (2019) in-depth investigation into how Holocaust memory is ignored, appropriated and obfuscated in the making and remaking of the Serbian, Croatian and Lithuanian collective identities in the post-Second World War and post-Cold War era, challenging the Western narrative of the Holocaust and acting as a political strategy to resolve those countries' ontological insecurities. We are interested in seeing how memory is distributed within a community, and how people who view themselves as belonging to certain groups work together when constructing a narrative about the past, thereby engaging in what has been referred to as collaborative remembering (Weldon, 2001 cited in Wertsch, 2002). In our view, collective memory is hence fluid and ever-changing. This fluidity is influenced by many contextual factors, such as political climate, opportunity structures, hopes and aspirations.

Even though often manifested in material and spatial terms, the politics of memory is never still. Salient topics can be transformed, fade into the periphery or be abruptly reinterpreted through shock or rupture; they emerge in the present and shape how the past is interpreted retrospectively. In this context, for instance, scholars working on notions of nostalgia have contributed to our understanding of practices of memory-making as illustrative of present feelings of loss, expressed as a 'yearning for what is now not attainable' (Pickering and Keightley, 2006: 920). We are interested in how this process changes over time, with new actors joining and older ones disappearing, with various agents forming an entanglement of memory, and how this affects the quality of peace.

In many cases, collaborative memory actions make use of material and non-material sites. These sites of memory (*lieux de mémoire*) comprise 'any significant entity, whether material or non-material in nature, which by dint of human will or the work of time has become a symbolic element of the memorial heritage of any community' (Nora, 1996: xviii). They thus include places, objects and ideas that are vested with historical importance for a particular nation or community. Memorials, monuments and various activities of remembrance are perceived as sites for the telling of a stabilising, nation-building narrative for the fractured post-conflict state. These insights resonate with studies that assume a strong link between commemoration and nation-building (Blackburn, 2010; Kuzio, 2002). Sites of memory may include references to past violence, such as war memorials or commemoration events, but also national symbols, such as flags or national holidays. In cases where memory is highly disputed, memorials may be challenged by counter-memorials that publicly question the meaning of the initial memorial or serve as a comment that critiques its political stance. Frictions emerge around questions about how and what to remember, so that memory is also often contested. These frictions between remembering and remembering differently are crucial to memory politics and thus for understanding the quality of peace.

To overcome frictions, memory politics often aims at education. It is hoped that people will be sensitised through memorials and museums so that a repetition of atrocities will be avoided (Bickford, 2014: 394; Buckley-Zistel and Schäfer, 2014b) and peace may prevail. In this context, public debates about memorials may foster a dialogue about the past and help the parties to the conflict understand the experience of others. These debates, if successful, shape collective remembering by increasing the number of people who coalesce around a particular narrative or render the boundaries between communities more permeable by accepting competing narratives.

At the same time, commemorative activities may be central to the need for acknowledgement among survivors, so that truth commission reports, and more recently court rulings, recommend erecting memorials as part of reparation measures (Buckley-Zistel, 2020: 10). With the strong increase in concerns for victims over the past decades, acknowledgement of their harm and vindication of their dignity has come centre-stage and is frequently expressed in memorials. This is based on an understanding of the quality of peace that includes dignity – as will be discussed in the following chapter. Against this backdrop, victim associations have become powerful agents in many societies transitioning from violent conflict to peace.

It is important to recognise that key to the politics of memory and the construction of peace is not just how past violence and atrocities are remembered, but first of all whether they are remembered at all (Mannergren Selimovic, 2013; Temin and Dahl, 2017). Memory politics is just as much about social forgetting as it is about social remembering. Silences and voids are intrinsic to memory politics (Mannergren Selimovic, 2020a), so we also must attend to what is not commemorated, or what is actively forgotten (see Buckley-Zistel, 2006b; Chandler, 2008b). The shifting work of erasing topics from collective memory – to 'unsee' and 'unhear' – as well as the reactive labour of bringing the forgotten to public attention are of relevance for understanding the constitution of peace too. What is remembered and forgotten is at the centre of political authority. In such struggles, national governments and other political authorities often attempt to maintain power in the present by controlling the past (McDowell and Braniff, 2014). Yet silences do not necessarily stem solely from a lack of agency or political power; they may be actively chosen by certain actors as a coping strategy (Buckley-Zistel, 2006b; Mannergren Selimovic, 2020b).

In particular, we are concerned with narratives, rituals, myths, practices and so on that bring together past and present within a particular local context (Drozdzewski et al., 2019: 253). These generate symbolic capital of key interest for agents involved in transitions from war to peace. Importantly, memory politics in conflict-affected societies draws on a rich symbolic vocabulary (Brown, 2013: 497) to promote political communication. It is through commemorative activities and narrative accounts of particular events that places, groups or persons may be constructed as a form of political currency.

Victimhood, in particular, is a positionality that enables political and moral claims (Winter, 2006: 62). Identifying with a victim or perpetrator position (or both), attributing or dispelling responsibility, acknowledging or denying harm – all of this has an effect on how we see ourselves as well as how we see our (former) enemy. Advocacy groups such as victim associations may gain recognition and leverage through commemorative activities (Nettelfield, 2010), giving marginalised groups a platform from which to articulate their particular grievances and political claims for acknowledgement, compensation or simply recognition as a group.

Commemoration can thus be a site for agency for marginal or informal actors. Women's organisations that mobilise around memory, for example, may manage to give voice to silenced memories, reclaim collective memories that have been misrepresented in official narratives and challenge gendered hierarchies (Altınay, 2019). In Cyprus, many women on both sides of the divided island have internalised the mainstream prejudice that women cannot be a source of knowledge on the issue of the Cyprus conflict, and their experiences and memories have been forgotten, silenced and marginalised. In contrast, an oral history project recalls, collects and mobilises these women's shared memories of traumatic displacement, of daily lives and home-making disrupted, in a powerful collection that challenges gender hierarchies in memory-making while both stabilising and destabilising the mnemonic formations of nationalism (see Aliefendioğlu and Behçetoğulları, 2019). Such memory work has important repercussions for the ways in which peace is discussed and negotiated.

The quality of peace

Peace is a social phenomenon and as such it is related to the memories of communities. Peace can be either challenged or supported by commemorative practices, memory work, and various ways of remembering and forgetting.

Civil wars in the post-Cold War era most often end with a negotiated outcome and an ensuing peace accord; however, most post-war countries fail to live up to the provisions of such negotiated peace accords (Joshi and Wallensteen, 2018). The limited success rate of peace accords, and the risk of a recurrence of violence, calls for a deepened understanding of how to build peace beyond ensuring the mere absence of direct violence. In addition, peace-building missions have tended to conflate peace-building with state-building, and peace with the securing of states, institutions and rule of law, without considering local strategies for coping with violence and the making of peace (see Balthasar, 2017). An example of this is the United Nations Mission to Kosovo, where the international community in effect governed a state in the making, and where the peace-building process was contingent on meeting the standards for independent statehood. This has led peacebuilders to privilege a form of peace that tends to be empty, shallow and inherently unstable. Clearly, the 'one size fits all' blueprint of international peace-building has not been as successful as was hoped. A realisation has grown that peace needs to be emplaced and thus locally owned. How conflict-affected societies decide to build their peace will have different repercussions depending on the various local contexts (Loyle and Appel, 2011; Salehi and Williams, 2016).

In light of these developments, peace research has over the last decade profoundly changed our understanding of what a durable and just peace entails, raising questions such as peace for whom, by whom and in what spaces (e.g. Björkdahl and Kappler, 2017; Mac Ginty, 2010; Mac Ginty and Richmond, 2013; Paffenholz, 2015; Richmond and Mitchell, 2011; Shinko, 2008: 489). Recent developments in Peace and Conflict Studies have come to question the distinction between war and peace, as well as the assumed linear development of transitions from war to peace. The conventional understanding that peace is the opposite of war, and that where war is present, peace is absent, has been challenged (Flint, 2011; Mac Ginty, 2006). Instead, war and peace are seen to be intertwined and if there ever was a clear line between them, it has become increasingly blurred. This is expressed in the continuation of violence after the formal ending of a war, (Pain, 2015). The way in which memory politics in transitional or post-conflict societies links past violence to power struggles in the present also reflects how conflict dynamics persist once peace has been formally negotiated.

In order to challenge perceptions of peace as an abstract idea, an absent architecture or an ambiguous aspiration, a rich body of work has unpacked various components that affect peace. Some have paid attention to the link between democracy and peace (Doyle, 1983), between justice and peace (Allan and Keller, 2006) and between equality and peace (Hudson et al., 2012). Moreover, local dimensions of peace (Kappler, 2015), everyday peace (Mac Ginty, 2021; Williams, 2015) and emplaced peace (Björkdahl and Buckley-Zistel, 2016; Björkdahl and Kappler, 2017) have been proposed as more fruitful concepts, assuming that such peace is potentially hybrid (Mac Ginty, 2010) and produces a so-called peace dividend. Such peace anchored in the everyday can in turn strengthen the peace constituency and facilitate the crucial buy-in from the subjects of peace. Richmond (2016), for example, argues that peace processes often focus too much on the state and state institutions, thereby failing to understand the localised power dynamics that drive peace. To him, the constitution of peace is an agential practice that stems from the representation and participation of local communities, peace movements and other alliances, which cooperate in order to end violence and address social, economic and political problems (Richmond, 2016: 3–5). Others have been concerned with understanding obstacles to peace as they explore the multidimensionality of the process, the power dynamics between various agents, and the interplay between micro and macro scales, in formal as well as informal contexts (Millar, 2020; Richmond, 2022).

We are moving beyond the understanding of peace as merely negative peace, that is, an absence of direct violence, observable from the moment direct hostilities have come to an end whether through peace agreements, military defeat or international intervention. Such a negative definition may be contrasted with a positive understanding of peace as suggested by Johan Galtung (1964). A positive peace includes not only the absence of direct and organised violence but also an end to structural and cultural violence. This form of peace is utopian in the sense that it encompasses everything: social, economic and political justice, the satisfaction of basic human needs, and the recognition of identities. Positive peace is also abstract in its universal ambitions, and therefore affects people in different ways in their everyday lives. In the everyday the distinction between positive and negative peace often becomes blurred. The everyday peace, research shows, is socially produced and reproduced through everyday acts of tolerance, solidarity, hospitality, inclusion, but also of indifference, omission and tension as people go about their daily lives (Mac Ginty, 2021; Mannergren Selimovic, 2022a; Richmond, 2010; Williams, 2015). Thus, the everyday peace is intimate, tactile and real. It is emplaced among, and produced by, ordinary people, and as such is a crucial element of positive peace.

A number of approaches have tried to define positive peace by referring to certain qualities. The notion of quality peace has specifically been elaborated by Joshi and Wallensteen (2018). They view quality peace as encompassing five key factors: security, governance reforms to allow for dispute resolution, economic opportunities for marginalised groups, reconciliation promotion and a strong civil society. These five elements serve not only as indicators for quality peace, but also as policy prescriptions on how to achieve it.

The quality of peace is also often linked to democracy and is influenced by values and norms underpinning democratic societies and thus relations between liberal democracies (Doyle, 1983). The democratic peace thesis provides the logical reasoning as to why the global spread of democracy is expected to result in greater international peace, assuming that democratic political institutions make it difficult for governments to initiate war without the consent of their electorates. Cultural norms observed by democracies are understood to mean that they will favour peaceful means of resolving conflicts with one another. Yet although democracy may have pacifying effects, the process of democratisation, which often emerges as part of the peacebuilding process, tends to be conflictual, competitive and characterised by struggles for power (Paris, 2004).

The notion of equal peace, meanwhile, relates to the quality of peace as regards the status of women in society (Hudson et al., 2012). It compares micro-level gender violence with macro-level state peacefulness in global settings. A key argument is that gender inequality is a form of violence regardless of how invisible it may be or how normalised it may appear (Hudson et al., 2012: 5). Gender inequality, then, is understood as one type of subordination of those who are different and lacking in power and status. The main conclusion from this research is that 'there will never be peace for our nations unless there is peace between the sexes' (Hudson et al., 2012: 208). The concept has therefore emerged of a gender-just peace. This gendered understanding of peace diverges substantially from liberal peace, as it renders peace visible in the everyday and built from below. It brings to the fore equality, social welfare, equity and, by virtue of its emancipatory claims, it also provides for shifts in existing power and gender relations (Björkdahl and Mannergren Selimovic, 2016b).

This debate over the content of peace has its roots in the notion of a just peace as discussed by Allan and Keller (2006: 117–19). Just peace is understood to be locally and inter-subjectively constructed, somewhat in contrast to positive peace, which carries connotations of universality. It is, similarly, not simply about the absence of direct, visible violence, but requires underlying structures, drivers and dynamics of violence to be addressed (Allan and Keller, 2006). Just peace is an intersubjective and reflexive understanding of peace that is shared by the parties to the conflict, and relates the quality of peace to understandings of justice and equality. To cite but one example, from Bosnia and Herzegovina: many commentators on the Dayton Peace negotiations predicted that the peace agreement would not produce a just peace. It was stated that 'the Bosnia peace agreement … is a shabby compromise'. Today, that seems not far from the reality, although as Bosnian president Alija Izetbegović claimed at the time of the signing, peace is 'more just than continuing the war' (quoted in *New Statesman and Society*, 1995: 5). Almost thirty years after the signing of the Dayton Peace Accord, the shortfall between the actual experiences of the internationally negotiated peace and people's expectations of the peace challenge the idea of a just peace. Thus, for a peace to be just, a peace dividend must materialise in people's everyday lives.

These important conceptualisations of peace have formed the background to our investigations into how memory politics affects peace. We suggest that to rethink peace is to recognise that it means different things to different people in different places and times. Thus, peace is not an abstract, mythical singular, because as such it becomes unobtainable (Dietrich and Sützl, 1997). Instead, by taking into consideration intersubjective or subjective understandings of peace it becomes possible to observe fragmented, co-existing, fleeting, plural peace(s). Such peace(s) is and are understood as constantly 'becoming' and are best characterised as a process rather than an outcome. By thinking of peace in its plural, that is, peace(s), we are able to recognise the different ways in which peace manifests itself in conflict-affected societies.

Our approach suggests that peace is value-laden, fleeting, contested and ever-changing (see Richmond, 2008). We view peace simultaneously as an institutionalised system, a discourse, a practice and a utopia. It can be seen as both a process and a goal, following multiple parallel paths, always unfinished, always aspired to and unlikely to converge on a single agreed understanding. Multiple processes, including memory politics, can result in a complex peace architecture, building on frictional interplays between traditional top-down and bottom-up perspectives of peace processes as well as between international and local actors.

Bridging memory politics and peace

Peace and Conflict Studies and Memory Studies have both links and tensions, and we are concerned with the processes of memory-making and the construction of just peace at the intersection between the two fields of study. As we have outlined, contemporary approaches to peace research call for more comprehensive and finely grained methods for understanding how and why transitions to peace either develop into a just peace or deteriorate into deeply divided societies (or somewhere in-between). It is thus to be expected that an analysis of how memory politics affects the quality of peace will produce insights that are more sensitive to local and dynamic developments.

Research has long had an implicit focus on dominant hegemonic narratives and their effects on the constitution of peace, often based on a rather homogenising understanding of society (Renan, 2018). It has been assumed that there is some unity in remembering – without taking into account the fact that societies are necessarily plural and diverse. There have been calls to challenge the assumed homogeneity and unity of national memory, and to open up the gaze to the different and, at times, contradictory memory dynamics of a society. In our endeavour to conceptualise the link between memory and peace, we have found the notion of entangled memory particularly (Feindt et al., 2014).

Entangled memory emphasises that remembering is always dynamic and heterogeneous; it emphasises memory plurality. A mnemonic formation is therefore always a junction of various interpretations of the past that hang together, interlace, touch yet also separate, disconnect and break away. To Feindt et al., '[t]his insight calls for the analysis of detectable *entanglements*, taking into account multiple perspectives, asymmetries, and cross-referential mnemonic practices' (2014: 35, emphasis in original). It is to this approach that our study contributes.

Surprisingly, the Memory Studies literature has been remarkably silent on the connective link with peace. One important exception is Manuel Cruz's nuanced study of memory and trauma, which ties memory to politics and defines the forms, uses and political meanings of memory and forgetting (Cruz, 2016). He develops five memory models that link memory to, respectively, values, the present, retributive justice, mourning and revelation, in order to investigate methodologically how traumatic events are remembered, and in so doing to reveal the difficulty of living together (Cruz, 2016). Another noteworthy exception is Kristian Brown's work, which argues that by analysing memory politics one can attend to more fine-grained and dynamic assessments of peace processes than by relying on attitudinal indicators (Brown, 2013: 505). Thus, by closely studying memory work it is possible to trace on-going tensions – both between and within communities – in relation to how the peace process is developing. In this sense, the analysis of memory politics serves as a seismograph for peace. It serves to 'uncover tensions, ambiguities, and sometimes the plainly counter-intuitive' (Brown, 2013: 503–5), allowing for insights into social and political dynamics as relevant to understanding how memory affects the quality of peace.

Apart from this, one of very few systematic comparisons of memory politics is Bernhard and Kubik's (2014) edited volume on how the twentieth anniversary of the revolutions of 1989–1991 were officially commemorated in seventeen post-communist states. In their volume, the politics of memory is key to the establishment of the new political regimes in the region, as well as for new national and collective identities. They present a typology of memory regimes and mnemonic actors, characterising them variously as fractured, pillarised or unified, and make some preliminary observations as to the respective impacts of these types on democracy (Kubik and Bernhard, 2014: 10–11). Their interest is focused on official actors in the transition from communism to democracy.

We, on the other hand, are above all interested in patterns of memory politics as part of the complex interactions that peace processes generate. To pursue our endeavour to bridge memory politics and peace, we employ the SANE framework, which allows us to study comparatively and in depth how the politics of memory in conflict-affected societies affects the quality of peace. As illustrated in the empirical chapters of this book and synthesised in Chapter 7, we thus argue that the quality of peace is linked to justice and manifests itself in how memory is entangled. To contribute to a just peace, this entanglement needs to display particular dimensions that show that the parties to the conflict are moving away from antagonism and towards peaceful living together. The empirical investigations of selected mnemonic formations, through the conceptual entry points of sites, agents, narratives and events, show that a just peace is inclusive (in terms of ethnicity, religion, age and gender, among other things), plural (in terms of encompassing diverse memories and commemorative practices) and contributes to embracing dignity (in terms of acknowledging the injustices committed).

Structure of the book

In Chapter 1 we introduce the analytical framework, which conceptualises the mnemonic interplay of sites, agents, narratives and events. By grounding our analysis of evolving mnemonic formations in this framework, we provide an alternative to instrumentalised readings of memory politics, to studies that only depart from material manifestation, such as a memorial, and to research that only focuses on specific agents, such as victim groups. The framework gives us access to the entanglement of memory in mnemonic formations and makes visible the fluidity of memory as well as the frictions between competing memories. We posit that research needs to take on the challenge of analysing how these intricate processes interact and unfold over time and in space if we are to understand how and why remembrance impacts on the quality of peace. We suggest that memory cannot be understood through an analysis of sites, agents, narratives or events alone, but only through looking at the complex interplay between these. In addition, we show that there is added value in studying memory politics in a cross-case way, in order to identify patterns regarding the impact of memory politics on the quality of peace.

Chapter 2 presents the first case study, exploring how the mnemonic formation of competing nationalisms in Cyprus has turned memory-making into an obstacle to peace-making. In Cyprus, contested memories of past national struggles have become a foundation for the (re)constitution of the two nations. From a Greek Cypriot perspective, nationalist memory-making relates to the colonial struggle for independence from Britain, while Turkish Cypriots' nationalist memory-making is primarily about obtaining independence from the Greek Cypriots. We observe two oppositional tendencies. On the one hand, the process of memory-making in Cyprus is complex and multi-layered. On the other hand, this complexity has largely been overridden in public discourse by a binary process in which the memories of Greek Cypriots and Turkish Cypriots have been separately institutionalised as dominant forms of remembering. The chapter suggests that a key realm for negotiating a shared, emplaced peace on the island of Cyprus is the politics of memory, so as to mediate the strong mnemonic attachments to the nation.

Chapter 3 focuses on the 1992–1996 siege of Sarajevo. Studying this mnemonic formation gives us access to a memory politics that has wider implications for the quality of peace in Bosnia and Herzegovina, where the peace has been characterised by unresolved tensions and a deeply divisive political climate. The chapter studies the clashes between everyday and elite practices of memory, demonstrating that the diverse forms of memorialisation of the siege display a lack of consensus regarding the ways in which the siege should be commemorated, by whom and in which spaces. Political elites are constantly challenged by other agents. Memory politics in the Bosnian capital is thus less consolidated than in other parts of the divided country. A close examination of the mnemonic formation of the siege allows us to see the tactics of those memory agents that challenge hegemonic memories, suggesting that a fluid memory politics can provide for a more inclusive and plural peace.

Chapter 4 focuses on the role of international actors in the 1994 genocide against the Tutsi in Rwanda. To analyse the mnemonic formation that resulted, it explores various sites related to the role of internationals during the genocide, including the Kigali Genocide Memorial, which clearly articulates the government's official narrative, and the Murambi Genocide Memorial, which expands this official narrative with a more detailed condemnation of French complicity in the genocide. Various Rwandan and international memory agents have been key in attributing meaning to the role of the internationals in the run-up to, and during, the genocide, highlighting the preparatory role of colonialism, international inaction by the UN and the international community during genocide, and even a collaboration of the French state with Hutu extremists. Memory politics in Rwanda is hegemonically structured, and the chapter shows how these narratives can support legitimacy for the government, even at the expense of some facets of the quality of peace.

Chapter 5 investigates the memoryscape of South Africa as it is shaped by the legacy of colonialism. It argues that the mnemonic formation of colonialism has been sidelined as a result of the primary attention paid to apartheid and suggests that apartheid should be viewed as an extension of colonialism, rather than separate from it. The chapter therefore illustrates the mnemonic contestations around the ways in which colonial violence is represented and remembered, and points to two sets of divisions. First, there are social dynamics glorifying European colonial rule in South Africa as an honourable conquest which are countered by dynamics that identify colonialism as a brutal system of systematic oppression, especially of the non-white population. Second, each of these two camps has internal divisions, so that there is a multi-layered fragmentation of the mnemonic landscape pertaining to colonial rule. The complex and differentiated forms of victimhood and oppression as they have been experienced by, and are remembered from, different societal positions complicate the negotiation of the past as well as questions of acknowledgement and redress as they relate to colonial forms of violence.

Chapter 6 discusses the mnemonic formation of the dead in Cambodia, exploring how the bones and spirits of those killed by the Khmer Rouge are used in memory politics today and how this impacts peace. Government politics regarding the non-cremation of bodies in the aftermath of the Cambodian genocide is based on an understanding that these remains constitute evidence of the violent past and are needed to keep the memory alive and to educate future generations. But not cremating the bones has spiritual consequences for survivors in their interactions with the spaces of memorial sites. The chapter discusses various sites of local and national memorials, focusing particularly on the Tuol Sleng Genocide Museum, with a discussion of how the display of skulls there is indicative of broader memory politics. The chapter reveals how the political interests that have successfully advocated the dead being preserved for display in order to bolster their own legitimacy may in fact have undermined the quality of peace in the country, as the dead are not afforded the dignity the surviving population would expect. This chapter also looks at how the resulting presence of spirits has a detrimental impact.

Chapter 7 brings together these five empirical chapters to identify overarching patterns in how the politics of memory may affect the quality of peace in conflict-affected societies. Bringing our empirical case studies into conversation with each other, we compare across cases, identifying and systematising patterns, similarities and differences. We reflect on the complex ways in which the politics of memory conditions the quality of peace, accounting for the temporal ruptures and reconnections that make the politics of the past relevant to the present. We show that where memory is configured in a way that allows for plurality, dignity and inclusivity there is a stronger chance for a durable peace; the resulting peace will embrace a larger societal base in a sustainable way, as well as enabling productive encounters with the past. Where these conditions are scarcely or only partially fulfilled, on the other hand, the emergent peace suffers from a lack of traction and remains wedded to the emergence of mutually exclusive, competing peace(s), or an overall peace that is shallow.

The book concludes with our reflections on what a just peace may look like. A just peace is, a function of entangled memory, and stresses the key importance of plurality, dignity and inclusivity. Such entangled memory is fluid and dynamic, and is constantly renegotiated, thus allowing for adaptations over time. The chapter closes by looking at new avenues for future research in the field of Peace and Conflict Studies.

1

Mnemonic formations: an analytical approach to memory and peace

How can we grasp the effects of memory politics on the quality of peace? How can we instil peace with meaning so that it can be analysed empirically? This chapter lays out our comparative methodology for analysing memory politics, elaborates on the idea of mnemonic formations, and introduces an analytical framework for investigating mnemonic formations through four conceptual entry points: sites, agents, narratives and events.

With the unfolding of the so-called memory turn in the social sciences over the last couple of decades, a rich body of literature on individual case studies in and of conflict-affected societies has emerged. So far, however, there has been little research that attempts to draw out some generalisable observations across different cases and across time and space concerning the relationship between memory politics and peace. The analytical framework elaborated in this chapter allows us to take this step and compare across cases, look for patterns, similarities and differences, and to systematise and assemble emerging knowledge.

As outlined in the Introduction, mnemonic formations are thematic clusters of particular salience around which sites, agents, narratives and events gather and thicken. Mnemonic formations provide a multidimensional link between memory politics and peace, functioning as diagnostic sites; it is through interrogating these that we discern patterns of memory politics that allow us to understand better the relationship between memory politics and the quality of peace. While we search for patterns, we are cognisant of the fact that any comparative endeavour inherently and necessarily poses 'a threat to replace thickness with universal concepts or standards' (Niewöhner and Scheffer, 2010a: 533). Inspired by ethnography's key strengths, that is, detailed, nuanced and thick description *à la* Geertz (1973), we use soft comparison, allowing the cases to speak to each other by combining within-case analysis with cross-case comparison (George and Bennett, 2005). There is thus a balance between the depth of interrogation of a case and the comparability between cases, allowing for insights to be generated within cases, as well as teasing out what this can mean conceptually, through comparison. There is of course a trade-off between, on the one hand, the depth of contextualisation necessary to describe a phenomenon adequately in order for its meaning to be rendered understandable, and on the other the generality necessary for the concept to be applicable in other contexts. Our point of departure resembles comparative ethnography (Simmons and Smith, 2019: 341–2). We are therefore interested in the specificities of each of the five cases of mnemonic formations not only in and of themselves, but also with regard to how the insights from each individual case stand in relation to the other cases.

In line with the idea of thick comparison, the object of comparison is 'produced through *thickening* contextualisations, including analytical, cross-contextual framings that are meant to facilitate comparison' (Niewöhner and Scheffer, 2010b: 3, emphasis in original). Yet with what degree of precision should this thick comparison be drawn (Prus, 2010: 502)? The framework developed in this chapter enables a nuanced, thick description of individual cases as well as subsequent cross-contextual comparison by reading the mnemonic formations through the four conceptual lenses of sites, agents, narratives and events. While the optimal level of abstraction (see Sartori, 1970) is possibly unclear in general in ethnographic comparison (Prus, 2010: 503), we believe the framework we propose strikes the right balance for the study of mnemonic formations. It allows us to draw wider conclusions about how the quality of peace is intrinsically connected to the ways in which memory is configured and entangled, moving beyond the particularities of each case and enabling concepts and insights to be extended across cases and to generate theory.

Five different cases of mnemonic formations are explored, derived from Cyprus, Bosnia and Herzegovina, South Africa, Cambodia and Rwanda. The conflict-affected societies focused on are indeed diverse, and each displays its own unique historical trajectory and conflict dynamics. Nevertheless, they all share the characteristic that a violent past continues to be a divisive issue, with memorialisation emerging as a potential tool for building peace and/or perpetuating conflict. There are contestations around the ways in which the past could and should be remembered which translate past violence into present conflict. Importantly, the selected mnemonic formations are situated within a wider societal context of a number of topics that are commemorated – as well as some that are not. It is our close familiarity with these cases that allows us to select significant mnemonic formations within this broader context.

Reading mnemonic formations: sites, agents, narratives and events

The framework for the five case studies brings into play the theoretical traction of the conceptual lenses of sites, agents, narratives and events. We posit that the dynamic and frictional characteristics of peace processes are not fully captured by separate studies of these key elements and that we need to study their mutual constitution.

Through the emphasis on sites of memory, such as memorials, monuments or museums, we are able to capture that 'matter matters' for memory politics. Since memory politics is a process with, and a result of, the work produced by individuals and organised groups, it is crucial to acknowledge the role of agents in our understanding of mnemonic formations. Given the power of language and discourse and its substantial effects on societies, we bring to the fore narratives of memory. A focus on memory events, lastly, recognises the importance of performativity in effecting social relations. All these conceptual entry points are combined in the SANE framework, which can be systematically applied to either individual or comparative cases.

In what follows, the four interrelated elements are unpacked to bring out their relevance for a systematic analysis of mnemonic formations and how they relate to the quality of peace and the potential for a just peace. For the sake of heuristics, they are here analytically separated, but we understand them to be in constant productive interaction with each other.

Sites: pinning memory politics to place

In the most general sense, sites are places where something is commemorated. They may take the form of cemeteries, memorials, museums or artefacts. They fix meaning to physical locations and material structures, and pin memory politics to place (see Buckley-Zistel, 2020; McDowell and Braniff, 2014). Sites are, in our understanding, material representations at particular locations (Björkdahl and Buckley-Zistel, 2016; Kappler, 2017). Sites become invested with a particular meaning through social practice and by being tied into narratives about past events, present conditions and future aspirations. They are thus important nodes for memory politics as they enable a group to congeal around them (Halbwachs, 1992: 204). To make the link to the past tangible in the present and to give it a sense of permanence, groups tend to produce topographies of memory so that sites not only frame memory but 'situate and spatially constitute group remembrance' (Till, 2003: 291). Hence, sites where memory takes place are not per se places of memory; rather, it is through the social practices of placemaking that they become meaningful for memory, politics and peace.

At the same time, geographic locations of atrocities are often turned into sites of memory. Keeping alive the ostensibly authentic aura of an original site of atrocity – often despite decay and degeneration – is part of memorial aesthetics and has a strong emotional impact on visitors. Some sites are presented as museums or memorial museums (often at 'authentic' places such the Tuol Sleng Genocide Museum in Cambodia), with household objects, texts, videos and/or other displays to educate visitors about the past. These locations may appear as physical scars on the landscape, in the form of mass graves, buildings or areas previously used for confinement, torture or execution, or ruined religious buildings. They may include traces left by explosions, or remnants of divisive walls and crossings. To mark these locations and to invest them with meaning, museums and memorials are built, commemorative events held or burials performed, providing an important reference point for narratives and for the construction of collective identities. The materiality of objects at memorial sites, moreover, shapes collective identities, communicates particular norms and values, and transmits certain narratives about the past (Beckstead et al., 2011: 194). Here, too, social, material and spatial elements mutually constitute each other, in that people may construct memorial objects but at the same time their identity is (re)constructed as they engage with these objects. Memorial sites contain information and produce meaning in a metaphorical way, but also in a highly material way (Buckley-Zistel, 2021). They may serve as archives of facts and artefacts, or as storage spaces for documents and images and sometimes also for victims' clothing and bones, as at certain sites in Rwanda and Cambodia. Here, ostensible authenticity is linked to truth and material evidence, conveying a powerful narrative about the horror of the violence. Other sites consist of objects that are highly symbolic and culturally situated, such as statues, crosses, Buddhist stupas, abstract figures or walls filled with names, which may all be very meaningful to visitors.

The focus on sites of memory allows us to explore the social construction of sites and how they are linked to the efforts or needs of particular groups to construct a collective identity. A spatial analysis enables us to explore what effect sites have on particular groups and how different groups may compete over the interpretation of a site and its narratives. Sites, to us, are thus not fixed topographic entities but constructed locations and the result of place-making, where place-making refers to 'the set of social, political and material processes by which people iteratively create and recreate the experienced geographies in which they live' (Pierce et al., 2011: 54).

Beyond what the eye can see, memorial sites are affective by making us 'feel' the past (Buckley-Zistel, 2021; Tolia-Kelly et al., 2018: 3). Their display and design might trigger emotions such as sadness, a sense of loss, despair and despondency. Even though this is always personal and may differ widely from visitor to visitor, it is by no means random; it is situated in the wider commemorative practices of a society and the way a society remembers. These emotions are often beyond representation and cannot be captured by words. They expand the effect of these sites from what is visible to what is invisible, or from what they mean and what they do (Waterton, 2014).

Some sites are not formally marked but still form part of the cultural heritage of conflict. They may entail empty yet meaningful spaces, voids where individuals, families or communities once lived; places of pain where terrible things happened yet the crimes committed are collectively denied by new inhabitants. Rape camps may not display any acknowledgement of the past crimes. Physical gaps may remain in the townscape after the erasure of religious buildings. These voids are not meaningless, yet they may disrupt hegemonic remembering and forgetting. One particularly interesting example that we analyse is the so-called Sarajevo Roses, a citizens' monument in the shape of red colourings on the city's pavements and streets. These mark the craters left by mortar shells that killed residents during the siege of the city and are present in the cityscape for people to engage with or not in their everyday comings and goings (Björkdahl and Kappler, 2017). In that sense, people's movement across sites of commemoration, their reluctance to cross bridges or their determination to cross into areas of the other can be important markers of how they engage with the landscape of memory. Such a memoryscape necessarily carries the past into the present, where it can be re-engaged with in various ways.

Where and how memory is manifested spatially has a strong influence on how it is politicised and who can access it (Buckley-Zistel and Schäfer, 2014a). For instance, memorial sites may be erected to obtain some recognition, to draw attention to past atrocities and to serve as symbolic reparation. For victims, they become moments of assertion of their rights – rights they were deprived of in the past – giving them back at least some form of agency and dignity. For many, having their voices heard may be of great personal and collective significance. At the same time, these sites may be used for personal, quiet mourning (Viebach, 2014). Their material, style and form may provoke sentiments such as sadness, intimidation, despair or claustrophobia, turning them into places where heritage 'hurts' (Sather-Wagstaff, 2017; see also Mannergren Selimovic, 2020).

Agents: exercising memory politics

Memory politics after war and violence is driven by multiple agents with varying capacity to impact on the memoryscape. Agency is essentially about a person's or a collective's capacity to act, and is thus always about power relations. To exercise agency is to bring about an effect of some sort on the world through one's actions or, in the words of Anthony Giddens (1984: 9), agency is present if an 'individual could, at any phase in a given sequence of conduct, have acted differently. Whatever happened would not have happened if that individual had not intervened'. However, this agency is not exercised in a vacuum but in a spatial and temporal context that can enable and disable agency in various ways (Björkdahl and Mannergren Selimovic, 2016a; Giddens, 1984). Agency is further constructed in a social world that shapes the opportunities and resources available, in a constant interplay of practices and discourses (Ahearn, 2001: 112). We thus locate agency in the intersubjective relations between people and groups, rather than as a possession contained within individuals. To exercise agency is thus to engage in activities that form fields of relationality (Ahearn, 2001: 130; see also Arendt, 1985), involving varying degrees of friction.

Agency is essential for the making of the world that we inhabit. Its construction is mediated by social relations that provide 'a shifting set of possibilities that ha[ve] as much to do with objective realities as subjective and intersubjective understandings of changing conditions and pressures' (Fujii, 2009: 18). These shifting constraints or enabling opportunities are key to understanding agency at different points of time because they condition if and how memory agents can influence the memoryscape. When agents are constrained in their mnemonic agency, their narratives can become silenced and they may be absent from sites deemed meaningful by them. At the same time, though, constraints on agency may shift in time and absences and silences can ultimately be overcome by agents, affecting the structure of the memoryscape accordingly.

Even if not all memory agents' voices are equally heard or perceived, their practices not equally visible or their memories not afforded the same degree of legitimacy, in any memoryscape we can identify a whole host of different agents. They may have considerably diverging levels of power and understandings of the past, but they share an interest in shaping how that past is remembered. The array of different agents participating in memory politics may include politicians, victim associations, museum curators, international peacebuilders, media and tourist entrepreneurs, representatives of the international community and ordinary citizens. These agents may be formal or informal; they may be organised in a coherent, professional manner or they may collaborate in a less official way. Furthermore, while agency is located within social relations, the agents of interest here can be both collective and individual. While individuals can sometimes speak on the behalf of groups and even be endowed with a high level of legitimacy, it often happens that collective agents are able to position themselves more prominently in the memoryscape. We can find both elite or grassroots agents, with the former strongly embedded in state and civil society structures, while the latter can challenge this – for instance by developing a certain agency of resistance through practices of broader social mobilisation.

Agents can be located at a local, national or international level yet transgress these scalar levels (Björkdahl and Kappler, 2019). In any given mnemonic formation global agents – various UN agencies such as UNESCO, as well as peace-building agencies – are frequently present and influential, as memory work becomes increasingly global and transnational.

The international is also represented in a more transient sense by tourists. While tourism entrepreneurs are important in shaping the memoryscape in a way that is economically viable for their businesses, tourists themselves as agents are meaningful above all through their presence or absence at specific sites (Buckley-Zistel and Williams, 2022). The importance afforded to a certain site can legitimise certain narratives over others or expand the agency of particular individuals or groups.

Besides this multitude of memory agents, there are ideas on how agency can have a mnemonic effect beyond human agents, even though any agency attributed to non-humans remains controversial. Most frequently this is discussed with regard to the agency of objects (see, for example, Lindstrøm, 2015, 2017; Ribeiro, 2016; Sørensen, 2016, 2018). Proponents of this idea suggest that materiality can also possess agency, in the sense that objects participate in processes and affect social outcomes and thus one could argue that they are imbued with agency (Feldman, 2014). This is particularly pertinent as objects – like people – have different agentic capacities in differing (cultural) contexts, structuring the relationship between the individual and the object in ways that allow agency to unfold. Others have suggested that the most useful way of thinking about object agency is with respect to their emplacement in biographies (Hoskins, 2006). This is a particularly useful suggestion in the context of this book, as events of remembered violence can be tied to specific parts of an individual's life and associated with specific material objects. The affective personal objects on display in the War Childhood Museum in Sarajevo are a powerful example. However, any rendering of objects possessing their own intentionality is controversial, as it weakens the conceptual clarity of the term agency and its differentiation from concepts such as effect (see Lindstrøm, 2015). This is in line with our approach to the relational nature of agency, as discussed earlier in the chapter. We adhere to the idea that objects are imbued with agency primarily through the mnemonic significance they assume for certain individuals or the meaning they have in social relations.

Agency is by no means fixed over time, but we can see a constant struggle for, and reconstitution of, agency in social relations. Agents participate in an on-going making and remaking of the memoryscape, engaging in memory work both in formal settings and in the everyday. While agency exerted in the construction of a site may be seen as fixed, the everyday work of upholding the meaning of the site, as well as the maintenance of the site, requires agents' on-going commitment (Viebach, 2014). Moreover, the organising of events requires agency, and in the case of recurring events this requires on-going agency so as to allow the memory work to be performed and repeated.

It is in the upholding of such structures and compliance with them, or resistance to them, that the limitations of agency become visible. We recognise the fact that agents are to a lesser or greater degree embedded in relations of power and interdependence (MacLeod, 1992: 533–4). The analyses of agency must therefore also look at its constrained and restricted nature in order to understand when there are limitations on a full exercise of agency; for example, gendered notions of acceptable practice or gendered access to spaces and voice might be inhibitive for women (Björkdahl and Mannergren Selimovic, 2015).

And yet we find that it is important to recognise not only reactive but also proactive agency, which exercises power of initiative. In other words, the 'ability to act in an unexpected fashion or to institute new and unanticipated modes of behaviour' (McNay, 2000: 22) is crucial in understanding possibilities of change. A search for agency and agents in unexpected, ignored or hidden spaces discloses that transformation can take place even if it does not assume overt, organised forms. The creative dimension of agency hints at the shortcomings of the rationalist and determinist notions of agency; it alludes to the expressions of agency that do not reify or reproduce but which instead challenge structures and make something new.

Narratives: making meaning and coherence

Narratives are texts or speech acts that create particular meanings. In addition to spoken or written language, narratives can be communicated through exhibitions, symbols, and other spatial/emplaced and performative expressions. They can be produced and recounted through material objects and through sites, or expressed through commemorative events. They may be visually, sonically and viscerally experienced through performances and artefacts functioning as manifestations that the narrative can be pinned on, such as a bench, a museum photograph, a video recording or the displayed bones referred to earlier in the chapter.

Historical events as well as experiences of everyday life are turned into stories that can be told and retold, yet also changed. Narratives thus 'impose a structure, a compelling reality on what we experience' (Bruner, 2002: 89). Telling a particular narrative in a particular way is constitutive of identities, both individual and collective. These narratives connect the past with the present in that they refer to events and experiences of the past but are told and retold in the present. We thus understand narratives not as a reflection of reality 'out there', but as a meaning-making instrument. To explore memory narratives in the context of the framework we have adopted is to ask what is distinctive about a particular narrative, why it is narrated in this way and not another, and how it helps people make sense of their world. At the same time, we recognise that dominant narratives especially are rarely presented in a pure form. They are mediated, edited, translated and curated (Fernandes, 2017). They must, therefore, not be viewed in isolation from the power structures that produce and promote them (whether those cement a hegemonic or a transformative narrative). Some narratives will gain more traction than others, depending on the power of the narrative agents. Some become more or less ritualised and stabilised in society, while others may be prevalent but tend to be expressed and circulated in the everyday and through informal practices. The state has an unmatched capacity to shape narratives about the past by employing the various tools and resources at its disposal (Wertsch, 2008: 128). It has the power to institutionalise collective narratives through textbooks, statues, museums and other inscriptions in public space. The divided memoryscape of Cyprus is a case in point, demonstrating the power of the state in shaping mnemonic narratives. In Rwanda, moreover, the state has almost exclusive authority over the way the country's past is narrated and the events around the genocide interpreted. Nevertheless, as we also see in the deeply divided societies that we study, other collectives can create their own narrative realms below or parallel to that of the state. In this process, some stories and experiences are deemed irrelevant, shameful or even dangerous, so that they become marginalised and silenced. Denial and revisionism are the most blatant expressions of silencing in post-war societies, but it can also take more subtle expressions. When it comes to remembering victims (with ensuing acknowledgement and reparations), some crimes are given more importance than others. Moreover, even though many victims experience multiple harms, memory work tends to construct narratives that concentrate on select, easily defined crimes while silences grow around other pains. Indeed, sometimes the narrative power of silences can tell us at least as much as public vocalisations (Eastmond and Mannergren Selimovic, 2012; Mannergren Selimovic, 2020). Conflict-related sexual violence, in particular, is a crime often shrouded in silence, for multiple reasons. By being cognisant of narrative silences in memory work we can trace how such forms of marginalisation have consequences for the quality of peace. The degree to which such largely silent narratives are entangled with the wider mnemonic formation is telling for their particular role in the construction of peace.

With respect to the politics of memory, the power of narrative to shape our understanding of the past and of ourselves as a group is well documented (Bell, 2006: 5; Buckley-Zistel, 2014; Hammack and Pilecki, 2012; Wertsch, 2008: 122). Collective mnemonic narratives often aim to uphold boundaries between a collective us and a collective them, and attempt to weave plural and heterogeneous experiences and expectations within a particular group into a coherent story. Individual memories can thus merge into larger cultural and social frameworks that follow some generalised patterns (Wertsch, 2008). In Hannah Arendt's thinking, storytelling is what connects the individual experience to the public sphere at the centre of politics. Individual experiences are 'transformed, deprivatized and deindividualized, as it were, into a shape to fit them for public appearance' (Arendt, 1985: 50). Narratives thus produce certain generalised templates for remembering that bring meaning and coherence as they powerfully narrativise 'the experience of the social category to which the individual belongs' (Richardson cited in Elliott, 2005: 13). Some narratives bring forth commonly used tropes such as the role of victimhood in constructions of guilt/innocence that centre on 'chosen traumas' (Volkan, 1991) – a concept that suggests a group remembers a traumatic event in order to reproduce its collective identity. Another key trope is the idea of 'never again' which, originally coined by Holocaust remembrance, attempts to create narrative moral coherence by drawing a line between an atrocious past and a more peaceful present and future.

Crucially, while collective narratives may provide meaning for some, they are often juxtaposed with competing narratives that have a very different understanding of how to make the past, present and future morally coherent. Negotiations between competing stories are always on-going, as individuals attempt to make sense of and narrate their own experiences of trauma, upheaval and fragmentation. Individuals or collectives without the power to hegemonise the discourse may embrace, resist or transform collective narratives, sometimes (partly) producing and using them, sometimes (partly) rejecting them (Whitebrook, 2001: 10). These other voices may be difficult to hear, and we may have to listen more carefully and be prepared to listen to silences, as some agents who have little power over the collective narratives that dominate may choose silence as a way of navigating through polarised environments. To understand more fully the narrative work of memory politics, it is therefore important not to listen only to the 'privileged story-tellers ... to whom narrative authority ... is granted' (Campbell cited in Milliken, 1999: 236).

Given that narratives bring the past, present and future into a meaningful order, we are interested in detecting how memory work is inherently non-static and constantly evolving. Our case studies therefore look at narrative developments over time. For example, we explore how the narrative of South Africa's collective past has moved from a near-total exclusion of colonialism to a tentative inclusion, uncovering the connections between the country's colonial past and its apartheid era. This temporal dimension of narrative is also evident in the frictions between memories of Sarajevo pertaining to the last war and the present-day city, and how negotiations between these different identities affect the possibilities for a just peace.

Events: performative mnemonic practices

We understand events as meaning-making performative mnemonic practices that forge collective identity. They are not permanent but temporary, even though they might be planned, regular and repeated at particular intervals. They may be rooted in one place – often in relation to a memorial – or may lay claim to wider spaces, as in the case of peace walks or parades. They may be solemn and quiet, as with the reburial of excavated bones, or violent and loud, like a riot. Importantly, these mnemonic practices are assigned significance that is recognised by relevant agent groups. In this book, we are interested in events of remembering and commemorating past atrocities. Importantly, these atrocities can themselves be referred to as events: the event of the Rwandan genocide, the event of the siege of Sarajevo, and so on. We are not examining the remembered event, however; instead, we are interested in remembering as an event. This analysis recognises that events are part of a wider memory structure which they constantly reproduce (Wagner-Pacifici, 2015) yet potentially also challenge. Mnemonic practices only become relevant when they are infused with meaning which they (re-)produce through performance. They may involve some form of embodied practice such as gestures, movements or articulations enacted by an individual or several people, or an installation or art intervention. Events can take the form of parades, ceremonies, public protests and burials, special media broadcasts of a public ceremony, tourist tours, peace marches or national days of commemoration. They may be highly ritualistic or ephemeral and fleeting as people come together for political action. They are visual and may involve the display of flags, coffins and other material objects. Recurring events become rituals – as happens with anniversaries or holidays – that help maintain mnemonic continuity.

The event of remembering is intrinsically linked to a remembered event, as is the case with memory more generally. The event as a performative act therefore 'rehearses and recharges the emotion which gave the initial memory or story embedded in it its sticking power' (Winter, 2010: 12). Atrocities are commemorated in the present to mark their significance and to reinforce particular narratives about this past. In this sense, '[e]ach commemoration focuses on an event and the events are linked into a story whose meaning lies in the whole, rather than in any commemoration (or the historical event commemorated) by itself' (Papadakis, 2003: 253–4). For instance, in Cyprus, Greek Cypriots celebrate Greece's War of Independence from the Ottoman Empire by observing Greek Independence Day on 25 March. Here, a war that began in 1821 is a past event transported into the present by a national holiday.

In memory politics, events are frequently repetitive, as with annual commemorations, lighting candles or laying wreaths, and are embedded in, or borrow from, a long symbolic tradition (which often has its origin in religion). They often have the character of a ritual, including activities that have symbolic meaning and follow certain rules; they circulate around objects of thought and feeling that are of great value to participants (Lukes, 1975: 291). Drawing on shared objects or performances helps to form and sustain deep emotional bonds among those taking part or watching (Etzioni, 2000: 45). These kinds of rituals are therefore a crucial mechanism for the recreation of a collective identity for victim groups, citizens of a nation and the international community. As mnemonic practices, events can be understood as predictable occurrences that build on foreknowledge and previous experience, with the aim of reinforcing certain narratives of collective memory and re-establishing individuals' bond to the group as well as to the narrative (Drozdzewski et al., 2019: 261).

Events also require recognition and participation to be visible in the public sphere. A family member praying quietly at a memorial site receives little attention, yet a head of state visiting the same site and laying a wreath gains a large audience. A lone perpetrator in the Rwandan genocide mumbling softly 'I'm sorry' goes unnoticed, while the pope's visit and public apology for the role of the Catholic Church in the massacres generates headlines. Events as mnemonic practices require an audience for which they are performed, with the audience being part of the meaning-making process.

Many mnemonic events offer the opportunity for participation, mass enrolment and emotional purchase. They are often transmitted by television, radio and social media to reach a wider audience. This participation is important because it 'connect[s] participants together in commemorative moments, and provide[s] a sense of connection to people they imagine have performed or will perform the same ritual in the past or future' (Drozdzewski et al., 2019: 263). There is a strong physical aspect to participating in events that moves beyond their cognitive effect. The intensity of an event experienced through many people coming together, getting excited, feeling powerful, singing songs and chanting declarations strongly affects participants beyond words (Jerne, 2020), again contributing to forging a sense of community based around a particular memory.

Events may serve to maintain the existing memory narrative they reflect, but they may of course also be transformative in how they attempt to challenge dominant mnemonic structures. While memorial events may serve to (re)create a community they might also be used for the opposite purpose: to be divisive and to disrupt the community fabric, to question remembrance in and of itself, or to provide an alternative performance. Similarly to memorials, they are open to (conflicting) interpretations and can be subject to contestation. This is apparent in the case of South Africa, where, after apartheid, the ANC government decided to do away with the old national holidays linked to colonialism or apartheid and instead introduced new public holidays such as Youth Day and Reconciliation Day, with Mandela Day marked as a global observance day.

Events are often organised by elite memory entrepreneurs and are therefore potentially highly effective for the production of hegemonic collective memories. As identity-shaping mnemonic practices, however, they need to be re-enacted time and again, which requires resources. Forms of power, such as access to the media or control over national holidays, are necessary to mobilise larger groups to participate in an event. Nevertheless, other events can take place more spontaneously, as when a piece of art is created or a dance performed, or as with a light spectacle, graffiti or a flash mob. They are then not placed in the *longue durée* of repetitive performances but instead challenge those by breaking out of ritualised structures. This might take the form of competing events that confront the hegemonic role of more recurrent practices.

Events hence have a high potential for mobilising large numbers of people and can therefore become highly political. Such events may trigger conflict as much as they foster expressions of solidarity and belonging. They are often what holds a memory landscape together in terms of serving as a constant reminder of the importance of honouring the dead, keeping memory alive and establishing a sense of unity. At the same time, they can also hinder transformation as they keep performing the past and projecting its assumed significance onto the present.

Sites, agents, narratives, events: productive interactions

In this chapter, we have separately discussed sites, agency, narratives and events as conceptual entry points through which we can investigate mnemonic formations. Again, this can only be done heuristically for analytical purposes, as all four points relate to and constitute each other. The next step is then to demonstrate the dynamic interplay between these four elements.

We view sites as material representations that fix meaning to physical locations and material structures, make the link to the past tangible in the present, pin memory politics to place and underpin a mnemonic formation (see Björkdahl and Buckley-Zistel, 2016; Kappler, 2017; McDowell and Braniff, 2014). Memorials, museums or marked structures are invested with particular meaning by being tied into narratives about past events, present conditions and future aspirations. Such sites are important to memory-making as groups may congeal around them (Halbwachs, 1992: 204), although these groups are never static and are always in flux. Hence, we argue, through social practices of place-making such as commemorative events memory agents make particular sites meaningful for memory, politics and peace.

We also suggest that in any given mnemonic formation an array of memory agents that may be formal, informal, local, national, international, transnational, collective or individual participate in memory politics. Such agency is relational and reconstituted in social interactions. It can be exercised through formal, public actions with political objectives or through fleeting action in the margins of the mundane to uphold or challenge existing power relations. Agents participate in an on-going making and remaking of mnemonic landscapes.

The narratives we focus on are specific articulations of the past that are evoked in memory politics and underpin the mnemonic formations. Such narratives connect the past with the present in that they refer to events and experiences of the past but are told and retold in the present. As such they are constitutive of individual and collective identities, so that they are a meaning-making instrument. There are hierarchies of memory, as narrating memory involves deciding what to remember and what to forget. Some narratives will through this process gain more traction than others.

Finally, we understand events as the performance of memory in a set of enactments using speech, movements and gestures to make reference to past events. They are meaning-making performative mnemonic practices that are part of a wider mnemonic formation. Such events may be ritualistic, or organic and fleeting as people come together for political action, and they are attributed significance recognised by the community. Events may serve to maintain existing memories, but they also have transformative powers.

It is precisely the relational constitution of these four conceptual elements that we are interested in. It is only in an analysis of their interplay that the full complexity of the mnemonic formation becomes visible. The synthesis through the SANE framework is dynamic and allows these elements to be examined for their mutual constitution of each other, as well as for how they may change each other. Ultimately, the application of this framework to the mnemonic formations means that empirical insights from each case can be compared and contrasted, as we do in the final chapter. Based on the analysis of the interplay between sites, agents, narratives and events in each mnemonic formation, and informed by an entangled understanding of memory, the final chapter is where we present our conceptual findings on the impact that politics of memory has on the quality of peace.

2

Cyprus: parallel peace(s) and competing nationalisms

As the past continues to be an integral part of the 'Cyprus problem', Cyprus serves well as a case study through which to explore how mnemonic formations of nationalism can render memory-making an obstacle to peace-making. The traumatic experiences of the 1950s, 1960s and 1970s have left deep scars in the two communities. Memories of national struggles, intercommunal conflict, oppression, the creation of enclaves, a coup d'état, invasion, displacement and loss have become part and parcel of community remembrance. Contested memories of the violent past have also become a foundation for the (re)constitution of the two separate nations of the Greek Cypriot nation and Turkish Cypriot nation and for mnemonic formations of nationalism. From a Greek Cypriot perspective, nationalist memory-making relates to the colonial-era struggle for independence from Britain and a union with Greece as a motherland. For Turkish Cypriots, nationalist memory-making is primarily about obtaining independence from the Greek Cypriots. The competing narratives that each side often employs to tell the history of the island are a means of continuing a mnemonic battle that constitutes a barrier to any lasting resolution of differences (Papadakis, 2005; Papadakis et al., 2006). Although nationalism-inspired memories and recollections of the past predominate in the mnemonic formations, there nevertheless do exist some counter-memories within and beyond the Greek Cypriot and Turkish Cypriot communities that attempt to challenge these hegemonic mnemonic formations. Oral histories and multiple stories as well as individual memories narrated by eyewitnesses, and other grassroots accounts,[1] recall a different past that includes also peaceful everyday practices, co-existence and a shared Cypriot identity, narratives that both complemented and challenged official discourses (Aliefendioğlu and Behçetoğulları, 2019; Briel, 2013; Demetriou, 2012).[2] Some of these counter-memories have, in the context of Cyprus, sometimes been referred to as 'cross-border memory' (Briel, 2013: 34). Thus, two oppositional tendencies can be observed. On the one hand, memory-making in Cyprus is complex, multi-layered and entangled, reflecting a multiplicity of intersectional identities and memories. On the other hand, this process has largely been publicly overridden by a binary process dividing the memories into Greek Cypriot and Turkish Cypriot forms of nationalised memories. Memory politics in Cyprus therefore tends to revolve around the on-going construction and contestation of the two sets of collective identities, collective memories and interpretations of the past. These narratives have to a large extent gained hegemony on both sides, while counter-narratives have been constructed in the margins (Aliefendioğlu and Behçetoğulları, 2019; Hadjipavlou, 2007).

The Cyprus conflict was at its peak before transitional justice became a commonly used tool to address the legacies of conflict. Unlike South Africa, Rwanda, Bosnia-Herzegovina and Cambodia, Cyprus has not been through any transitional justice process. As a consequence, there have been no judicial or non-judicial measures to address past wrongdoings, nor has there been a truth commission or a fact-finding report to search for the truth about the past, and reconciliation and reparations measures have likewise been lacking. According to Bryant (2012: 341), past conflicts and their aftermath have left a trauma or a wound, 'visible in the rupture of partition as well as in politicized personal suffering'; traumas remain unaddressed and victims are left without dignity. Thus, the quality of the present peace can be said to lack notions of justice.

In Cyprus, divisive memory work on both sides represents stumbling blocks in a peace process that seems never-ending. In fact, it is perhaps more appropriate to speak of peace(s) in the plural, as peace is experienced and manifested differently on the two sides of the buffer zone. Many Cypriots seem sufficiently content with the ceasefire, the absence of direct violence and the negative peace that is upheld on the island and do not feel any direct need to push for further peace talks. Thus, memory-making seems inevitably to have an impact on the quality of peace in Cyprus, which suggests that a key realm for negotiating a shared peace on the island of Cyprus will be in the area of the politics of memory. Clearly, the violent past is a divisive issue, and how history is recalled has become a potential tool for the perpetuation of conflict. Yet, if entangled memories are allowed to surface, they may soften or modify the strong mnemonic attachments to the nation.

With the aim of contributing to the research on the interplay between memory-making and peace making in Cyprus, this chapter will map sites, agents, narratives and events and their interactions as they shape the memoryscape of the two post-conflict societies on the island. Through the SANE analysis, this chapter compares and contrasts the Greek Cypriot and the Turkish Cypriot museums and commemoration practices to cast light on how nationalism predominates in the way in which memories are publicly articulated. We also map memory agents who uphold the officially endorsed mnemonic formations and those who challenge them. We review the events where such memory work is performed and the counter-memories that are not represented in the hegemonic mnemonic formations. We find that the competing mnemonic formations of nationalism centre around the two struggles for independence, and it is by looking at these that we can draw wider conclusions regarding how memory politics impacts the quality of peace in Cyprus.

The divisive past of Cyprus

The volatile recent past of Cyprus has divided the society and transformed the island into a frozen conflict sustained by competing nationalisms, divisive historical narratives and a bifurcated memoryscape. The study by Yiannis Papadakis and others (2006: 1) summarises Cyprus's turbulent past in a poignant way: 'Cyprus has experienced anticolonial struggles, postcolonial instability, the divisive effects of opposed ethnic nationalisms, internal violence both between the two major ethnic groups on the island and within each one, war, invasion, territorial division, and multiple population displacements, all facets of the notorious Cyprus Problem.' This violent past has produced traumatic memories and unhealed psychological wounds that affect the present and threaten to colonise future mindsets.

The nationalist struggle turned violent when Greek Cypriot armed combatants formed the National Organisation of Cypriot Fighters (EOKA) in the late 1950s (Papadakis, 2005). EOKA represented a drive for *enosis*, or union with Greece, that was led by Archbishop Makarios on the political front while General Georgios Grivas headed the military organisation. The idea of *enosis* for Cyprus was opposed by the significant Turkish minority, which in 1958 embarked on its own armed struggle, calling for taxim of the island. This struggle was led by the Turkish Resistance Organisation (TMT), a paramilitary organisation created in 1958 by Rauf Denktaş and a Turkish military officer, Rıza Vuruşkan. The TMT's focus was on combating Greek Cypriot attempts to unite the island with Greece, and subsequently on advocating independence for Northern Cyprus as a separate state (Papadakis, 2005). However, the two sides failed in their respective aims which paved the way for the creation of the Republic of Cyprus, headed from 1960 by Archbishop Makarios as president. This represented an end to British colonial rule.

Three years after independence, violence between the Greek Cypriot and the Turkish Cypriot community erupted in Nicosia and spread throughout the island. In the tumultuous years of 1963–1967, the Turkish Cypriot community experienced the brunt of the conflict, enduring a majority of the human toll with casualties and approximately 20 per cent of its population being displaced to refugee camps (Bryant, 2010; Hadjipavlou, 2010; Papadakis, 2005).[3] The interethnic conflict led the British, who still maintained military bases on the island, to create the Green Line, a boundary intended to separate the two communities.

The lines of division deepened in 1974 when the Greek fascist junta, in collaboration with EOKA B, headed by General Grivas, launched a coup d'état to topple the Makarios government (Hadjipavlou, 2010). This event in turn prompted Turkey's military intervention, which resulted in the division of the island as Greek Cypriots fled to the south and Turkish Cypriots subsequently sought security in the north. The Green Line became a de facto border, with a UN-endorsed buffer zone later added to it; few crossings were allowed until restrictions were relaxed in 2003. The Turkish intervention was celebrated as a peace operation by the majority of the Turkish Cypriots, but it was interpreted as an act of aggression and a violation of human rights and international law by many Greek Cypriots (Bryant, 2010; Hadjipavlou, 2010). This time, the Greek Cypriots bore the heaviest casualties, in terms of people killed, missing and displaced. The events of 1974 paved the way for the unilateral declaration of the Turkish Republic of Northern Cyprus (TRNC) in 1983. The TRNC gave the Turkish Cypriots a sense of security in that they finally had a state of their own as well as a place of belonging. For Greek Cypriots, however, the declaration of independence in the north meant that the island was socially, politically, ethnically and spatially divided (Navaro-Yashin, 2012).

After 1974, rapprochement between the two communities became an official Greek Cypriot policy. This policy emphasised the common Cypriot identity and also meant active expressions of goodwill towards Turkish Cypriots in the present, in order to enable the future reunification of Cyprus. This connection between the past, the politics of the present and the future orientation was a result of an official re-evaluation of the past that took place after 1974 on the Greek Cypriot side (Papadakis, 1998: 152). The historical narrative that 'people used to live together peacefully in the past' provides the impetus for the Greek Cypriot demand for a future united Cyprus where everyone would live together peaceably once more (although this position does not specify how power should be shared). The historical narrative also provided a counter narrative to the equally selective official Turkish Cypriot reading of the past as a 'past of animosity and oppression'; that historical narrative implies that 'the two peoples in Cyprus can never live together' (Papadakis, 2003: 261) and suggests continued partition will be necessary in the future (Bryant, 2012).

The United Nations has had a long commitment to the Cyprus peace process. As Cyprus was to enter the European Union, renewed efforts were undertaken by the then Secretary General of the United Nations,

Kofi Annan. After several rounds of talks, a plan for Cyprus reunification, the so-called Annan Plan, was drafted, which proposed the establishment of the United Republic of Cyprus. It was a peace plan for Cyprus based on a bizonal and bi-communal federal structure that included a federal constitution and constitution for each constituent state, federal laws and a suggestion for a national flag and anthem. In the two separate referendums held in 2004, the Turkish Cypriots voted in favour of the plan, but the Greek Cypriots rejected it (Heraklides, 2004; Vassiliou, 2003). The results of the referendums added yet another event to the divisive history of the island and perpetuated the agonistic peace on the island.

As Bryant suggests (2012: 337), 'the Cyprus Problem is a dispute over the future of partition', but 'it is necessarily also one over how the island came to be partitioned in the first place'. Thus, the on-going conflict 'requires a constant mobilization of memory, and rejection of the present state of partition makes it impossible to "put the past behind us" ' (Bryant, 2012: 337). Today, many Turkish Cypriots argue that the legacy of the past legitimises the continued division of the island, while many Greek Cypriots, on the other hand, claim that this past legitimises the striving for reunification of the island.

The Cyprus memoryscape

The memoryscape shows Cyprus as a divided island captured in history, and the landscape is scattered with mnemonic traces of its violent past used as political tools in the continued production of the conflict. Abandoned cities, museums, monuments of heroes, colossal statues and flags are dedicated not only to the memory of what are regarded as heroic struggles, but also to the traumas and tragedies that have befallen the Cypriot people.

There are monuments that materialise the memories related to the Greek Cypriot struggle for independence from Britain (1955–1959) and *enosis* and the Turkish struggle for *taksim* and the military invasion of Cyprus in 1974, as well as to the two declarations of independence: for an independent Cyprus and for an independent TRNC. Most prominent in the memoryscape is perhaps the sealed-off city of Varosha, a suburb of the city of Famagusta located in the north of the island. It has been held by the Turkish military since the Turkish military invasion, and it is a testament to the division of the island. Previously, Famagusta was a tourist destination inhabited by both Greek and Turkish Cypriots. The Turkish invasion changed this and the Greek Cypriots fled in fear to escape the violence. Today, the city is known as a ghost town (Björkdahl and Kappler, 2017: 37–40) and it has become a dismal legacy of the Turkish military intervention.

The memoryscape is shaped not only by material legacy but also by narratives of the past. One of the most divisive elements in the Cyprus conflict is the writing of the island's history, a history invoked by both communities to justify and explain their politics in the present (Bryant, 2012; Bryant and Papadakis, 2012; Papadakis, 1993, 1994, 1998; Toumazis, 2014). The divisive memory work and the partition of memory in Cyprus have been thoroughly researched and well documented (Bryant, 2012; Bryant and Hatay, 2019; Papadakis, 2003). For example, Bryant (2012) explores the role of remembering and forgetting in maintaining a partition line that divides the island into the Greek Cypriot south and the Turkish Cypriot north. Her research further demonstrates that former spaces of interaction have been transformed into sites of past violence and that such spaces are marked by the absence of groups who once lived there. The partition line is also a legacy of the colonial past. Constantinou and Richmond's investigation of the continuities and discontinuities of British rule in Cyprus highlights the partition line and underlines the diffusion of colonial power post-independence while discussing the tensions faced by the competing narratives and practices of post-colonial emancipation (Constantinou and Richmond, 2005). Also concerned with the bifurcated memoryscape, Papadakis (2003) maps the commemoration events that divide Cyprus, both across the partition line, but also within each community, while Bryant and Hatay (2019) reveal that commemoration practices and events wax and wane over time.

Constantinou et al.'s (2012) examination of the politics of cultural heritage within the two communities and across the ethnic divide clearly demonstrates what is at stake in terms of who belongs, whose heritage is to be preserved and whose is to be demolished. Traces of the shared past and memories were destroyed through everyday acts such as occupying houses left by Greek Cypriots, as well as through demolishing cultural heritage sites (Constantinou et al., 2012; Hadjipavlou, 2007). The destruction of material heritage tainted by having belonged to 'the other' was part of the intimate and emplaced violence of the conflict, and its traces are still visible in voids, empty spaces and ruins in the mnemonic landscape. As argued by Constantinou et al. (2012: 178), it is 'quite common to see vandalized and ruined Greek Cypriot cemeteries, churches and houses in the north, and similarly to see destroyed Turkish-Cypriot cemeteries, mosques and villages in the south'. Such actions against cultural heritage help to promote exclusionary meanings to history as well as exclusionary ownership of the past (see Bryant, 2010).

Thus, the memoryscape of Cyprus has become bifurcated but also fragmented. Julie Scott (2002: 228) suggests that 'casting the history of Cyprus as the history of the Greek/Turkish Cypriot national struggle presents problems of narrativity on both sides'. These 'problems of narrativity' are derived from a lack of nuances and selective representations of the past reproducing moral categories of good and evil primarily attached to the competing nationalisms underlying the Cypriot conflict (Toumazis, 2014). Thus, there is a strong dominance of a binary set of narratives as they pertain to either the Greek Cypriot or the Turkish Cypriot community, respectively. The results are two very different consolidated mnemonic formations that are the foundation for the politics of memory to control the past in order to maintain power in the present (see Barahona de Brito et al., 2001: 38). Yet, it is also fragmented. There are cracks in the mnemonic formations of nationalism as counter-narratives absent in the official hegemonic narratives are present in the margins.

Prominent anthropologists like Yiannis Papadakis have mapped and analysed the partitioned memoryscape of nationalism. Papadakis's study of the two museums of national struggle in Nicosia is an excellent example of the selection and relationality of nationalist narratives presented and the material representations that reflect these narratives (Papadakis, 1994, 1998). His study is paralleled by an analysis by Toumazis (2014) of museum exhibitions in Greece and Turkey dedicated to displaying the Cyprus problem. The empirical analysis of this chapter builds on, develops and updates the important research on museums that display competing nationalist narratives, and on the mapping of commemorations in Cyprus, that has been carried out by Papadakis and Toumazis, while connecting it theoretically to the analysis of sites, agents, narratives and events as they reflect processes of memory-making and state-making in Cyprus.

Mnemonic formations: competing nationalisms

To understand the competing mnemonic formations of nationalism in Cyprus we need to explore the island's recent past starting from when Britain assumed control over Cyprus in the late nineteenth century after three centuries of Ottoman rule. The British colonial administrators began to distinguish between the Turkish and the Greek Cypriots and treated the communities according to their ethnicity – a social stratification that had previously not been salient on the island – a practice that strengthened the growing division, and created fear and suspicion between the two communities (Apeyitou, 2003). Greek Cypriot nationalism was expressed in the narrative of *enosis*, a will to unite with Greece, justified by the argument that the Greek Cypriots and Greeks of Greece were culturally one and formed one nation and thus one state. The Turkish Cypriots, as a reaction to the Greek Cypriot idea of *enosis*, struggled for *taksim*, the partition of the island (Bryant, 2010). Both *enosis* and *taksim* reveal extreme or 'blatant' nationalisms (Billig, 1995: 43). This type of nationalism is related to the idea of the nation-state and a collective ethnic identity that is based on a shared past and emplaced geographically. Neither side opened up for a pluralistic memoryscape (Feindt et al., 2014: 32). There are two dominant ways of remembering, one connected with *enosis* and one with *taksim*; this risks silencing marginalised voices in each society, as often happens where memory politics is heavily dominated by a hegemonic actor, such as the state, and where 'memory has been narrowed through hegemonic closure' (Feindt et al., 2014: 32). Thus, memory work recalling the past is important on both sides of the divide in a country where nostalgia has become a patriotic and nationalistic duty. Yet, the mnemonic formations of Turkism (referring to a shared Turkish identity and closeness to Turkey) and Hellenism (referring to a shared Greek identity and closeness to Greece) are not uncontested (see Papadakis, 2003: 265) as each society reveals its own tensions. Thus, memory politics is linked to contemporary politics and is contested not only across the buffer zone but also within each of the two communities.

The mnemonic formations of nationalism shape a narrative aimed at fostering nation-building, designed for consumption by one's own faction. This narrative is actively promoted by the states involved and influential memory agents. In the subsequent analysis, the SANE framework, encompassing sites, agents, narratives and events, serves as a guide to explore the mnemonic formations of Cyprus's contrasting nationalisms. Additionally, it delves into counter-memories that challenge the dominant mnemonic structures, thus highlighting the complexities within the national narrative.

Sites: museums of national struggles

Museums representing the state are sites that can produce social ensembles of agents, narratives and events to present the foundational myth of the state. The museums of national struggle in Cyprus have therefore been sites of national representation. They inevitably refer to collective identities, the nation, nationalism, as well as the myth of the origins of the state and the becoming of the state (Papadakis, 1994: 400). They are similar to traditional war museums in the sense that they are part of the state propaganda, represent the state's historical narrative and, as such, participate in processes of memorialising past conflicts. The museums refer to material representation in which artefacts bring something absent to the fore. These museums can be seen as 'mnemonic signifiers' as they refer to 'socially relevant figurations of memory' (Feindt et al., 2014: 31). They freeze the conflict in time and space, Pozzi (2013: 10) remarks. The two museums focus on the legacy of the two national struggles for independence – the Greek Cypriot struggle for independence from British rule and reunification with Greece, and the Turkish Cypriot struggle for Northern Cyprus to be independent from the south of the island. They demonstrate that a conflictual cultural heritage may transcend pure historicity. The two museums of national struggle on either side of the buffer zone in Nicosia certainly fail to engage with counterhegemonic narratives of the past. As we shall see, they do not unsettle the hegemonic narrative of nationalism and do not provide space for multiple voices. Other museums, however, display a more complex, historical narrative that may challenge the hegemonic nationalist ones at the museums of national struggles.

The Greek Cypriot Museum of National Struggle

The Greek Cypriot Museum of National Struggle was founded to reflect the Greek Cypriots' struggle for independence from British colonial rule and to commemorate the EOKA fighters who fought and lost their lives during that conflict.[4] According to its own publications, the museum is also to serve 'as an inspiration to future generations with regards to the duty to participate in liberation struggles' (Karyos, 2013).[5]

The museum is located in the square near the Archbishopric (the Greek Cypriot ecclesiastical centre) and parts of the museum are located on premises owned by the latter.[6] It displays documents, photographic material and some personal belongings of leading figures of the struggle, as well as other memorabilia related to the period. At its entrance, the aim of that struggle is defined as that of *enosis*. In prominent display are the volumes from the 1921 and 1950 referendums, when Greek Cypriots voted in favour of unification with Greece. Nationalist leaders Archbishop Makarios and General Grivas feature prominently in the museum's displays, alongside the EOKA fighters. The EOKA oath sworn by all the EOKA fighters is also introduced. At the centre of one of the exhibition halls is a replica of a hideout, as an illustration of how brave EOKA fighters in the island's Troodos Mountains were able to use surrounding vegetation as camouflage.[7]

The focus on the violent deaths of combatants denies visitors the opportunity to learn about their individual lives and collective actions. In a sense, it conditions visitors to view the soldiers as victims or heroes throughout the exhibition. On display are collections of personal belongings, mostly clothes, books and guns that belonged to dead fighters. Exhibiting emblematic photographs of violent deaths is aimed at triggering nationalistic emotions among local visitors and empathy with the Greek Cypriots among international visitors (Toumazis, 2017). The armed combatants are portrayed as 'protectors of the nation, heroes and finally as martyrs and icons after their deaths' (Toumazis, 2017: 84). The exaggeration of stereotypical male

Figure 2.1 Sign at the Greek Cypriot Museum of National Struggle (photograph by Annika Björkdahl, February 2020)

behaviour, with an emphasis on physical strength, aggression and heterosexuality, demonstrates a hypermasculinity that is closely connected to the performance of war and the ultimate sacrifice for the cause. It silences other forms of masculinity that exist in parallel and suggests that masculinities are fixed rather than fluid.[8] Moreover, it teaches young schoolboys who are taken to the museums as part of their history curriculum a toxic masculinity that is scarcely conducive to inclusion and empathy with 'the other', or reconciliation and a respect for human dignity.[9]

In the exhibition space, symbols connected to ancient Greece and Orthodox Christianity, such as the sacred lamp, candles or the photos on the wall of the dead, honour the men that died in the struggle against the British. The structure of the museum space and its curation lead the visitor down a path to a room with a replica of a gallows. This is, as pointed out by Papadakis (1994: 402), 'the most emotionally charged room in the museum'. Accompanied by letters written by EOKA fighters executed by the British, with some portraits, it is a powerful symbolic statement of nationalism.[10]

Certain absences and presences are interesting to analyse in this space. Although the British are narrated as the enemy, few photos actually portray British soldiers or other representations of colonial power. Instead, the British presence comes to the fore through their actions, that is, the destruction of property, evictions and killings. While the Turkish Cypriots, or Turks as they are referred to in the museum, are given less attention and space than those of the British, the way in which they are represented in the museum as British collaborators is significant. As Yiannis Papadakis so poignantly points out, the British are 'symbolically represented as "soldiers" who "kill", while the "Turks" are represented as "barbarians" who "slaughter"' (Papadakis, 1994: 406). Such representations shun nuances and subtleties and reinforce the other as a historical nemesis.

The Turkish Cypriot Museum of National Struggle

Let us now turn to the Turkish Cypriot Museum of National Struggle; built in 1978 on the Venetian Walls of Nicosia, just east of Kyrenia Gate, it is located next to a Turkish Cypriot army camp. Its declared purpose is to commemorate and educate about the struggles undertaken by Turkish Cypriots from 1878 to the present day.[11] It is organised in chronological order, with different spaces assigned to different periods. The exhibition has a documentary character and uses mostly two-dimensional material such as newspaper articles, documents, books, posters, photographs and maps. A limited number of three-dimensional objects, such as guns and other firearms as well as personal belongings, are on display as the museum presents visitors with a tightly curated narrative.[12]

The first section of the museum covers the period 1878–1955. The year 1878, when the British took over the island, is generally considered to be the start of the Turkish Cypriot struggle. However, very little information is on display from that period. The second exhibition space covers the period

Figure 2.2 Sign outside the Turkish Cypriot Museum of National Struggle: 'How happy is the one who says he is a Turk' (photograph by Annika Björkdahl, February 2020)

1955–1974. There, much emphasis is placed on the Turkish Cypriot trauma, tragedy and killings at the hands of the Greek Cypriots and the honoured heroes and martyrs among the TMT fighters. In contrast to the Greek Cypriot museum the British colonial power is basically absent, which stands in contrast to the prominent presence of the Greek Cypriots. The exhibition closes with the end of the struggle, that is, the declaration of independence on 15 November 1983 and the establishment of the Turkish Republic of Northern Cyprus, as well as the military intervention by Turkey in 1974. These are important events highlighted through photos, documents and written statements.

Nationalist ideas are clearly reflected in the ways in which events are selected and represented, for example through an emphasis on massacres, but also in the choice of themes to remember traumas and struggle, that is, with an emphasis on overcoming a strong enemy (Papadakis, 1994). The brave TMT fighters are in the spotlight as the heroes of the permanent exhibition and there are several stories of individual heroism by the fighters. The soldiers killed in struggle are referred to as martyrs, and the names of the fallen soldiers are listed on a stone wall that visitors pass as they leave the exhibition. Unlike many contemporary museums of war around the world, the exhibition that weaves together the artefacts on display at the Turkish Cypriot museum does not attempt to restore the human dimensions of the soldiers or to emphasise their vulnerability.

Similar to the Greek Cypriot museum, the Turkish Cypriot museum also mirrors the nationalistic sentiments of its motherland. While both the north and the south of Cyprus have their respective flags, these flags are conspicuously absent within the museums; instead, the museums prominently display the flags of Greece and Turkey. In the Museum of National Struggle in the north, symbols, representations and narratives of the past clearly express continuity with the Ottoman past and identification with Turkey and the Turkish nation. When the museum was inaugurated, it also reflected ambitions in Turkey at that time to modernise and westernise the Turkish state. The content of its displays has an anti-religious character that reflects secularising aspirations at the time of its inauguration. This content has not changed, despite the increased Islamisation of Turkey's politics under Recip Erdoğan as president. The secularism and absence of religious symbols contrast with the presence of such symbolism in the Greek Cypriot museum. The fact that the Turkish Cypriot museum is situated adjacent to an army camp and the Greek Cypriot one is located just next to the Archbishopric also reflects this (Papadakis, 1994: 404).

Women are strikingly absent from the exhibitions and the nationalist narratives in the two museums. Nationalism often tends to portray women as vulnerable, as mothers of the nation, as widows or as grieving victims. Yet here women are denied even this type of presence. Only a brief recognition of women is accorded in the Turkish Cypriot Museum of National Struggle, through a photo of a few women in uniform fighting in the TMT ranks. In the Greek Cypriot museum, a bullet that killed one of the very few female EOKA fighters, Loukia Papageorgiou, is on display.[13] Other women activists are forgotten, one such being EOKA member Androula Kouspetri, whose code name was Agamemnon. Kouspetri was a messenger and organiser who also undertook traditional care work for EOKA. Her importance in the struggle is recognised in a collection of personal short stories by EOKA fighter Renos Lyssiotis (2016), as the woman behind the idea of having a donkey surrender to the British – an incident captured in a photo that appeared on the front page of all the newspapers. Although the photo showing the donkey surrendering is given prominence in the exhibition, Kouspetri is not mentioned by name in the text that explains the item.

Both museums focus on the experiences of individual soldiers, the trauma and sacrifices of the civilians, and the heroic struggle against a stronger enemy. The museums also act as memorials for the soldiers who lost their lives in battle. Museums like these are clearly institutions that care for and conserve the past through the careful curation of selected mnemonic narratives. The two museums are little inclined to serve as spaces to explore potentially divisive issues within their respective communities or to openly criticise the Greek Cypriot state or the de facto Turkish Cypriot state. They do not provide space for counter-memories. Thus, these two museums hold in place the memory of past struggles and trauma and exhibit the nationalism that persists in Cyprus, which represents an obstacle to efforts to move towards the unification of the island and a durable peace.

Alternative sites for alternative memories

Other museum spaces, such as the Nicosia Municipal Arts Centre, present contemporary art projects that at times engage with and destabilise these mnemonic formations by exhibiting work from both sides of the Green Line. In February 2020 a temporary exhibition at the Ledra Palace Hotel in the buffer zone, a building which had been the UN peacekeepers' base until 2019, included works by Greek Cypriot artists that had been left behind in the north as a result of the Turkish invasion. After being exhibited the works were to be returned to their former Greek Cypriot owners.[14] In this context it is worth highlighting a two-part documentary film entitled *Parallel Trips* by Cypriot directors Panikos Chrysanthou and Derwis Zaim, which is intended to give a voice to survivors of the 1974 Turkish invasion of Cyprus. It addresses issues of the interconnectedness of such complex processes of remembering, and how these are mobilised as symbolic resources in political manoeuvres (see Briel, 2008, 2013). It is an example of how independent initiatives and creative activities outside the curated official institutions of memory and history may contribute to opening up spaces for voices and memories not currently acknowledged within the dominant mnemonic formation.

Figure 2.3 The Nicosia Municipal Arts Centre (NiMAC) (photograph by Annika Björkdahl, February 2020)

Agents: selective memory-making

Memory agents are actively involved in a discerning process of making memories, converting specific individual memories into collective ones. Simultaneously, they endeavor to translate these collective memories into political narratives. These agents wield significant influence, possessing the capability to mold, modify and solidify political memories to serve specific objectives. As frequently emphasised, agency is intrinsically tied to power dynamics. The exercise of agency is either enabled or disabled by the prevailing material and immaterial structures (Ahearn, 2001: 112; Giddens, 1984). As we will see in this section, memory agents have rarely been inclined to explore issues that are potentially divisive within their own communities or to openly criticise the state through these museums as venues.

Memory agents in the south

Memory agents uphold the mnemonic formation of Greek Cypriot nationalism, but this is not necessarily a homogenous group as past and present memory politics showcase. Papadakis (2003) has pointed out that there is left–right dimension in memory politics in Cyprus. Since the events of 1974, Greek Cypriot politics has been sharply divided between the left and the right in the south of the island. Within the Greek Cypriot community, the two dominant parties, the left-wing party the Progressive Party of Working People (AKEL) and the right-wing party Democratic Rally (DISY), each read the history of the island through different lenses. They also present different narratives of a complex past and hold different views of the future. The mnemonic formation of nationalism is largely challenged by the political left, including AKEL, and by the bi-communal movement, a citizen-led reconciliation movement (Papadakis, 2003) that provides a space for counter-memory work. The right is closely connected with EOKA and tends to be the party of choice for EOKA veterans (Papadakis, 2003). The exclusionary mnemonic formation of nationalism is mainly upheld by the political right including the DISY, associations of former EOKA members, the Archbishopric of Cyprus, as well as associations of displaced Greek Cypriots. However, over time DISY has changed its politics from being a staunch supporter of a Hellenic Cyprus to being the only party that openly campaigned for the Annan Plan in 2004 (Yakinthou, 2012: 237).

The left and the right consequently also have different views on the importance and role of the Museum of National Struggle, which is sometimes also dubbed the EOKA museum. Among agents on the right of the spectrum is the Association of EOKA Fighters, which makes its contribution to keeping memories of the struggle alive by organising and taking part in anniversary events, often side by side with DISY. The association is one of the main stakeholders influencing the Museum of National Struggle, as its members provide the objects, letters, photographs and narratives on display there. The former curators of the museum have all been EOKA members and have seen their main task as being to protect the memory of the fallen heroes and commemorate their struggle.[15] The association therefore continues to be an important pillar of the mnemonic formation of nationalism in the south and exerts the strongest influence over the narrative communicated by the museum's permanent exhibition. Moreover, the Archbishopric of Cyprus, which owns parts of the museum premises, has indirect influence over the museum. The Cypriot Orthodox Church has for some years engaged in memory work on its own account to consolidate collective memories of past suffering and to uphold the hegemonic nationalist narrative. Government institutions, such as the education ministry through its Cultural Department and Cultural Services, are important stakeholders in the Greek Cypriot Museum of National Struggle. The ministry funds the museum, and the funding has been maintained irrespective of whether a left-wing or a right-wing political party is in power.[16]

Memory agents in the north

Turkish Cypriot memory agents have been key to making memory out of the suffering of their community. Similarly to what happens in the south, the nationalist memory politics is produced mainly by right-wing politics, the former TMT fighters' association, the army and of course the strong influence of Turkey. The Democratic Party (DP) and the National Unity Party (UBP) constitute the dominant right-wing political force in the north, collectively securing a substantial majority of the electoral support (Papadakis, 2003). The political right narrates the history of Cyprus as one of Greek expansionism, beginning under the Ottoman Empire, continuing with the persecution of Turkish Cypriots in Cyprus and culminating in the 1974 coup d'état aimed at the annexation of Cyprus to Greece, which provoked Turkey to intervene. Thus, it is the Turkish Cypriot right that is promoting its own nationalist reading of history, drawing on the mnemonic formation of Turkism, which in a way mirrors the historical narrative of Hellenism adopted by the Greek Cypriot right (Papadakis, 2003: 264). There is a prevailing sentiment among the political right that the eventual establishment of the TRNC represented a triumphant outcome after a protracted period of struggle, and there seems to be a determination to persist in advancing this cause. This form of nationalism and othering may appear old-fashioned and out of step with the times, yet the representations of the Turkish Cypriots' suffering are visible at the museums and at the crossings where you enter the buffer zones, and not just to the casual visitor but also to those who do not agree with this interpretation of the past. This materialisation of memory also contributes to freezing the past and perpetuating the conflict.

The Turkish Cypriot left, including the largest left-leaning party the Republican Turkish Party (CTP), the smaller Communal Liberation Party (TKP), trade unions and activists in the bi-communal movement, as well as individual academics within the Turkish Cypriot community, have attempted to provide alternative histories of the past, contesting the nationalist narrative (Papadakis, 2003: 263). However, those who challenged the hegemonic narrative, expressing criticism of Turkey or sympathy towards the Greek Cypriots, were labelled as traitors ungrateful to Turkey.[17] Despite these harsh circumstances, the bi-communal movement continues to bring to the fore memories, testimonies and voices that provide recollections of the past where peaceful co-existence between the two communities was not uncommon, and that challenge the dominant nationalistic one.

The mnemonic formations of nationalism have proved difficult to challenge, contest or dismantle, even for those in political power. The election of two left-wing candidates – Demetris Christofias of AKEL as president of Cyprus in 2008 and Mehmet Ali Talat of the socialist Republican Turkish Party (CTP) as leader of Northern Cyprus in 2005 – was seen as a significant break with the past. The leaders were regarded as a clean slate who had no previous relationship with, respectively, EOKA or the TMT, nor with the Greek Cypriot or Turkish Cypriot nationalist movements (Yakinthou, 2012: 234). Although in power at the same time and sharing some views about the future of the island, both leaders were trapped in the hegemonic nationalist mnemonic formations and were unable to challenge the nationalist narratives that permeated politics and society in the north and south of the island.

Memory agents in the margins

Civil society actors have occasionally tried to destabilise the mnemonic formations of nationalism, whether in cooperation across the divide or separately. The bi-communal movement has been most effective in encouraging different readings of the past and promoting alternative understandings of the Cyprus problem. Bi-communal activists, along with academics, are often unacknowledged memory agents whose work gives voice to silenced and forgotten memories. Examples of such memory work that challenges hegemonic nationalist narratives are two major initiatives: *The Life Stories Project* by Olga Demetriou and Rebecca Bryant and the oral history project entitled *Completing the Incomplete History of the Turkish Cypriot Community: Portraits Drawn through the Narratives of Women*. Through such projects memory agents focus on reconciliation through remembrance and by doing so interrupt official history with unofficial histories. In some ways, these memories have all found a way into the public memory-making. Moreover, the Association for Historical Dialogue and Research (AHDR) has been at the forefront in trying, through education and by supporting revisions of history curricula and textbooks, to provide a less nationalist version of history.[18] The AHDR is developing the Cyprus Critical History Archives as a unique digital resource containing digitised and catalogued Greek Cypriot and Turkish Cypriot newspaper articles on intercommunal relations and conflict-related violence during the 1955–1964 period, providing different perspectives on specific events so as to better understand the complexities of the Cyprus conflict (CCHA Website).[19]

Memory work by members of minority communities in the north and in the south reveals cracks in the hegemonic mnemonic formations of nationalism. One example is the Armenian–Cypriot writer Nora Nadjarian (2006), whose poetry attests to the fractured memories of the Armenian diaspora in Cyprus, a community whose memories and past have been marginalised by the hegemonic formations of nationalism on the island. As Nora Nadjarian claims, 'memories are not an amorphous mass, they are not experienced equally by their subjects and they always represent what has been called "inherited labour"' (Stoler, 2006 cited in Briel, 2013: 33).

Often missing from memory politics are women's recollections of the past. Collected micro-narratives of displaced women in the north and in the south contribute both to upholding the mnemonic formations of nationalism and to revealing cracks in the hegemonic metanarrative. The narratives and memories of Turkish Cypriot women who had lived much of their lives in the mixed villages of Cyprus, and had experienced displacement or segregation as a consequence of conflict, hardly mentioned any hostility or antagonism between them and their Greek neighbours until the mid-1950s. Instead, they recalled helping each other with domestic duties, childcare and farming (Aliefendioğlu and Behçetoğulları, 2019: 1480; see Hadjipavlou, 2007, 2010). When the crossings opened in 2003, new experiences with 'the other' brought the past to the present, and helped to reinterpret the past in the light of new experiences (Hadjipavlou, 2007: 60). Greek Cypriot women who crossed the Green Line to see their homes and villages returned with reconstructed memories, experiences, stories and feelings.[20] Hadjipavlou (2007: 61) cites a Greek Cypriot family who visited their old home in the north after almost thirty years and were sad to find that a Turkish settler family from Turkey had been given their house. 'The people who now live in our house are very nice. They kept these photographs of my family and some valuables, like embroideries, and have now given them to us. I wonder if they knew that one day we shall return' (Hadjipavlou, 2007: 61).

Figure 2.4 Graffiti by the Green Line (photograph by Annika Björkdahl, February 2020)

Other marginalised voices in memory-making are youth on both sides of the divide. In interviews with Turkish Cypriot youth, they recognised that nationalism shaped everyday lives in the TRNC. For example, they went on school excursions to the Turkish Cypriot National Museum of Struggle and to the smaller Turkish Cypriot Museum of Barbarism as part of the history curriculum, and they revealed that they felt uncomfortable when they visited these museums. Similar sentiments were found among Greek Cypriot pupils and their parents visiting the Greek Cypriot Museum of National Struggle.[21] Many young voices have been at the forefront challenging the mnemonic formations of nationalism in the north and in the south, calling for a more nuanced form of remembrance.[22] In their view, 'putting the past behind us' should include acknowledging the suffering on both sides and moving towards the future. Although these micro-narratives can contribute to challenging the binary of 'us' and 'them', it has proven difficult to acknowledge and incorporate minorities, youth and women's narrated memories and experiences in the nationalist meta-narratives.

Narratives: nationalist stories

Struggle is a prominent feature in the official nationalist mnemonic narrative of the recent history of Cyprus. While the island was under British colonial rule, both Greek and Turkish nationalist ideologies gained ground. The national struggle-narratives play a significant role in commemoration and state-building as they have political purchase in the present. There is a nationalist narrative highlighting the Greek Cypriot struggle to unite the island with Greece and the Turkish Cypriot narrative of partition of the island.

Greek Cypriot nationalist narratives

The emergence of nationalisms in Cyprus is a consequence of a range of processes, including the nineteenth-century Greek War of Independence from the Ottoman Empire, modernisation and an emerging Greek national consciousness that impacted on traditional Cypriot society. The development of a Greek national consciousness and identity, and the emergence of a nationalist middle class among the Greek Cypriots, led to the formation of two ethnic communities of Greek and Turkish Cypriots (Kizilyürek, 2002).

The hegemonic historical narrative that reinforces nationalism refers to the Turks and the British as foreign rulers of Cyprus. The narrative indicates that the island was Greek from the fourteenth century BC. In this narrative, Cypriot clearly means Greek, while the 'Turks' and the British are regarded as foreign conquerors (Papadakis, 1994). This implies that the Turkish Cypriots do not share the collective Cypriot identity and are thus not proper Cypriots, but newcomers to the island. The nationalist narrative constructs a symbolic divide between Cypriots, meaning Greek Cypriots and the Turkish Cypriots. However, when rapprochement developed, the notion of a common Cypriotness was revisited and the memories renarrated to also include memories of peaceful co-existence. For a long time, Greek Cypriots suppressed and silenced stories of Turkish Cypriots' actions during the 1974 war, and portrayed the Turkish Cypriots as having likewise been victims of the Turkish army (Bryant, 2012). According to Bryant, this was, in turn, part of a forgetting of the violence perpetrated by Greek Cypriots against the Turkish Cypriots between 1963 and 1974, and served to undermine suggestions that the acts of Turkish Cypriots in 1974 might have been motivated by a desire for vengeance. The knowledge that there had been intercommunal conflict between Greek and Turkish Cypriots did not challenge the narrative of 'peaceful coexistence' between the two communities in the official Greek Cypriot narrative (Bryant, 2012).

The Turkish Cypriot nationalist narratives

Turkish Cypriot nationalism can be understood as a response and a reaction to Greek Cypriot nationalism and was thus conditioned by it. Identifying with the island's Ottoman past, this nationalism developed into a monolithic national force, partitionist in nature, and became increasingly uncompromising and militant as a consequence of the violent conflict of the 1950s and 1960s (Apeyitou, 2003). The hegemonic nationalist narrative depicts the history of Cyprus to begin under the Ottoman Empire, then challenged by Greek expansionism, continuing with the persecution of Turkish Cypriots in Cyprus and culminating in the 1974 coup d'état aimed at the annexation of Cyprus to Greece, which provoked Turkey to intervene. Thus, Turkey and the Turkish Cypriot political elite were fully committed to the idea of *taksim* or partition. A Turkish Cypriot nationalist cited in Apeyitou (2003: 89) observed that the new generation of nationalists changed the slogan from 'Cyprus is Turkish' to 'partition or death'. Thus, nationalism was firmly established in the north as well. As Turkish settlers immigrated from Anatolia, Turkey, bringing a different more rural, religious culture to the island, the Turkish Cypriot narrative changed slightly to emphasise the difference between the Turkish from Turkey and the Turkish Cypriots. At the same time, the government in Turkey led by the AK Party provided funding to build new mosques in the TRNC to strengthen the connection with Islam and contemporary Turkey. This development was perceived by many Greek Cypriots as a 'Turkification process', and by leftist Turkish Cypriots as a process of Islamization of secular Turkish Cypriots endangering Atatürk's historical secularisation reforms (Constantinou et al., 2012). Such tensions within the nationalist narrative demonstrate the multi-layered and contested dimension of nationalism.

Silences in the nationalist narratives

The many absences and silences in the historical narratives amount to the marginalisation of certain actors and their narratives by the mnemonic formations of nationalism and their dominant nationalistic narratives. Among these are memories of Cyprus's minority communities, of Turkish migrants to the TRNC, of migrant workers and refugees. All these voices are silent. Needless to say, both museums deny the existence of any bi-communal Cypriot nationalism, or Cypriotism, a nationalism that highlights the shared Cypriot culture, heritage or economic, political and social rights. Contemporary tools and strategies of information and communication technologies, which would allow for interactive practices and multiple perspectives, and assist visitors 'in the construction of the museum's narratives' as well as to 'accommodate conflicting voices' are typically absent (Bull et al., 2019).

Events: political commemoration of nationalist anniversaries

Nationalism is not only narrated or on display at the museums but is also performed at a number of commemorative events organised by the political elites on either side of the divide. Such events are meaning-making, performative, mnemonic practices that aim to forge collective identities. The political divisions evident in Cyprus are often related to the commemorations of the past and political memory, and commemorations remain an important ritual in a context of nationalism. Commemorative events attain their significance when integrated into a narrative that articulates a certain history (Papadakis, 2003: 253–4). The Greek and the Turkish Cypriots' commemorations continue to feed antagonism between the two communities. These nationalist commemorative events are, however, not cohesive and unchallenged, nor are they always bought into by their target audiences.

A closer investigation of the commemorative events in the north and in the south reveals that the two communities are less homogenous and cohesive than they might at first appear. Yiannis Papadakis's (2003) comparative analysis reveals a distinct left–right division within both communities, in addition to the north–south divide. In a sense, the commemorative events are not merely reflections of the two exclusive nationalisms that run through the communities on either side of the divide.

Greek Cypriot commemoration practices

The Greek Cypriots have a tradition of observing Greek Independence Day on 25 March, the date the Greek War of Independence from the Ottoman Empire began (Katsourides, 2017). The date is an official national holiday in

Greece and in Cyprus, and is observed in the Greek Cypriot south. This commemorative event has, however, over time come to be mostly associated with the right-wing DISY (Papadakis, 2003). The right also independently organises a highly controversial commemoration of the 1974 death of General Grivas on 27 January each year.[23] These commemorative dates are performative events that reproduce annually a combination of a will for independence and *enosis* (Papadakis, 2003: 257). Thus, the right aims to unite Cyprus's ritual commemorations and national anniversaries with the commemorative calendar of Greece. One nationalist anniversary celebrated by both the right and the left in Cyprus (as well as throughout Greece) is *Okhi* Day ('No' Day) on 28 October, commemorating the 1940 event when Greece refused to bow to an ultimatum from the fascist regime of Italy during the Second World War. In the southern part of Cyprus, this date is also used to express protest against the Turkish invasion of 1974. The date is also commemorated by the Greek and the Greek Cypriot diaspora around the world, and one can find parades and festivities in major cities in the United States, Canada and Australia. This meaning-making event is a nationalist performance where some political parties connect the historic event to present-day politics in Cyprus (Andreou, 2020). Since 1960, 1 October has been a public holiday in Cyprus, as the anniversary of the independence from Britain after the EOKA struggle of 1955–1959. This day sees the most important commemoration event organised by the Greek Cypriot left, although the mnemonic practices of Independence Day parades are a performance of Greek Cypriot nationalism by the military. Instead of a display of Greek flags, however, the Republic of Cyprus flag features prominently. This commemoration therefore revisits and re-evaluates Cypriot history, challenging nationalistic narratives of the past to provide a positive view of a shared future. After 1974, the left began to organise an event series called 'Ten-day Event for Rapprochement' to commemorate the time of peaceful co-existence, promoting goodwill against the Turkish Cypriots in support of the idea of reunification of Cyprus (Papadakis, 2003: 261). In contrast to the controversial commemoration of General Grivas's death, the left, AKEL and the United Democratic Youth Organisation (EDON) organise an annual commemoration of Archbishop Makarios, honouring also the Resistance Fighters for Democratic Associations who fought against the EOKA B in the 1974 coup. This event, which takes place on 19 January, is intended to counter the commemoration of the death of Grivas organised by the right. All in all, the commemorations organised by AKEL provide a different historical narrative of Cyprus's recent history, challenging the nationalist, right-wing narrative. The left-wing narrative puts the blame for the Cyprus conflict on the two motherlands, Greece and Turkey. Still, most of these Greek Cypriot commemorative events are clearly offensive to the Turkish Cypriot community (Papadakis, 2003).

Turkish Cypriot commemoration practices

The Turkish Cypriots' commemoration events are also highly nationalistic, although it is clear that the Turkish Cypriot community is not as cohesive as is often presented; here too, as in the south, there is a left–right dividing line. Many commemorative events are connected with and coincide with similar events in Turkey. The Turkish Cypriot right devotes one week in July to celebrating thanksgiving to Turkey and on 20 July marks the celebration of peace and freedom (Yakinthou, 2009). In the south, this date is a significant day of mourning. Three different historical events are commemorated on 1 August: the 'Birth of the TMT', 'Foundation of Our Security Forces' and the 'Conquest of Cyprus' (Papadakis, 2003: 264). At these commemorations official politicians from the political right are present, there is much right-wing rhetoric and flag-waving and the controversial symbol of the Grey Wolf, which stands for Pan-Turkism, is used, as the events are organised by the government, the security forces and the TMT fighters' associations (Papadakis, 2003: 264). Thus, the competing nationalisms are performed in parallel, in a sense reinforcing each other. Another day of celebration in the north is Republic Day on 15 November, when events are organised by the right-wing parties, the Northern Cyprus government and the TMT fighters' organisation to commemorate the declaration of the independence of that territory and the creation of the TRNC in 1983. Throughout the north of Cyprus, celebrations of this day frequently involve air displays and military parades, with a gun salute fired (Yakinthou, 2009). They are often attended by the leader of Northern Cyprus, foreign diplomats and journalists, and are a clear illustration of how official public events commemorating a national struggle may be instrumentalised to reinforce the mnemonic formation of nationalism. The 15 November date is meanwhile marked by protests in the south (Yakinthou, 2009).

As the left-wing parties in the north have not exercised political power at government level, they have had little influence on the commemorative calendar and its annual anniversaries. While left-wing politicians take part reluctantly in some commemorative events, they do not tend to organise them. Turkish Cypriots leaning to the left often find that these events raise tensions between the two communities, creating animosity towards Greek Cypriots and limiting the possibilities of finding a durable and just peace.

On 21 December both the Turkish Cypriot left and right commemorate the Bloody Christmas of 1963, an event that ignited interethnic fighting, and those who died during the violence of 1963–1974. The Turkish Cypriot slogan 'We Won't Forget' is used during this commemoration. This event urges the Turkish Cypriots not to forget the sacrifices of their martyrs, the brutality of the Greek Cypriot enemy and the purported constant threat from this enemy. It is jointly organised by the TMT fighters' associations, the right-wing parties and the TRNC government, with some participation from leftists. Without exception, these days are characterised by nationalism and militarism, with political elites opting to attend, demonstrating solidarity with their community and cause (Papadakis, 2003: 264).

We cannot, however, assume that public commemorations are accepted by all in a society and that no contestation or challenge is presented to the nationalist narratives and commemorative events. It should not be assumed that the state's intentions come to be endorsed by the public at large. In fact, during some of the commemoration events celebrated in the north many Turkish Cypriots use the day off work to cross to the south to go shopping, for instance, thus demonstrating that these politically instrumentalised commemoration events do not necessarily resonate widely.[24] Similarly, in the south, many of the official commemorative events attract limited attention and are widely ignored, although not necessarily actively opposed.[25]

The SANE analysis: memory and the quality of peace

Where hegemonic mnemonic formations of nationalism disguise contestation, agonistic narration, competing voices and alternative pasts, they may prove to be an obstacle to a just and durable peace. Cyprus provides a clear example of this. The bifurcated peace or peace(s) that we observe on the island is in part a production of struggles around what to remember and what to forget, as the two dominant communities continue to stake their claims for power based on ethno-nationalist and divisive politics. On the surface, the quality of the Cypriot peace(s) may seem sufficient in terms of manifesting as an absence of violent conflict; the ceasefire is still in place despite occasional challenges to it. The Turkish Cypriot peace and the Greek Cypriot peace may co-exist on the island, but there is no shared peace and there is no agreed vision for the future of the island and its communities. The peace(s) we can observe has emerged from competing imaginaries of the past, whereas the mnemonic formations of nationalism continue to dominate the peace in the present. As manifested through sites, agents, narratives and events, these mnemonic formations tend to serve as a tool of state propaganda. They combine nationalistic, religious and political memory in a mix that can be regarded as antagonistic memory.

The nationalist interpretations of the two national struggles provided the points of departure for this analysis of the mnemonic formations of nationalism produced by the two respective state actors and demonstrate the absence of counter-narratives. As sites, the museums of national struggle function in a way that inscribes a sense of stability around received information on what happened in the past and the meanings of that information. In that sense, the museums become a means of inscribing time upon space, while stabilising the associated narrative. Through material inscriptions of the past at these museums the two dominant nationalist narratives find expression. At each site they remain uncontested and pass unchallenged. The representation of the two independence struggles in the museums has the potential to arouse affective reactions and strong emotions, even after several decades.

Neither the sites emplacing the hegemonic nationalist narrative nor the conventional memory agents and nationalist commemorative events emphasise the suffering of all victims on both sides of the buffer zone, or the shared experiences of fighters on the two sides, nor do the exhibitions at the museums convey for visitors an anti-war message or a peace message. The memories on display at the museums, and the narratives into which they are woven, support a toxic nationalism that tends to apply moral terms to specific roles and characters, in the form of heroes and enemies. Thus, it is fair to say that the mnemonic formations of nationalism in place in Cyprus are obstacles to reconciliation. They are divisive, self-absorbing and exclusive. They function as obstacles to peace-building and raise concerns as to the quality of the peace. The sites, agents, narratives and events that are the cornerstone of the mnemonic formations of the two competing nationalisms perpetuate a divided, ethnic peace(s) at the expense of a potential to construct a shared, just peace. The analysis supports Aliefendioğlu and Behçetoğulları's (2019: 1474) argument that 'the negative collective remembering fed by nationalism(s) of two communities maintains the unresolved situation of not being reconciled and intensifies the in-betweenness and uncertainty on the island'.

Despite the dominance of the mnemonic formations of nationalism, there are sites, agents, narratives and events that reference a different past and attempt to remember a past that is otherwise often actively forgotten. Indeed, memory work by left-wing political parties, academics, civil society, trade unions and women's organisations have tried to construct counter-memories by focusing on the shared past and the loss of still missing persons. These counter-memories are nevertheless often depicted as self-contained, despite circumstances that suggest intricate interconnections with each other and with the mnemonic formations of nationalism.

When we investigate the Greek Cypriot collective memory and unpack the narratives and commemorations of the past, we can actually observe three interwoven yet different narratives promoted by different memory entrepreneurs. One set of narrated memories may be seen to romanticise the past by highlighting the peaceful co-existence between Greek and Turkish Cypriots said to have prevailed previously. Memory work along these lines may, nevertheless, contribute to bringing to the fore positive community relations, which in turn may be supportive of peace-building activities to construct a shared peace. This understanding of the past is in part supported, promoted and performed by the bi-communal movement of Cyprus. A second set of memory work connects with nostalgia. It captures Greek Cypriot memories of their lives in the north and their desire to return to their former homes. Such nostalgia, as the visits to the other side have revealed, may create disappointments, contributing to upholding exclusionary practices that perpetuate processes of othering the Turkish Cypriots. When nostalgia can be turned into a constructive force for peace, co-existence and cohesion, it may contribute to peace-building. A third Greek Cypriot narrative, also absent from the mnemonic formations of nationalism, captures the more recent past of the referendum on the Annan Plan, Cyprus's membership of the European Union, and the acceptance of the separation and of building a Cypriot state on half of the island (Bryant, 2012). This parallel and contemporary narrative connects with a peace that only reflects the absence of conflict and with the existing status quo where the buffer zone functions as an international border. These memories are clearly entangled within the Greek Cypriot community, but tend not to be entangled in the same way in the Turkish Cypriot remembrance of the past.

Moving on to examining the Turkish Cypriot practices of remembrance and forgetting, we can discern three narratives that destabilise the mnemonic formation of nationalism. The first is a narrative that recalls a horrific past, highlighting insecurity, vulnerability and the marginalisation of the Turkish Cypriots in previous decades. This is the pillar of the mnemonic formation of nationalism as supporting *taksim* (partition) and the sovereignty of the TRNC. Similarly to the Greek Cypriot narrative of nostalgia, a second, less dominant Turkish Cypriot narrative highlights the Turkish Cypriots' aspiration to return to their lost homes in the south. This narrative may have been gaining strength with the increased influx of people from Turkey, so-called settlers, with political developments in Turkey and with Turkey's growing influence in the TRNC. This has made some Turkish Cypriots recall the past in terms of nostalgic recollections of co-existence, of Cypriotness and a former collective Cypriot identity, as well as of a shared island rather than agonism and division (Bryant, 2012). A third Turkish Cypriot narrative is similar to its contemporary Greek Cypriot equivalent and accepts the partition, conveying a sense of pride in the TRNC. These mirroring narratives uphold the current negative peace on the island, a peace that is divided and has ethnicity as its basis. In this sense, nostalgia may facilitate the envisioning of a future peace built on shared experiences as refugees, shared experiences of oppression, as well as of individuals' experiences of personal autonomy, dignity and mutual respect.

Both the Greek Cypriot and the Turkish Cypriot mnemonic formations of nationalism comprise memories that are narrated, emplaced at sites and performed at events commemorating the past. In both cases, there are various memory agents that in different ways make efforts mainly to stabilise, but at times to destabilise, the dominant mnemonic formations. The mnemonic formations of nationalism clearly do not overlap in Cyprus and, as this analysis has demonstrated, memory work is bifurcated and lacks a genuine entangledness of memory entrepreneurs, memory work and remembering. The counter-mnemonic activities challenging nationalist recollections of the past may unsettle the otherwise settled mnemonic formation of nationalism. However, at this point in time these do not seem sufficiently interconnected or dynamic to contribute to reconciliation and peace-building and thus to a quality peace.

Conclusions

As explored in the Introduction, history and memory are more concerned with the future than the past, and history is constantly reinvented to legitimise claims to power in the present. It is in this context that we can read the competing disentangled singular mnemonic formations of nationalism and their representations. The bifurcation of the memoryscape in Cyprus demonstrates a kind of homogeneity within each of the commemorating communities and privileges tangible manifestations of memory, such as the museums. At the same time, however, individual acts of remembering or seeking out the past help to explore what lies underneath the seeming homogeneity within the two communities.

The Greek Cypriot and the Turkish Cypriot nationalisms have shaped sites of memory, the narratives presented and the artefacts on display, and they have shaped the work of the agents of memory. The representations at the museums of national struggle reflect and enhance nationalist ideologies; both display violent and traumatic events. The museographic representations used in their spaces, as examined in this chapter, aim through various practices to incite visitors' potentially nationalist emotions, not least through their focus on traumatic memory and the aesthetisation of death. Such sentiments rest not only on nostalgia for the past – its fictionalisation – they also rely on a perpetrator/victim dichotomy and the victimisation of one side against the other. The exhibitions function principally on an emotional level to incite nationalist sentiments, which at the same time produces polarisation and alienation.

The SANE analysis of the mnemonic formations of nationalism thus makes visible the difficulty of an entity that is as historically heterogeneous as Cyprus to serve as a proper singular subject of collective identity and shared political memory. Whereas the hegemonic narratives, performed commemorations and memory agents underpinning the mnemonic formations aim to represent the correct singular history of the island, they more accurately represent the history of two nations and two respective state entities. Both mnemonic formations show the tragic and often denied aspect of state-making, that is, the massacres, atrocities and ethnic cleansing that were part of the two national struggles for independence. Hence, there are competing understandings of what counts as the struggle for independence. The mapping of the memory agents of Cyprus reveals how such mnemonic agency is present across scale and is fluid and frictional as well as trans-scalar, stretching from the individual to local communities, national and transnational politics and diaspora communities. Some of the everyday, mundane memory work takes place under the radar and goes unquestioned, for example through school visits to the museums of national struggle. Other memory work is more high profile, such as when the respective authorities encourage visiting dignitaries and foreign correspondents to visit their museums of national struggle. What is made visible is that memory politics on both sides of the island is hegemonic, lacks acknowledgement of the other and is stuck in the state framework – a reflection of how memory-making is closely connected to state-making.

In an effort to gender the history of Greek and Turkish Cypriots and provide alternative histories to respond to the officially engrained masculinised versions of nationalism, researchers have collected and curated women's memories of the past. Although these individual memories are not necessarily divorced from collective remembrance, and are often a mixture of official and informal histories, at times they also make visible a different past. It emerges as a past in which women as neighbours shared the everyday in a casual, carefree way, and it provides a more nuanced version of a past that is shaped by a variety of intersectional identities. Thus, gendering the past helps advance the plurality of memory, and the memories of the everyday may also contribute to the entangledness of memories.

In summary, the partition of the island has led to the memory of the 'other' becoming disentangled from 'our' memory, and this has been turned into a political strategy. The bifurcation of memory does not reflect a plurality of memory in the sense of entangled memories. Rather, the Greek Cypriot and the Turkish Cypriot memories are portrayed through a tunnel vision of the past, where the influence of, and entanglements with, the other's collective memories are marginalised. Memory in Cyprus is dominant and hegemonic, and state-centric political memories evidently enhance separateness, revealing a lack of acknowledgement, plurality and inclusivity. Such selective, politically motivated cultures of remembering the war are an impediment to meaningful dialogue across a divided Cyprus. Today, memory-making does not contribute in any meaningful way to peace-making in Cyprus. This is mainly due to the fact that memory production is divisive and memories are compartmentalised between the two communities rather than entangled.

Notes

1 In 2009–2012, the Cypriot Oral History project aimed to add its voice(s) to the cultural conversations taking place across the island of Cyprus by making them publicly accessible. The Turkish-initiated oral history project entitled *Completing the Incomplete History of the Turkish Cypriot Community: Portraits Drawn through the Narratives of Women*, at the Eastern Mediterranean University, also contributed to this effort.

2 Today, the issue of mixed villages is one of the thorniest and most contested in Cypriot history and perhaps the only mixed village today, Pyla/Pile, is often used (and abused) in contemporary politics. Only very few Turkish Cypriots live on the Greek side of the island, and vice versa.

3 At the time, the Greek community comprised 80 per cent of the island's population, while the Turkish represented only 18 per cent.

4 Interview, curator, Nicosia, February 2020.

5 The museum was founded after the end of the 1955–1959 national liberation struggle by EOKA fighter Christodoulos Papachrysostomou, among others.

6 The museum was initially housed at 25 Hera Street in Nicosia, in a building donated by Zenonas Sozos. Its inauguration ceremony there, on 1 April 1962, coincided with the annual commemoration of the start of the EOKA campaign in 1955. The cost of refurbishing the museum in 2001 was covered by the Archbishopric of Cyprus, the Cyprus education and culture ministry, and a grant from Anastasios Leventis, a Greek Cypriot businessman and philanthropist. Interview, curator, Nicosia, February 2020.

7 Fieldnotes, Nicosia, February 2020.

8 Fieldnotes, Nicosia, February 2020.

9 Interview, peace activist, Nicosia, February 2020.

10 Fieldnotes, Nicosia, February 2020.

11 Interview, curator, Nicosia, January 2019.

12 Fieldnotes, Nicosia, January 2019.

13 Interview, curator, Nicosia, February 2020.

14 Interview, director, Nicosia, February 2020.

15 Interview, curator, Nicosia, February 2020.

16 Interview, director at the Cultural Department and Cultural Services, Nicosia, February 2020.

17 Interview, scholar and bi-communal activist, Nicosia, February 2020.

18 Interview, civil society representative 1, Nicosia, February 2020.
19 Interview, civil society representative 2, Nicosia, February 2020.
20 Interview, peace activist, Nicosia, January 2019.
21 Interview, peace activist, Nicosia, January 2019.
22 Interview, civil society representative, Nicosia, February 2020.
23 Interview, peace activist, Nicosia, January 2019.
24 Interview, scholar and bi-communal activist, Nicosia, February 2020.
25 Interview, civil society representative 2, Nicosia, February 2020.

3

Bosnia and Herzegovina: remembering the siege of Sarajevo

The siege of Sarajevo began in April 1992 and lasted for 1,425 days, making it the longest siege in European history. Intensive shelling and sniper fire over that time killed more than ten thousand inhabitants and left the Bosnian capital largely in ruins. This chapter analyses commemoration of the siege as a key site for memory politics and one that has wider implications for the quality of peace in Bosnia and Herzegovina. After nearly three decades of uneasy peace, Bosnian society is defined by unresolved tensions and a deeply divisive political climate centred around incompatible narratives as to who was a victim and who was a perpetrator. The memorialisations of many of the gravest atrocities of the war, such as the genocide in Srebrenica, tend to feed into such dichotomies. In many ways the memory politics of Bosnia and Herzegovina follows the same logic as that of Cyprus, with separatist understandings of the past serving to maintain divisions in the present. However, the mnemonic formation of the siege of Sarajevo is relatively unsettled; the several contestations of the dominant ethno-nationalist understanding of peace that have emerged there make it a very interesting case to study for the purposes of this book.

As outlined in the Introduction, a mnemonic formation is a topic of particular salience around which sites, agents, narratives and events gather. Analysing the mnemonic formation of the siege renders visible frictional lines and contentions, and thus deepens our understanding of how these shifting dynamics bring with them possibilities for transformation. This chapter shows that elite institutions and political agents use commemoration of the siege as a means for exclusionist nation-building through efforts to 're-remember' the siege through a militaristic, ethno-nationalist lens that focuses on dichotomous positionalities of 'us' as victims and the 'others' as perpetrators. Nevertheless, the mnemonic formation is by no means stable, as memory activists have resisted the ethno-nationalist rhetoric. Independent curators, artists, tourism entrepreneurs and other agents have produced narratives about the resilience shown by civilians and their defence of multiethnic values and practices. They argue that the siege was an attack on universal values of humanity, and they insist on telling everyday stories of what it was like to live through the daily danger and hunger of those years.

This focus on the siege as the topic under analysis highlights a particular phenomenon of warfare and its concomitant memorialisation, namely urbicide. Urbicide is a particular form of political violence that seeks to destroy urbanity, defined as conditions that enable heterogeneity as an existential quality of life (Coward, 2008). Urbicide entails the destruction of urbanity through, for example, targeting the public buildings and spaces that make such heterogeneity possible. Urbicide is not only, or even foremost, an attack on material infrastructure in a defined territory; it is above all an attack on the social texture and human plurality generated through people interacting in a shared urban space (Folin and Porfyriou, 2020). The civilian lived experience of urbicide is thus anchored in the mundane realm, a realm that may not so easily lend itself to formalised commemoration with single-focus messages. This chapter understands the siege of 1992–1996 as having been a form of urbicide, and examines how the dignity of survivors can be recognised through mnemonic activities and sites that encompass the entanglement of multiple memories of tangible and intangible losses caused by this particular form of violence. A focus on the mnemonic formation of the siege of Sarajevo thus brings insights that are clearly of relevance as we investigate what a just peace entails.

The Bosnian war and post-war challenges

When the Socialist Federal Republic of Yugoslavia collapsed in the early 1990s, it set off a wave of extreme violence and warfare across its constituent republics. These wars were driven by leaders and elites who embraced aggressive ideologies with the aim of creating ethnically homogenous, independent states. Their politics were embraced by large parts of the population, which often had both economic grievances and memories of previous violence based on ethnic and religious differences during the Second World War. That earlier violence had been followed by decades of enforced silences that prevented discussion of it. The aggressive political moves by leaders and elites had devastating consequences across much of the territory of the former Yugoslavia, with the war in the Republic of Bosnia and Herzegovina at the epicentre of violence. The war there broke out following a referendum on 29 February 1992 to decide whether the new republic should declare independence or not. The result, in favour of independence, was rejected by the Bosnian Serbs who instead supported the idea of a ‘Greater Serbia’. The Bosnian Serbs, led by Radovan Karadžić and supported by the Serbian government of Slobodan Milošević and the Yugoslav People’s Army, mobilised their forces and began fighting against the newly formed Bosnian army. The war soon spread across the country; eventually fighting would also break out between Bosnian forces and Bosnian Croat forces – whose leadership likewise envisioned a 'homeland' for their own community (Donia, 2006; Malcolm, 1996).

In terms of demographics, Bosnia and Herzegovina is made up of people from various ethnic and religious backgrounds, a factor that has had a strong influence over its identity and history. Within Yugoslavia, it was designated a federal unit, as Bosnia-Herzegovina, and no one group had an absolute majority. Its population was a multi-ethnic mix, with (Bosnian Muslim) Bosniaks as the largest group, followed by Orthodox Serbs and Catholic Croats (Moll, 2015a).[1] It therefore represented 'a contradiction of the logic of nationalism' (Bringa, 1995: 33). The ethno-nationalist war, on the other hand, sought to separate out ethnic groups and create ethnic homogeneity within designated territories (Donia, 2006: 290). Horrific methods were used to pursue this vision. At least 100,000 people were killed and over 2.2 million displaced (Tokača, 2012) in a war of massive destruction. Civilians were targeted in a drive to 'cleanse' villages and towns of those deemed undesirable. People were killed and forced to flee, thousands of women were raped in camps set up for that purpose, tens of thousands of men and women were kept in detention camps where they underwent torture (including sexual violence), towns were shelled and besieged for months and years, and more than 70 per cent of all private homes were destroyed, as well as a very large part of the cultural heritage and infrastructure (e.g. Bassiouni, 1994; Donia, 2006; Stiglmayer, 1994). In the final months of the war, the country became the site for the first genocide on European soil since the Holocaust. The ad hoc UN tribunal set up for addressing war crimes, the International Criminal Tribunal of Former Yugoslavia, would later rule that genocide had been committed in and around the town of Srebrenica, with more than eight thousand men and boys killed and executed in a matter of a few days. The key figures of Bosnian Serb leader Karadžić and Bosnian Serb army leader Ratko Mladić were sentenced for genocide, as well as for crimes against humanity for the siege of Sarajevo and other deeds.[2]

The atrocities in Srebrenica led to an intervention by NATO and following its targeted bombing of the Bosnian Serb Army, the fighting stopped (Holbrooke, 1998). A US-brokered peace agreement, known as the Dayton Peace Agreement (DPA), was signed in December 1995. It confirmed the ethnically based lines that resulted from the war and a complex system was created for consociational power-sharing between the constituent groups in order for peace to be accepted by all parties. The DPA thus divided the country, to be formally known as the State of Bosnia and Herzegovina, into two semi-autonomous entities: the Republika Srpska, which is dominated by Bosnian Serbs, and the Federation of Bosnia and Herzegovina, which is subdivided into ten cantons and is dominated by Bosniaks and Bosnian Croats.[3] In addition, the city of Brčko is a self-governing district. There is a system of ethnic checks and balances in place within all political organisations and even beyond. The presidency of the country is three-headed and must include a Bosniak, a Bosnian Serb and a Bosnian Croat.[4]

The construction of peace is thus built upon the same logic of ethnic divisionism as the war, and the ethno-political centrifugal powers of the war are continued by other means, as ethno-nationalist agents benefit from a political framework that emphasises the protection of group interests and identities (Bose, 2002; Donia, 2006). For example, the Bosnian Serb member of the tripartite presidency, Milorad Dodik, has repeatedly blocked the formation of a central government and his outspoken goal is full independence for Republika Srpska.[5] Further, the process of addressing war crimes is slow and partial; nearly ten thousand people are still missing and mass graves continue to be found with some frequency (Dzaferovic, 2021). The economic situation is dire and the social fabric has been irrefutably changed by the large displacements of people through so-called ethnic cleansing (Kondylis, 2010). The political situation is further complicated by the fact that the country is still under partial international control, as the massive international peace intervention included both a military and a civilian component. The Office of the High Representative for Bosnia and Herzegovina (OHR), an ad hoc diplomatic body created under the DPA and in line with UN resolutions, is in charge of overseeing the implementation of civilian aspects of the accords. The OHR has extensive powers and can impose laws if the legislative bodies of the country refuse to do so in breach of the agreement.[6]

Bosnia and Herzegovina is thus in the present day a fragmented and divided society, and this is strongly in evidence in its politics of memory. The country and its inhabitants are split between several conflicting stories of the past and there is little agreement as to who was a perpetrator and who was a victim, what actually happened or why.

The Bosnian memoryscape

Bosnian memory politics has been the subject of several studies that discuss how its fractured nature is a result of the mass killings and forced transfers of population as well as the subsequent ethnic reorganisation of the country (Bădescu et al., 2021; Božić, 2017). One factor often stressed in explaining the persistence of divisions is the fact that the state-level administration of the reconstituted Bosnia and Herzegovina is more or less absent from the field of cultural heritage, leading to a construction of memory and identity 'within a particular and potentially exclusivist perspective', as noted by Stevens and Musi (2015: 67). Legislative decisions about monuments and memorials are taken at the local political and administrative level, which means that the memoryscape is spatially defined as 'part of *renationalization policies* … focusing on dividing memories, values and practices' (Dragićević Šešić cited in Musi, 2021: 56, emphasis in original). While earlier studies of Bosnian everyday life pointed to the dangers of a 'reduction of Bosnian realities to its ethnic dimensions' (Bougarel et al, 2007: 13), decades of excluding memory politics have in fact reified simplified stories of the past. Opposing narratives exist side by side in this small state, upheld by mnemonic cycles that celebrate different commemorative days, using different flags. Streets are renamed to celebrate military heroes, figures regarded by others as war criminals, and schools teach three different curricula (Moll, 2015a). The genocide in Srebrenica has understandably attracted a lot of scholarly interest, including around what role the commemoration of the genocide in Srebrenica plays in contemporary Bosnia and Herzegovina and beyond (e.g. Duijzings, 2007; Fridman, 2022; Jacobs, 2017; Nettelfield and Wagner, 2014). It is the most visible commemorative event in the country, with tens of thousands of people taking part every year, travelling to the burial site in Potočari outside Srebrenica, which is located in Republika Srpska. In Republika Srpska, in contrast, the genocide is actively denied and, for example, high schools and streets have been named after the imprisoned war criminals Karadžić and Mladić, who are serving life sentences for the genocide.[7]

Overall, the victimhood narrative is very strong on all sides and mnemonic claims about victim exclusivity are made by all (Barkan and Bećirbašić, 2015; see Demirel, 2023). No politician in power in Bosnia and Herzegovina has worked actively for reconciliation, and there has been no truth commission beyond important but still limited civil society initiatives (Moll, 2015a; Touquet and Vermeersch, 2016).

Further, research on Bosnian memory politics points to a temporal fracturing of memory in addition to the spatial fracturing of memory. Temporal fracturing is brought about by the fact that generations remember differently, as the older generation was born into socialist Yugoslavia and can experience a disconnect with younger generations who know little about that period (Maćek, 2018; Palmberger, 2016). Young people coming of age today have no personal memories of the war of the 1990s, and many in the generation that lived through it keep silent about their experiences, often motivated by a desire to 'protect the young'. Stories of a multi-ethnic past tend to be downplayed in the face of increasingly homogenised ethno-nationalist collective identities (Eastmond and Mannergren Selimovic, 2012).

In contrast, as will be discussed, a number of mnemonic activities do challenge such spatial and temporal breaks. So, while the centrifugal powers tending towards division remain strong, the upholding of ethno-nationalist memory spheres is nevertheless a contingent and unstable undertaking. The dichotomy between us as victims and them as perpetrators is destabilised through social relations that continue across space and time, as many people continue to navigate and be part of webs of relations that cross ethnic boundaries. The multiple layers of Bosnian society – including class, rural–urban identities and gender to name but a few – mean that moral categories often do not follow ethno-nationalist logic (Bougarel et al., 2007: 2). While the war left a legacy of major demographic changes, interrelational practices across ethnic boundaries are still in evidence in Sarajevo, where the urban fabric of the capital city has been woven through centuries of religious and ethnic interaction.

Mnemonic formation: the siege of Sarajevo

Surrounded by steep, green hills, the silhouette of Sarajevo reflects a history shaped by the Ottoman Empire, the Austro-Hungarian Empire, two world wars and a socialist state. The cityscape includes mosques, synagogues, Serb-Orthodox churches and Catholic churches. Elegantly decorated Ottoman bazaars nestle next to grand, nineteenth-century buildings that evoke the Austro-Hungarian period, while vast concrete housing estates are evidence of the more recent socialist past. No wonder that the city has captured the imagination of people across the world, and that many Sarajevans themselves have related to this multi-cultural heritage as a matter of pride, expressing a deep sense of identity as *Sariljelje* (Stefansson, 2007). When the war broke out, this identity would come under vicious attack. The Bosnian war had just begun in April 1992 when the Yugoslav National Army and Bosnian Serb forces belonging to the newly proclaimed Republika Srpska initiated a blockade that would last for four years. The mixed urbanscape of about 400,000 inhabitants was transformed into a giant prison. Several hundred mortar shells a day were fired from the green hills surrounding the city (Bassiouni, 1994). People were shot at every day, living under terror of snipers and shelling. People engaged in mundane practices were 'moving targets' (Ristic, 2018: 51) as streets, tram stops, schoolyards and markets became danger zones. The insides of homes were not safe either as bullets and shrapnel tore through living rooms. UNICEF estimated that of the approximately 70,000 children living in the city during the period nearly half had been shot at and had witnessed one or more family members killed, and nearly all had spent time in underground shelters. In addition to the approximately 10,000 people killed, an additional 56,000 people were wounded, including nearly 15,000 children (Bassiouni, 1994).

Throughout the siege there was a desperate shortage of food and Sarajevo residents relied on humanitarian aid mainly delivered through (insufficient) airlifts by the UN High Commission for Refugees (UNHCR). People went out foraging for weeds and snails to eat. The trees in the parks were felled to be used for heating and cooking. Getting water meant queuing for hours at pumps, in grave danger of being shot at (FAMA, 1993; Maček, 2009). One of the harshest aspects of siege life was the rupture of communications with the outer world as telecommunications and the postal system broke down, and many survivors have testified to the feeling of 'living in a cage'. In the words of Jasenko Selimović, a writer who lived through the first year of the siege, the aim of the aggressors was not to take over the city; the point was to humiliate people and make them lose their dignity (Selimović, 2020). In response, the city's inhabitants displayed resilience and ingenuity in protesting the urbicide. Cultural expressions symbolically transmitted the pain, as for example when the musician Vedran Smailović played Albinoni's 'Adagio in G Minor' in the ruined National Library and during burials in makeshift graveyards.[8] The images of 'the cellist of Sarajevo' have become emblematic for their insistence on human dignity in the face of violence. The attackers also targeted the city's cultural and social memories in their material form. Some of the buildings that represented the city's key institutions were destroyed, including the National and University Library Vijećnica, whose library of 1.5 million volumes was burnt to ashes (today the renovated building is used as City Hall), the Houses of Parliament and the building of the city's main newspaper, *Oslobodjenje*. Overall, it is estimated that about a third of all buildings were damaged or destroyed (Bassiouni, 1994). This violence against physical architecture and infrastructure, public spaces, streets and squares had both symbolic and material consequences for the sense of urbanity (Maćek, 2018).

When the siege officially ended on 6 January 1996, large parts of Sarajevo were in ruins and it had gone through some dramatic population shifts. In addition to the thousands of refugees who had fled the city, most of Sarajevo's Serbs had left for the newly formed entity of Republika Srpska. The dividing line between Republika Srpska and the Federation of Bosnia and Herzegovina was drawn through greater Sarajevo, with the semi-rural municipalities on the city's eastern periphery designated 'Serb Sarajevo'. Nowadays this area is known as East Sarajevo and, with its own municipal structure, no longer looks to Sarajevo administratively. Many people born in East Sarajevo since the siege have never visited Sarajevo itself and have been brought up with a school curriculum that does not acknowledge the siege; memorial events celebrating Bosnian Serb leaders and victims are held regularly in East Sarajevo, in a mirrored, opposing reflection of the commemorations held in the city itself (e.g. Bădescu, 2015; Jansen, 2013). However, the particular memory politics of this area will not be discussed in this chapter, as the geographical area of East Sarajevo never came under siege.

Overall, Sarajevo emerged from the war as a far more segregated and politicised post-war space; it was now a contested, divided city with changed demographics. Its present spatial division influences people's actions as they navigate their way through the city, whether upholding or attempting to transform segregation (Jansen, 2013; Kappler, 2017; see Björkdahl and Kappler, 2017: 93). The war in many ways feels distant in present-day Sarajevo, with its lively café terraces and office buildings of blue-tinted glass, but material remnants from the siege are ever-present. The tell-tale signs of extreme violence include ruined buildings that have yet to be rebuilt, apartment houses chipped by bullets or mortar shells, and gaping holes in the cityscape where a building once stood. There are also the makeshift cemeteries of the war years, when parks became burial grounds, and here and there in the residential areas one comes across the word *sklonište*, 'shelter', painted on a building. More subtly, material remnants still circulate in the daily life of the city, from bullet cases sold as keyrings to tourists hunting for war souvenirs, to sheets of UNHCR plastic used to patch up a backyard shed. There are also things and material places that are unmarked but which still hold affective and silent meaning for individuals; sites that bear no visible wounds but are forever connected to the war years in the minds of residents (Jansen, 2013; Mannergren Selimovic, 2021). The post-war city itself is thus in a sense an affective locale, as inhabitants and visitors move through today's cityscape and their actions activate the traces of war manifested in the scarred surface of the city.

Just as the violence of the siege ripped through and scarred the urban fabric, peacetime memorialisation of the siege also makes its own marks and shapes the city discursively, relationally and materially; it consequently also shapes the quality of peace. It is to this on-going memory work that we now turn to investigate the shifting terrain of the memory work carried out around the siege.

Sites: competing claims to the urban space

The sites in Sarajevo that we focus on in this analysis have been selected on the basis of a careful mapping of the whole city, and they have emerged from this as especially noteworthy and consolidated nodes in the on-going mnemonic formation of the siege. In the analysis in this chapter they are sorted into three categories based on their material manifestations in the cityscape. The first category comprises street memorials and plaques placed in the cityscape as markers at 'authentic sites', meaning the physical places where atrocities occurred. The second category is prominent and meaning-making memorials and monuments regarding the siege that have been constructed at various spots in the city. The third category comprises the three museums that deal specifically with the siege. This analysis is based upon repeated fieldwork carried out in Sarajevo over the last decade and also draws on the careful mapping of the city's memorial sites by Musi (2014, 2021) and Ristic (2018).

Importantly, these sites are understood as nodes in the living fabric of the post-war city – a city that itself is an 'authentic site', as the numerous scars on the cityscape testify. We need to bear this ever-changing memoryscape in mind when approaching the more formal sites of memorialisation, that is, the monuments, memorials and museums. As will be discussed, while the material sites in a sense pin down meaning, our analysis shows that the meanings constructed at these sites have shifted and developed over time, as mnemonic agents engage with them in various ways, eliciting sometimes conflicting narratives from them and using them for both memorialisation and counter-memorialisation events. In this sense the memoryscape emerges as fragmented, with the dominant ethno-nationalist understanding of the war in some ways growing in visibility in the city, yet often challenged by contending, more pluralist understandings.

Street memorials and plaques: the power of the 'authentic site'

Someone strolling through the city will come across a number of plaques that mark authentic sites of particularly gruesome events during the war. These plaques have been commissioned through the Sarajevo Canton Assembly and give an indication of what the dominant political powers seek to emphasise. While unobtrusive in the sense that they are easy to pass by without always being noticed, they convey an unequivocal message. The wording on each plaque follows more or less the same formula: 'At this place Serb criminals on [*the date*] killed [*the number*] citizens of Sarajevo,' signed 'the Citizens of Sarajevo'. Sometimes these brief sentences are complemented with a list of names of individuals killed at the particular spot. One such plaque is found at the Markale open market in the centre of town, where on two occasions shelling took many lives ('on 5 February 1994, 66 people were killed and 197 wounded, and on 28 August 1995, 43 people were killed and 84 were wounded'). Another plaque bearing similar wording has been placed on the building of the reconstructed National Library Vijećnica (now City Hall). The explicit mentions of ethnicity on the plaques inscribes an ethno-nationalist reading onto the war and obscures the fact that victims of the siege included many Sarajevans of Serb ethnic origin.

Another plaque is found at one of the many bridges that stitch the city together across the narrow Miljacka river. It was on this bridge that the first civilians were killed in the war. On 5 April 1992 about 100,000 citizens gathered outside parliament in a peace rally to protest against the impending military threat. Serb forces were step by step tightening their encirclement of the city. When the protesters marched across the bridge the first shots rang out, killing two young women, twenty-three-year-old Suada Dilberović and thirty-four-year-old Olga Sučić (Malcolm, 1996). They were civilians belonging to different ethnicities, and would become symbols of the courage of peaceful protesters in the face of tanks and guns. The bridge is thus an authentic site that holds a central meaning in the history of the siege and of the war at large. It has been renamed the Suada and Olga Bridge, with a plaque marking the space in their honour. While the wording on this plaque is less blunt than on the above-mentioned plaques, the message is certainly not one of peace and co-existence. The poetic, nationalism-tinged text reads, 'A drop of my blood flowed. And Bosnia did not dry up,' framing the deaths as directly linked to the survival of the independent state of Bosnia and Herzegovina, and thereby obscuring the fact that the demonstration was for peace in a broad sense; it had no nationalist or patriotic agenda (Björkdahl and Mannergren Selimovic, 2016a). The bridge is in fact also famous for another horrific event. It was here that a young couple, Boško Brkić and Admira Ismić, were killed when trying to escape the besieged city. Photographs of the two university students – who were likewise of different ethnic backgrounds – dying in each other's arms spread across the world, turning a personal tragedy into one of the emblematic images of the war as they were dubbed the 'Romeo and Juliet of Sarajevo'. After the war, the couple was commemorated with a plaque which at some point was removed. There are several stories about why this happened. A common explanation is that the multi-ethnic love story was judged not suitable in the increasingly ethno-nationalist climate of the post-war era, as will be explicated later in the chapter in relation to the more cosmopolitan narrative about the siege.

The meaning of this particular site has thus been negotiated and changed over the years. Entangled memories at this spot are pulled in various directions, which illustrates a more general tendency in the memoryscape towards an ethnification of memory that links one group – the Serbs – to a collective perpetrator identity while excluding them from victimhood. However, the most recent marking of another authentic site in the city points to a shift in this respect. In November 2021 the Sarajevo City Council raised a memorial stone at the Kazani ravine, located on Mount Trebević just outside the city.

It commemorates some of the victims of Mušan 'Caco' Topalović, a criminal turned commander of a notorious unit in the Bosnian army of the early 1990s that tortured and murdered civilians, mostly those of Serb origin. Some of their victims were dumped in a mass grave in the Kazani ravine. Over the years, relatives, victims' associations and others have demanded that the victims be accorded recognition and commemorated. Finally, the memorial stone was raised. In contrast to the plaques initiated by the Sarajevo Canton Assembly in the city centre, there is, however, no mention of who was responsible for the killings. The fact that they were committed by a unit of the Bosnian army is ignored, an omission that has sparked further controversy, leading to political protests and activists boycotting the ceremony at which the memorial stone was unveiled (Dzaferagic, 2021). Through the official commemoration of the Kazani killings, the victim–perpetrator dichotomy has been destabilised, in so far as Bosnian Serb Sarajevans may now also be recognised as victims. But there is – at the time of writing – no willingness to open up the perpetrator identity to include Bosniaks and the Bosnian army.

So far then, we can see that the authentic sites have to a large degree been harnessed to ethnic imaginations. But this is not the full story. What is arguably the most moving type of authentic site markers in the city offers an alternative, more pluralist spatial message. The attentive wanderer will soon notice an occasional red floral pattern in the concrete of pavements, on streets or squares. The patterns are known as Sarajevo Roses and are in fact the splattered scars left by mortar shells and grenades; these marks have been filled with resin and then painted red. There are about a hundred such roses all over the city and while the red splashes are hard to miss, they are at the same time unobtrusive. As such, they belong to the same category of pavement memorials as the so-called stumbling stones that mark the homes of Jews murdered in the Holocaust in cities across Europe and Russia; they are an organic part of the urbanscape and seek to 'transform the largely instrumental practice of walking into an encounter with urban history' (Stevens and Ristic, 2015: 274). Like the stumbling stones, the Sarajevo Roses remain open to interpretation, as you may walk across them obliviously, notice them for a fleeting second in the course of your shopping, or you may stop for a moment of remembrance without explicitly seeking out a specific area designed for commemoration. They heal the torn fabric of the city by smoothing out the craters, making the pavement possible to walk on again. At the same time, they keep the wound open, as the red colour of the roses reminds passers-by of the blood spilt on the very site of the crater, thus refusing to allow the suffering and death of Sarajevans to fall into oblivion. As we shall discuss, they have a history linked to agents of memory activism.

Figure 3.1 Sarajevo Rose outside the Tunnel Museum (photograph by Johanna Mannergren, February 2018)

Memorial sites: military heroes and civilian suffering

A very different approach is taken at the most prestigious memorial site in the capital, the Martyrs' Memorial in the Kovači cemetery. The institutional fund that manages most of the commemoration sites in Sarajevo Canton is the Fund of Sarajevo Canton for the Protection and Maintenance of Cemeteries for Shahids and Killed Veterans, Memorials Centres and Monuments for the Victims of Genocide (Fond Memorijala for short).[9] Situated in the central neighbourhood of Kovači, the cemetery is considered to be the oldest burial ground in Sarajevo, possibly dating from the fourteenth century (Musi, 2014). In 1964 it was turned into a park and a sports centre, before the war brought it back into use as a burial ground. The 1,487 graves it contains make it the country's largest burial ground for soldiers who died in the 1992–1995 war. It also contains the grave of independent Bosnia and Herzegovina's first president, Alija Izetbegović, who led the country through the war years, as well as the grave of the chief of staff of the army of Bosnia and Herzegovina during the war. The complex includes an amphitheatre, an auditorium and a Wall of Memory with names. A recent addition to the site is the small Liberation War Heroes Museum, opened in April 2019, which celebrates the lives of nine Bosnian army soldiers who lost their lives in the war and who are designated heroes worthy of special honour. This memorial is intimately linked to mnemonic work to consolidate the Bosnian post-war state and to frame the state's existence in terms of liberation rhetoric, as demonstrated by a quote from Izetbegović that adorns his tomb: 'We swear to God that we shall not be slaves.' The site further engages with the dimension of religious identity through the use of Muslim symbolism, including the use of the word *shahid* (martyr), traditional tombstones (*nišan*) as well as other symbols such as a memorial pool in the shape of a half crescent, and so on.

Under one of the *nišan* tombstones rests the controversial figure Mušan Topalović, known as 'Caco', already mentioned above. The memorial stone at the Kazani ravine and Caco's grave at Kovači cemetery are not geographically far from each other. It makes sense that the relatives of the Kazani victims are still dissatisfied, as there is no admittance of guilt; the perpetrator is on the contrary honoured as a hero at his own site of burial.

Although the Kovači cemetery is centrally located next to the historical centre of town (Baščaršija), it is not a site you might come across accidentally, as you might with the Memorial to Children Killed in the Siege of Sarajevo. The Children's Memorial was erected in a central square next to a shopping centre and has quickly become part of the city's profile and is well visited. It was inaugurated in 2009 by the Sarajevo Canton in cooperation with the Association of Parents of Children Killed in the Siege of Sarajevo.

It consists of an abstract sculpture of green glass rising out of the centre of a fountain. Beside it are seven cylinders of aluminium bearing the names of 521 children. The cylinders can be twirled round so that the names can be touched and traced with your fingers, inviting the passer-by to engage in a tactile way with the monument. On the edge of the fountain are shapes of footprints left by siblings of the children killed. It has been suggested that this monument, created by sculptor Mensud Keco, conjures up images of children playing in the sand, building sandcastles, or the abstract forms of a mother sheltering her child. The water lapping across the footprints brings to mind both the vulnerability of life as well as the eternity of memory.[10] In this sense, the monument is highly symbolic and works with affect to communicate its message about the innocence of child victims. Nevertheless, at the time the memorial was built it was a subject of heated debate, especially around whether it represented all the children who had been killed or solely children within those areas of the city that had been under siege by the Bosnian Serb forces, hence excluding children killed in adjacent areas – mainly what has now become East Sarajevo in Republika Srpska and some other neighbourhoods that were under Serb occupation during the war. Critics argue that this exclusion, if that is what it is, implies that some children were less innocent than others (Musi, 2021). Thus, it can be argued that even the death of children is ethno-nationalistically commemorated. The debate seems to have lost its heat over recent years, as the monument has gradually become emblematic of the city and is now a common stop on tourist itineraries.

Some memorial sites have been created with artistic ambitions. In general, the art scene in Sarajevo and in Bosnia and Herzegovina is a lively one, and a number of artists have made their marks locally and globally with works dealing with themes linked to memory and loss. The permanent, material imprints have so far been few, however, as artists have often worked with installations and other more temporary interventions in the cityscape. The few artistic monuments that have been installed permanently add a different tone to the memoryscape: more confrontational and often using irony as a tool. One of special interest to commemorations of the siege was produced as part of a project entitled 'De/Construction of Monument' that the Sarajevo Centre for Contemporary Art organised in the mid-2000s (Ristic, 2018: 191–2). This work by Nebojša Šerić Šoba stands on the city's main avenue, close to the History Museum. Known as the Canned Beef Monument, it is a scaled-up tin can of the kind that contained the low-quality food airlifted into the city during the siege. It bears the words 'Canned Beef' in English, with a sarcastic inscription below on its plinth: 'Monument to the International Community, from the Grateful Citizens of Sarajevo'. This is especially pertinent as the international community at the same time as sending food was enforcing an arms embargo, thus making it impossible for the city to defend itself. Hence, the 'grateful' inscription is doubly sarcastic (see Kappler, 2017: 8; Ristic, 2018: 195–6; Sheftel, 2012). The monument thus functions as a remembrance act regarding the inept gestures and the passivity of the international community, as well as a recognition of the hunger suffered by the Sarajevans. The fact that the artist chooses not to engage with the ethnic dimensions of the conflict, instead focusing on the urbicide and its transnational dimensions, is a statement in itself.

Museums: military heroism versus civilian everyday resistance

The third category of sites in this mapping comprises three Sarajevo museums: The Tunnel of Hope Museum, the Historical Museum and the War Childhood Museum. Each engages with the siege in a different way, but all three permanent exhibitions demand an active engagement from the visitor in ways that the markers and monuments in the open urbanscape do not (see Mannergren Selimovic, 2022b). They do this primarily through the display of objects, and thus we move our focus from more symbolic representations to material remnants and artefacts that can be seen, touched and experienced at a more visceral level.

The Tunnel of Hope Museum is actually partly an authentic site, partly a designed museum. The museum is centred around a reconstructed part of a tunnel that was built by the Bosnian army as an artery out of the besieged city and was used to transport weapons, food and other supplies. It was also used to help the severely injured out of the city. The tunnel, 1.5 metres in height and about one metre in width, ran for approximately 960 metres under the airport before ending in a private house on the outskirts of the city, at what used to be the frontline.[11] The house is severely damaged, and by its entrance a Sarajevo Rose marks one of the worst grenade hits during the siege, which killed dozens of people. About 15 metres of the tunnel have been reconstructed, offering the visitor a chance to crouch down and get the tactile, often claustrophobic experience of moving through the enclosed space. There is also an auditorium where footage from the siege and from the tunnel is shown, as well as exhibits of objects and artefacts related to the tunnel. There is an ambivalence in this exhibition between a focus on the military defence of the city and sufferings of civilians. The museum came into being as an act of activism by the Kolar family, who owned the house, turned the site into a museum and took care of it for fifteen years without any government support.[12] Some years ago, Fond Memorijala took over responsibility for it, although the owner of the house continues to act as director of the museum.

While the Tunnel of Hope Museum is by far the most visited museum in the city, and is highlighted as a must-see on tour operators' itineraries, the city's most comprehensive exhibition about the siege is actually found at the History Museum. The museum was built in the Yugoslav era in order to tell 'the history of antifascism during World War II and the cultivation of socialist state values',[13] but this focus has been overlaid by a new permanent exhibition concerning the siege. In this exhibition, the museum is evidently seeking to rectify dominant ethno-nationalist narratives by focusing on citizens' resilience and the individual and social cost of war. It does this from a position that can only be described as a counter-position, taking a stand against the divisive memory politics that prevail elsewhere at all political and administrative levels. This content appears to be the reason why it is starved of funding. For an outsider to Bosnian politics this situation, for a state institution, may seem somewhat surprising, but just like several art institutions that operate at the state level, the History Museum does not get any long-term funding. This reflects political paralysis at the state level regarding memory politics, as decision-makers are drawn from both the Republika Srpska and the Federation, with their divergent historical narratives. The museum hence mostly survives on small allocations of funding handed out on a yearly or even monthly basis. The lack of funding is manifested in the fact that the museum has not yet been properly renovated. The modernist-style building is situated on the broad avenue that was nicknamed 'Snipers' Alley' during the war and was badly damaged by incessant shelling. With its budget not stretching to heating, in wintertime a raw chill pervades the building.

On its website the museum states that its aim is to tell the story 'about the persistence, resourcefulness and creativity of Sarajevans, who lived 1,335 days without electricity, water, heating'.[14] Entering the exhibition area, the visitor is confronted by an abundance of objects and photos relating to everyday life under siege. There are staged reconstructions of, for example, a kitchen. The familiar situation of making a family dinner is easily recognisable, except that the details are skewed: the window is replaced by plastic provided by the UNHCR; dinner includes a tin of donated food aid that is to be cooked on a stove made up of parts of a can and a roof gutter. Close by, a bicycle leaning against a wall is loaded with the plastic canisters that were used to collect water. In addition to these references to very concrete experiences through simple but powerful displays, the museum provides space for temporary art exhibitions that address the memories of the siege in various ways.

The building that houses the History Museum is a testimony to the material damage caused by shelling and as such it is yet another authentic site in the urbanscape. In contrast, the recently constructed War Childhood Museum offers an entirely different experience, with the sleekness of its grey surfaces closely reflecting international trends in museum

Figure 3.2 Swing on display at the War Childhood Museum (photograph courtesy of the War Childhood Museum)

architecture. This independent museum, mostly funded by international donors, came into being through a call put out on social media by its director, Jasminko Halilović, in a move of social activism. Halilović, who spent his childhood in the besieged city, started a website where he asked a simple question: 'What was a war childhood for you?' After thousands of people shared their stories and donated objects from their childhoods, Halilović came up with the idea of a museum that would display these objects. They are the most ordinary things which formed part of many childhoods – a game of Monopoly, a diary, a Sony Walkman – each presented alongside a personal story told by its owner. Through the objects, and the stories that accompany them, the museum aims to portray how everyday life was for a child or teenager during the siege.[15]

To summarise, these three museums all provide spaces for engagement with objects and material markers of the siege that hold affective power generated by their authenticity. Some of them are strange to see in peacetime, such as a stove made from debris or an improvised stretcher used to carry the wounded through the 'tunnel of hope'. Others are shocking in their very ordinariness, such as the Monopoly board, and are therefore painfully relatable. All of them have the power to make us feel the past (see Buckley-Zistel, 2021; Mannergren Selimovic, 2022b).

In the above analysis, based on the mapping of the key mnemonic sites commemorating the siege of Sarajevo, a memoryscape emerges that shows a number of temporal shifts in meaning at the sites. These shifts are further explored in the next section, which investigates the role of mnemonic agents.

Agents: from institutions to activists

Agency is about power and the capacity to act, and this section maps the key agents who are involved in bringing the mnemonic formation of the siege into being. They include commemoration institutions, international political bodies and donors, curators, activists, artists and tourism entrepreneurs. In addition, the discussion in this chapter adds a crucial element to the analysis concerning the interventions and engagements of ordinary people, who have no set agenda and do not belong to any formal collective, but who seek individual recognition of their personal memories and objects of remembrance in various settings.

The influence of memory agents in the context of Sarajevo ranges from that of powerful hegemonic elite agents to the different kind of influence of those operating as grassroots organisations and/or taking up positions of opposition and protest. Further, one can see that many traverse local, national and transnational scales as they link up with various networks of memory agents. Another interesting aspect of the role of memory agents is derived from the sheer physical proximity created by the topography of the urbanscape, which makes agents without formal power more visible as they act in public spaces and intervene in the memoryscape, albeit fleetingly.

In the analysis of the mnemonic formation of the siege, certain categories of agents have emerged as of particular interest: the political and institutional agents as they control the formal politics of memory; the counter-agents who work in less formal spaces such as museums, civil society and art; ordinary citizens who engage with memorialisation activities; and tourism entrepreneurs and tourists, who play an important role in making certain sites visible and meaningful in the city.

Political and institutional agents: promoting and resisting ethno-nationalist yearnings

Fond Memorijala and the Sarajevo Canton have so far in this analysis emerged as key elite agents active at several of the sites analysed in the previous sections. When it comes to the formal monuments and memorials, most decisions are taken at the level of canton; Fond Memorijala, as a cantonal institution, is the leading actor in remembrance work. As a reflection of the complicated political system in Bosnia and Herzegovina, these actors are not situated at the state level as the state is weak given its highly decentralised structure. As noted above, the politics of memory follows these ethnically based dividing lines that underpin diverging and even opposing narratives about the war. Some political agents use commemoration of the siege as a realm for ethno-nationalist power advancement, speaking to the increasingly homogenous Bosniak population of Sarajevo. The fact that the Fond Memorijala, with its focus on military heroism and ethno-nationalist symbolism, is gaining control over an increasing number of memorial sites is a clear reflection of this mode of operation. Yet, it is a mistake to see the ethno-nationalist agenda as having complete dominance because there has been a gradual acknowledgement of victims from different ethnic groups, as has been happening in the case of the Kazani victims.

Furthermore, the political and institutional agents act under the auspices of the international community, which is still very much involved in day-to-day politics in Bosnia and Herzegovina. The Office of the High Representative (OHR), which has extensive powers to make laws and oversee the civilian aspects of the Dayton Peace Agreement, increasingly takes an interest in memory politics. At a national level the OHR has recently used its powers to ban genocide denial and any official celebration of war criminals. In the context of the commemoration of the victims of the siege, it is telling that at the installation of the memorial to the Kazani victims, the current High Representative participated in a gesture of active support (Dzaferagic, 2021). Further, a number of international actors have funded various commemoration initiatives. Here interests diverge. For example, Turkey has given support to the construction of the Kovači memorial site, whereas donors to the War Childhood Museum include Sweden, Germany and France, as well as the EU delegation to Bosnia and Herzegovina and the European Council.[16]

Curators, artists and activists: civic values and pluralism

It is notable that most of the memorials and museums discussed have not come into being through any top-down initiative by an official agency. The two most emblematic street memorials and monuments – the Sarajevo Roses and the Children's Memorial – were both instigated through pressure and activism from below.

The origins of the Sarajevo Roses are blurry. It is believed that they came into being through the ideas and work of individuals, and that later on victim associations and memory activists began actively engaging with them. The citizens' association Akcija Građana has been active in colouring in shell craters, as has the Youth Initiative for Human Rights of Bosnia and Herzegovina (Musi, 2021). There has also been an important change, as the Fond Memorijala in 2012 was entrusted with the task of maintaining the Roses. Subsequently, concerns have been raised that the grassroots counter-monument positionality of the Roses have been appropriated by institutional agents, and that they may potentially be used to endorse the more ethno-nationalist version of victimhood that is displayed at other authentic sites. Nevertheless, segments of civil society are continuing to use the Roses as important sites for a more open-ended and inclusive memorialisation of the siege, and so far have more or less managed to safeguard them as integral street monuments. For example, activists and others successfully protested when Fond Memorijala revealed plans to cover the Roses with glass in order to protect them from destruction (see Musi, 2021: 60). Thus, the sites of the Roses remain open for pluralist mnemonic work as well as continuing to be an integrated part of urban day-to-day life, exposed to all the usual wear and tear.

When it comes to the Children's Memorial, the parents' association was a key agent in bringing it into being. In the case of the monument at the Kazani ravine, likewise, it was an association for Kazani victims that drove the process forward. This is a reflection of the relatively strong agency and position of victims' associations in Bosnian society; as a matter of fact, the memorialisation of civilian victims of the conflict is one of the few civil society arenas where associations from both entities, the Federation and Republika Srpska, cooperate to a certain degree.

Sometimes the line can be hard to draw between activism and art, as many artists who have engaged with the memory of the siege do this from an activist positionality, supporting a counter-narrative that opposes the

Figure 3.3 The Children's Memorial in central Sarajevo (photograph by Johanna Mannergren, June 2018)

ethno-nationalist framing of the siege and of the conflict at large. Their work has left limited tangible traces in the urbanscape, with the Canned Beef Monument, mentioned above, as one of few exceptions. Their most important work has been in the form of installations that have instead left valuable intangible imprints by opening up intense discussions about the role of memory and its various power dimensions, including gender hierarchies. One such installation took place at the commemoration of the twentieth anniversary of the siege. This is analysed, as a significant event, towards the end of this chapter.

When it comes to curators, their positionality is likewise blurred. As discussed above, two of the main museums that have displays concerning life under siege have been unable to secure long-term funding from the state of Bosnia and Herzegovina, and see their work as running in opposition to the overall, officially sanctioned memory politics. All three museums have international funders and have also put a lot of effort into building transnational networks that link them up with other museums and institutions. The War Childhood Museum has an explicit agenda to cooperate and expand beyond Sarajevo; its collection is partly an international one, bringing together objects and artefacts from its temporary exhibits with children's artefacts from other conflicts such as those in Iraq and Afghanistan. Since 2020 the museum has had an office in Kyiv in Ukraine and in 2021 it opened an exhibition at the Kyiv History Museum, which focused on the experience of children in Eastern Ukraine since the war started there in 2014. The museum has also curated a travelling exhibition. The Tunnel of Hope Museum sits more seamlessly within the overall frame of militarism, as it is of course linked to the military defence of the city. Nonetheless, representatives of the museum who had been involved since its opening expressed concern that under its new leadership, that is Fond Memorijala, the courage and resistance of civilians against war might subsequently be obscured or downplayed.[17]

The agency of ordinary people

The agency of ordinary people has been instrumental in bringing together the key exhibitions on the siege. The Historical Museum's exhibition with its focus on everyday objects has come about through citizen engagement. As objects continue to be brought in, ordinary people are able to take an active part in adding to the narrative and filling in gaps in the knowledge of the siege. A number of people regularly act as storytellers in the museum, recounting their everyday struggles to survive during the siege. When Sarajevans who experienced the siege visit the exhibition they usually find themselves taking an active part, for example by spontaneously contributing more first-hand testimony about a particular event that they see in a photograph, or by providing a description on how the hospital organised surgery, or by explaining the war-time cooking recipes.[18] Similarly, the War Childhood Museum is continuously collecting oral testimonies and receiving items from ordinary people who remember their war childhood. The Tunnel of Hope Museum meanwhile employs as guides people who have a personal relationship to the tunnel. Some of them are former soldiers; others are civilians. The bloodied bandages on display actually belonged to one of the guides, who was wounded and carried out on the same stretcher that is on display in the museum.[19]

Tourism entrepreneurs: cosmopolitanism as a brand that sells

Sarajevo is increasingly a magnet for tourists, many of whom take an active interest in the city's multi-layered past. As part of a global dark tourism trend, the siege has become an object of tourism. Musi (2021: 59) notes that tourists are offered 'a variety of reminders of the war for consumption: from "survival guides" to maps of the siege, war paraphernalia and leaflets offering guided tours'. Tour operators and other actors in the tourism sector, such as for example travel journalists, are important agents in constructing outside perceptions of the identity of the besieged city. Tourists are giving more visibility to certain aspects of the past as they move through the city, stopping at certain sites and thereby demonstrating to inhabitants which are the sites that outsiders consider important and meaningful, and why. By visiting some places and not others they contribute to bringing certain sites into being, while letting others remain invisible. All of the war-themed tours of Sarajevo advertised on, for example, Tripadvisor, include a visit to the Tunnel of Hope Museum and the Children's Memorial, as well as a stop-off on Mount Trebević, so that the tourists get the same bird's-eye view of the city as did those carrying out the sniping and shelling during the conflict. The tours also tend to stop at the Suada and Olga Bridge in order to share the story about the four young Sarajevans Suada, Olga, Admira and Boško who lost their lives there (see Björkdahl and Mannergren Selimovic, 2016a). In addition, they often include a visit to the abandoned Winter Olympic sites from 1984, as well as to some memorial sites that relate to the Yugoslav Partisan defence of the city against Nazi occupation in the Second World War. As will be discussed, these ties to the pre-war period are beginning to emerge as part of a nostalgic connection to the Yugoslav socialist past in which ethnic divisions were downplayed instead of emphasised. Tourism entrepreneurs actively engage with this 'yugostalgia', linking it to notions of a cosmopolitan and multi-ethnic city.

Interestingly, there is an absence of international tourists at the Kovači cemetery memorial. While politicians and other official figures use the site as a backdrop for various events, other engagements with the site are limited. On repeated visits to the site, the lack of visitors in general has been noticeable and the site is definitely not on the tourist route. So, while a lot

Figure 3.4 Bullet cases from the war turned into souvenirs. Shop in the historical centre of town (Baščaršija) (photograph by Johanna Mannergren, February 2018)

of resources have been invested in this memorial site by a central agent, it seems that the resistance or lack of interest on the part of tourism entrepreneurs as well as the general public places it on the margins of the city's memoryscape. Elsewhere, meanwhile, tourist engagement provides an alternative space in which marginalised voices can be heard. Hence, tourism entrepreneurs shape the memoryscape in ways that are economically viable for them, whereas tourists themselves make meaning through their presence or absence (Buckley-Zistel and Williams, 2022).

Narratives: military heroism, cosmopolitanism and lived realities

In the above analysis, we can see that the meaning of the material sites shifts over time as various agents make their imprint, in line with Kappler's remark that '(t)he meanings of a monument can never be fully controlled from higher levels of hierarchy, but instead are subject to constant challenge, modification and resistance' (Kappler, 2017: 4). With this in mind, we turn our attention to the narrative aspect of the mnemonic formation of the siege. The narratives about the siege are told in relation to the larger narrative contentions about the war. Those larger narratives follow divisive and separate paths in ways that are constitutive of individual and collective identities at the same time as striving to impose a compelling structure onto a fragmented memoryscape (see Bruner, 2002: 89). Three main narrative strands emerge: an ethno-nationalist hegemonic narrative with a particular interest in military heroism; a cosmopolitan narrative that centres on urban identity; and a narrative of everyday resilience and civic values as performed by ordinary citizens.

Military heroism and ethno-nationalism

The memory of the siege has become increasingly ethnicised in a narrative construction of victims versus perpetrators, where the key message is that ethnic division and difference is the reason for the war and that, consequently, separate ethnic futures are necessary for peace. Exclusivity of victimhood and refusal to accept responsibility for the reprehensible deeds of one's own group have created a cemented dichotomy between '*heroj ili zločinac*' – 'hero or war criminal' (Moll, 2015b: 35). The narrative about the siege is thus fairly seamlessly linked to the larger discourse about competitive victimhood that dominates the Bosniak narrative about the war (Demirel, 2023). It feeds into the dynamics of remembering and is loudly expressed in, for example, social media, and also through televised commemorative events and in school textbooks, as already detailed.

It can be hard to isolate the specific narrative about the siege in the midst of such general contention, yet a reading of the material memoryscapes allows one to trace the key points of the ethno-nationalist narrative and the way it is organised with regard to remembering the siege. As part of

Figure 3.5 Tombstones at Kovači cemetery (photograph by Johanna Mannergren, February 2020)

the overarching narrative division, the Bosnian Serb narrative largely denies that there was a siege at all, and the Bosniak side makes it part of a nation-building narrative about the birth of the independent state of Bosnia and Herzegovina. The expressive linking of military battle, religious traditions, and the Bosniak nation's victimhood and struggle for survival is the main narrative frame of the memorials that the Fond Memorijala is in charge of. As already noted, the state is more or less absent in matters of cultural heritage, and memorialisation narratives are mostly formed at entity or canton level, meaning that the memory of the siege is surrounded by silence in Republika Srpska, including in East Sarajevo. In addition to the memorial plaques described in this chapter, this is in evidence in, for example, the renaming of streets after military (Bosniak) heroes, integrating the dominant narrative into the everyday of Sarajevo residents (see Azaryahu, 1996). It is telling that the Fond Memorijala, a key mnemonic agent in the city, has, as yet, not funded any exhibition exploring the everyday experiences of living through the siege.

Cosmopolitanism and commemorating the loss of universal values

There is a clear disconnect between the dominant narrative of ethnonationalism and nation-building and the narrative of the cosmopolitan city. This narrative is above all told to and by a globally oriented audience, including the diaspora, and is arguably losing some of its traction. Cosmopolitanism in the sense used in this narrative refers to a mixed, multicultural urban identity. The cosmopolitan identity of Sarajevo is understood as one of the very reasons for the relentless attacks launched against it, in order to create ethnically homogeneous states. Specific parts of the city such as public spaces, the National Library as well as religious buildings were singled out and attacked as symbols of this inter-mixing; it was the city's urban identity itself that was the target – hence an urbicide (see Coward, 2004). The cosmopolitan narrative is often referred to and endorsed by Sarajevans who lived in the city before the war, as well as by tourism entrepreneurs and the international community. Elite political agents may also on occasion deploy this narrative.

The narrative of cosmopolitanism has in fact played a key role in the engagement of the international community ever since the war. Lene Hansen (2013) has argued that this narrative of the relatable, urban, modern metropole came into being during the war and challenged predominant discourses of the Balkans as 'a dark place' seeped in 'ancient hatreds'. Through this discursive shift, the representation of Bosnia and Herzegovina changed from a place of no hope (meaning there was no point in any outside intervention) to a place of civic values under attack (eventually making intervention possible). The global narrative of cosmopolitanism is a good fit with the War Childhood Museum, as it speaks to these globally supported civic values. The key narrative of the museum appeals to universal ideas of human rights, peace and the innocence of children, arguing that the attack on the urbanscape is in fact an attack on humanity. The global branding of the city as cosmopolitan is equally important for tourism entrepreneurs who seek to uphold a romanticised imagery of the cosmopolitan city that fits with global discourses about universal humanity and the triumph of human goodness over evil. The prominence of sites such as the Suada and Olga Bridge on tourist routes through the city testifies to this.

In addition to multi-culturalism and diversity, the cosmopolitan narrative also alludes to a distinctive urban, self-ascribed, sophisticated identity that is often juxtaposed and contrasted with a supposed rural and 'uncultured' identity. According to this version, the forces attacking Sarajevo were drawn from the population of rural areas, who were an easy target for ethno-nationalist propaganda as they already were distrustful of the cosmopolitan city. In post-war times, this discourse translates into a contempt for newcomers from rural communities who arrive seeking a financially more viable life in the city. Bădescu (2020) calls this an exclusionary type of cosmopolitanism that takes little interest in ethnic identities yet draws up other boundaries and hierarchies.

The narrative of the unique identity of Sarajevo survives among many of its pre-war citizens despite their war experiences. It has also been adopted by activists and a younger generation who are critical of what they perceive to be an inward-looking political and administrative leadership, and who yearn for the state of Bosnia and Herzegovina to step up to play a role in international arenas, including in the European Union. While there are indeed mixed neighbourhoods, mixed families and de-ethnified social relations among many inhabitants, the insistence on cosmopolitanism may obscure the fact that the demographic changes caused by the war mean that today the overwhelming majority of Sarajevans identify as Bosniaks (Bădescu, 2020).

Everyday resilience and dignity

The director of the War Childhood Museum calls the stories that are circulated in the museum 'honest', and says they offer a different perspective from the state narrative; this 'partly answers the question regarding why we are not supported by the state, because we do not fit their narrative'.[20] Likewise, the director of the History Museum agrees that an ethno-nationalist narrative of the war is gaining ever more traction and that the aim of the museum's exhibition on the siege is to counter that with everyday stories:

> The whole idea [of the History Museum] is to promote life, creativity and resilience, how people coped with the siege by developing a strong will to live. Developing different creative skills and the importance of art and culture ... The circle of people still promoting and believing in this is getting smaller, and the nationalist narrative is prevailing ... It is getting louder and louder.[21]

Figure 3.6 Handmade sign that was posted at a particularly dangerous crossing, warning of snipers (preserved and displayed at the Historical Museum, photograph by Johanna Mannergren, February 2020)

To counteract ethno-nationalist narratives of the war the museums try to knit together a multitude of personal stories, inviting people to talk about their everyday experiences, as outlined above. The focus is on the civilian experience and the resilience and resistance of human beings who uphold civility in the face of death and suffering at the hands of others. The alternative spaces created at the museums provide openings for the telling of diverse experiences; for example, the gendered experiences of war can be narrated as well as the experience of being a child – perspectives that tend to go unheard. The museums thus avoid sticking to a closed and static narrative but rather let visitors create their own interactions and interpretations. This openness is promoted through the focus on objects as the carriers of meaning and emotions. By selecting the objects of the everyday as a valid point of reference, the museums resist the erasure of the terrible individual and social losses that war and violence entail. These stories are told through things that evoke emotions and affect. Indeed, the director of the War Childhood Museum insists that it is not really a museum of things – it is a museum of stories as told by the things.

Events: rituals and ruptures

As the capital city of Bosnia and Herzegovina, Sarajevo is the site for a curated cycle of commemorative events which through their very recurrence support and maintain a hegemonic memory. They are performative practices that are inscribed in the official calendar and as such they provide a sense of continuity and regularly remind citizens of the dominant narratives of the war. The event as a performative act 'rehearses and recharges the emotion which gave the initial memory or story embedded in it its sticking power' (Winter, 2010: 12). Events are thus a means to (re)activate the taken for granted and (relatively) stable material landscape of monuments and markers. The mnemonic event is not always a ritual, however. It may be a sudden rupture and shock that does not recur but nevertheless leaves a lasting impact. The urban memoryscape includes a dynamic stream of demonstrations, protests and artistic interventions that rely on urban public spaces to resonate and make an impact.

Recurring rituals instigated from above

An official 'Day of Remembrance of all the citizens of Sarajevo killed during the siege' is observed on 5 February. Every year representatives and officials at various political levels – the city, the canton, the federation and the state – pay homage on that day to the victims by laying wreaths at the 'authentic site' of the Markale market shellings. It should be noted that the commemoration of the (mostly) Bosnian Serb victims that were buried at the Kazani ravine now has its own official day of remembrance, on 9 November (Dzaferagic, 2021). There seems to be a missed opportunity here – the opportunity to commemorate all victims of the siege together on one date.

Another key recurring event in the city is the celebration of 6 April as the Day of the City of Sarajevo. In Yugoslav times, this was the date to mark the anniversary of the 1945 liberation of the city from the Nazi occupation. In relation to the latest war, the day commemorates the beginning of the siege of Sarajevo, turning the event into an occasion that makes a temporal move by connecting the latest war and the siege with Yugoslav history. On this day each year, politicians and officials stop by at a number of key monuments where flowers are laid down and speeches delivered. Usually, the first stop is at the well-known Eternal Flame memorial in the centre of the city, which honours the Yugoslav Partisans who fought the Nazis. The tour continues to a number of other memorial sites concerned with the Second World War, such as the Vraca Memorial Park just outside the city, which commemorates the anti-fascist struggle, as well as the Jewish cemetery. With regard to the latest war, the tour visits the Kovači graveyard, the Children's Memorial, and the Suada and Olga Bridge (Musi, 2014). The memorial sites connected with the Second World War are usually half-forgotten places and it is interesting how they are reactivated as significant places each year through these recurring visits. The linking of the two wars through a public ritual deepens the meanings of the sites, as the history of heroic resistance against the Nazis is used to support a present-day nation-building narrative of heroism.

Activist interventions for plurality and inclusivity

The inclusion of the Kazani victims in the mnemonic formation of the siege has been a recurring theme in this chapter. We can pinpoint a couple of key mnemonic events that ruptured the memoryscape and precluded the material manifestation in the form of a monument to those murdered and then buried at the ravine. One such event took place in 2015, when the activist initiative *Jer me se tiče*, 'Because it concerns me', installed a memorial plaque in a Sarajevo park in memory of the Kazani victims. The organisation works for a pluralistic memoryscape where all victims are commemorated and describes its activities as 'memory guerrilla tactics'. The plaque was destroyed very soon after, however – it is not known by whom (Ristic, 2018: 192). Thus, the event did not leave a lasting inscription in the physical space, yet it had made the fight for recognition at least fleetingly visible in the public space.

Another sudden event occurred when the then president of Bosnia and Herzegovina, Bakir Izetbegović, in June 2016 paid a visit to the Kazani site and said, 'I should have come here earlier'. The event became big news and was interpreted as an opening towards reconciliation (Orentlicher, 2018: 307; TV1 BiH, 2016). With hindsight it seems that these two interventions – one grassroots and the other top-down – had an impact on the politics of memory that eventually led to the actual instalment of the monument, as described earlier in the chapter.

Artistic commemoration of urbicide

There have been a number of artistic interventions seeking to express tangibly the intangible losses of sociality and diversity that urbicidal violence brings. One such installation stands out: the *Sarajevo Red Line* was an installation mounted in 2012 to mark twenty years since the siege started. Bosnian artist and theatre director Haris Pašović placed 11,541 red plastic chairs into rows stretching for 800 metres along the main street that runs through the city centre. There was one chair for each person killed and 643 of them were child sized. This huge artwork was shocking, as each empty chair represented a rupture in intersubjective webs of relations: family, relatives, friends, co-workers, neighbours, acquaintances. The empty chairs all faced a stage where dance and singing performances and poetry readings unfolded over the course of the day and evening. The dead were 'the audience and the living were transformed into bystanders on the sidelines'.[22] While there has been a debate around the artwork, specifically concerning the number of the dead that it alludes to and similarly to the debate around the Children's Memorial, the installation has been widely embraced and has become part of the recent historical memory of the city, both locally and globally. It was an event that conveyed the collective and individual loss resulting from an urbicide, a loss that for a moment was made visible and tangible. The installation did not come with a message to remember in order to heal, or to understand better, or to enrol the dead in a patriotic project. It was an acknowledgement of the enormity of the individual and collective loss caused by the siege.

The SANE analysis: memory and the quality of peace

The memory of the siege of Sarajevo is a wound that runs deep and is a challenge for peace in Bosnia and Herzegovina. How is the siege to be remembered? Was the siege a logical outcome of deep-seated ethnic hatred? Was it a reaction stemming from rural discontent with a cosmopolitan, urban elite? Should it be remembered as a military battle focusing on soldiers who gave their lives for freedom? What about the courage of civilians defending a multi-cultural way of life against the ethnic divisionism of political elites, and what about international passivity in the face of a humanitarian catastrophe? What about the loss of life, the loss of love, the loss of childhood? Who was a victim, who was a perpetrator? These questions and their responses are entangled in the memory of the siege. How they are voiced – and silenced – through commemoration impacts on the quality of peace in Bosnia and Herzegovina. The mnemonic formation of the siege is in many ways a reflection of the overall divisive memory politics of that country which has created parallel 'ethnic peace(s)'. Yet the SANE analysis of the mnemonic formation points to a number of openings towards a more just peace.

The sites that we have studied here leave their material mark in the form of monuments and memorials that pin down the mnemonic formation of the siege with at least a semblance of permanence. Importantly, the sites may seem to tell only one story, but this chapter asks, with Božić (2017: 17): 'What do war monuments apparently reveal to us? and … What do war monuments attempt to conceal from us?' Every new addition to the memorial landscape breaks some silences, whereas others are maintained or imposed. There are on-going fluctuations between silence and speech, recognition and erasure, as is illustrated by the case of how the Kazani killings are remembered.

It is also clear that sites come to life and generate meaning when someone engages with them. What happens to a site that is not visited? And does it matter who visits? The residents of Sarajevo shape the post-war city by their movements, activating some sites as meaningful by their presence and engagement, and deactivating others through withdrawal. Likewise, the visits by tourism entrepreneurs and tourists to certain sites and not others have an effect on their meaning and significance.

The on-going agential work in the city destabilises the seeming permanence of monuments, memorials and other material marks. At the time of writing, the ethno-nationalistic attempt to reinforce its appropriation of memories is on-going. The Suada and Olga Bridge is a point of reference in the shifting of meanings. However, victim associations, artists, activists, curators and tourism entrepreneurs provide plural perspectives which in the urban public spaces confront and challenge hegemonic storytelling, thereby making homogenisation impossible. These agents uphold memories of multiple entanglements and palimpsests of experiences (see Fridman, 2022).

Alternative commemoration activities engage with, instead of closing off, the experiences of ordinary people. The focus on people's everyday experiences of the siege allows for a more pluralist and inclusive mnemonic practice which challenges divisionism. The engagement of ordinary people with memory work in the museums points to a need that top-down commemoration cannot satisfy. In hegemonic accounts of the past that seek to erase ambivalence there is, after all, little space for the ambiguities and fine-tuned mechanisms of grief, dignity and co-existence. This chapter has noted the remarkable affective power of objects. The artefacts and objects representing a difficult heritage are evocative of plural emotions, ideas and narratives. Through the tangible objects, intangible losses to do with the fabric of everyday life are acknowledged. The acknowledgement of the everyday of war as a cultural heritage through the objects on display in the museums can contribute to dignifying civilians who experienced urbicide. The exhibitions in Sarajevo thus serve as valuable examples of how such difficult cultural heritage after conflict can be used to direct attention and motivate action towards a more inclusive narrative – one that recognises victims' experiences. They foster a dialogue about the past and open up new avenues towards understanding the experiences of others, thereby rendering the boundaries between communities more permeable.

This chapter has further investigated how open-ended sites and open-ended events can encompass pluralistic meanings. Aesthetic interventions can produce representations that intervene in the broader memoryscape. For example, the *Sarajevo Red Line* art installation spoke a language that communicated the ever-present loss, offering survivors an opportunity to be silent and letting art speak beyond polarising narratives. Art may thus reconfigure the political imaginaries of the past (the way we remember) and also the future (the way we envision where we go from here).

Finally, the mnemonic formation of the siege is particularly interesting as it renders visible the violence of urbicide and the concomitant memory politics that are formed in and by the urbanscape. The urban is a practice in heterogeneous pluralism and is therefore always in the making. Part of the impossibility of imposing a single narrative derives from the fact that urbanity is defined by heterogeneity as an existential quality of life (Coward, 2008), and thus the living space of the city is defined by its inhabitants. While Sarajevo today is structured along more or less ethnicised spaces and mnemonic practices, these patterns are in fact not inscribed through fixed borders or checkpoints. The materiality of the city is both a reflection of the society that has constructed it as well as a space that is continuously produced through the actions of its citizens (Lefebvre, 1996). The city is thus a living memoryscape and its memory politics is not confined to official remembrance spaces and orchestrated events. The social fabric of everyday life unfolds in relation to the material registers of memory, and it is through the spatial practices in the sites of the city that meanings are made and remade.

Conclusions

The urbicide carried out in Sarajevo attempted to erase a history of pluralism and co-existence and destroy public spaces of urbanity. The city's current demographics indicate that this attempted urbicide succeeded at least partially, since most inhabitants of post-war Sarajevo now share the same ethnic identity. But the prevailing ethno-nationalism does face a number of challenges. The above examples of commemorative practices and sites speak to possibilities of embracing memory in ways that can improve the quality of peace in Sarajevo, in Bosnia and Herzegovina, and beyond.

While analyses of Bosnian memory politics tend to focus on the silo structure of memorialisation, we can see that a plurality of mnemonic agents provide different narratives, activate a number of sites and participate in events that hold potential transformation. We have noted that there are changes over time as to how various victim groups are met with recognition, and that at times the contours of a more inclusive peace can be discerned. At the same time, this analysis has pointed to a number of moves by elite memory agents to increase control over memorial sites and events, which indicates that the divisive narrative of ethno-nationalism is in some respects gaining ground. The mnemonic formation of the siege of Sarajevo is thus restless; it solidifies, fractures and again solidifies. A shifting memoryscape emerges, in which the memory of the war is under constant formation.

Notes

1 Bosniaks is the name for the group formerly known as Bosnian Muslims, recognised as their own ethnic group in the 1960s (Moll, 2015a: 2).
2 The United Nations International Criminal Tribunal for former Yugoslavia (ICTY). *Radovan Karadžić Case – Key information & Timeline.* www.icty.org/en/cases/radovan-karadzic-trial-key-information (20 March 2023).
3 The country is often referred to in daily speech as BiH (where the 'i' means 'and' in Bosnian). Republika Srpska is often referred to as RS and the Federation of Bosnia and Herzegovina as just the Federation.
4 Office of the High Representative. *Annex 10. Agreement on Civilian Implementation.* www.ohr.int/dayton-peace-agreement/annex-10/ (20 March 2023).
5 For a collection of news articles about Dodik and his politics, see Associated Press. *Milorad Dodik.* https://apnews.com/hub/milorad-dodik (20 March 2023).
6 www.ohr.int/about-ohr/mandate/ (20 March 2023).
7 https://balkaninsight.com/2020/05/19/bosnian-streets-and-squares-named-after-war-criminals/ (20 March 2023).
8 For a portrait of Smailović, see the documentary directed by Roger M. Richards (2016): *Sarajevo Roses: A Cinematic Essay.*
9 Shahid is an Arabic-origin word usually translated as 'martyr'.
10 Centre for Non-Violent Action. *Kultura Sjecanja.* https://kulturasjecanja.org/en/sarajevo-memorial-to-children-killed-in-the-siege-of-sarajevo/ (20 March 2023).
11 Museums of the World. *Sarajevo Tunnel Museum.* http://museu.ms/museum/details/303/sarajevo-tunnel-museum (20 March 2023).
12 Interview, Historical Museum director, Sarajevo, February 2018.
13 Historical Museum. *About the Museum.* http://muzej.ba/collections-research/about-the-museum (20 March 2023).
14 http://muzej.ba (20 March 2023).
15 Interview, War Childhood Museum director, Sarajevo, June 2018.
16 War Childhood Museum. *Partners and Friends.* https://warchildhood.org/partners/ (20 March 2023).
17 Interview, museum staff member, Sarajevo, May 2018.
18 Interview, museum curator, Sarajevo, May 2018.
19 Interview, War Childhood Museum director, Sarajevo, June 2018.
20 Interview, Historical Museum director, Sarajevo, February 2018.
21 Interview, War Childhood Museum director, Sarajevo, June 2018.
22 East West Centre Sarajevo. *Sarajevo Red Line.* https://eastwest.ba/sarajevo-red-line/ (20 March 2023).

4

Rwanda: the role of the internationals

Beginning with colonialists and missionaries, followed by the United Nations and the international community more generally, international actors have had a significant and detrimental impact on Rwanda's national politics. Today, the role of internationals is a key component in the prevailing narrative around the 1994 genocide against the Tutsi, and that mnemonic formation is what we shall be examining in this chapter.[1] Importantly, we recognise the detrimental effect that international involvement has had on Rwanda in the past. However, we are interested here in how the internationals feature as a trope in current memory politics and what impact this has on the quality of peace. We argue that the creation of an enemy outside of Rwanda serves the function of forging a coherent identity in a country still heavily affected by the experience of genocide.

In the government's explanation of the genocide, internationals feature in three ways: they are attributed responsibility for having constructed and politicised ethnic identities under colonialism; for having failed to stop the killings in 1994; and for having actively supported the genocidal regime. By blaming colonialists for instigating the ethnic divisions that led to genocidal violence, the government locates responsibility with actors outside of the country, thus significantly reducing Rwandan responsibility for the massacres (Brehm and Fox, 2017: 121; Longman, 2017: 265). Through projects of civic education, training camps and public events, this version of history and of the causes for the genocide is systematically reproduced throughout the country. It seems to be successful in influencing how Rwandans narrate their past today (Bentrovato, 2017; Brehm and Fox, 2017; Buckley-Zistel, 2006a; Longman, 2004), and is a major influence on peace because it leaves prevailing social cleavages unaddressed and obstructs an open discussion about alternative narratives as to causes and consequences of the genocide. In particular, the framing of international responsibility for the genocide precludes any critique by the international community of the current government, headed by former military leader President Paul Kagame, despite this regime's autocratic nature. This framing explicitly emphasises that it was Kagame and the Rwandan Patriotic Front/Army (RPF/A) that ended the genocide, while the international community seemed indifferent.

There is a large body of literature concerning Rwanda's memoryscape that addresses a variety of contentious issues. Most prominently, the unifying narrative of the government and its stifling of alternative memories comes in for some criticism (Buckley-Zistel, 2009; Hintjens, 2022; Longman, 2017; Thomson, 2018), and the role of various constituencies in the memorial process has been analysed (Ibreck, 2010; Viebach, 2014). In this chapter, we take a slightly different approach and zoom in on the way internationals are depicted in memory discourses. We explore how current memory practices narrate the internationals' responsibility for genocide, and with what effect.

The 1994 genocide against the Tutsi in Rwanda

The 1994 genocide against the Tutsi in Rwanda is an unprecedented example of extreme and often very intimate violence between social groups, all the way to community members and their neighbours. On 7 April 1994, after the aeroplane carrying the Hutu president Juvénal Habyarimana was shot down, a well-prepared killing machine moved into action in an attempt to extinguish all Tutsi. In just 100 days around 500,000–600,000 Tutsi and moderate Hutu were killed (Meierhenrich, 2020).[2] The genocide was perpetrated by Hutu militias, most notably the *Interahamwe*, as well as by government troops and Hutu neighbours. Most victims were killed at roadblocks, in villages and towns, at home in their gardens, or in places that had been deemed safe by Tutsi fleeing the violence such as churches, school buildings or UN compounds that were then abandoned by UN peacekeepers (Straus, 2006). They were killed with machetes, clubs, spiked nail bats, grenades or small arms. In addition, about 350,000 women were raped or subjected to other forms of sexual violence (Bijleveld et al., 2009). More than 1.6 million people, predominantly Hutu, were later found guilty of having participated in the genocide (Nyseth Brehm et al., 2014), their crimes ranging from killing or instigating killings to property crimes, in a country that had been home to about six million people at the time.

The Rwandan genocide did not occur in a vacuum, though, but in the midst of a peace process that followed a three-year-long insurgency by the RPF/A under Kagame's leadership. At the time, the RPF/A mainly consisted of Tutsi refugees and their descendants; they had fled Rwanda after experiencing aggressive attacks during the so-called Social Revolution of 1959 and subsequent waves of violence, and now wanted to return to their homeland. As they were not granted a right to return, Tutsi forces of the RPA invaded Rwanda in 1990, starting a civil war that was only terminated by the Arusha

Peace Agreement three years later. The agreement promised democratisation, power-sharing, multi-party elections and freedom of speech – all in a highly volatile situation. This opened a space for radical politics, extreme hate speech and anti-Tutsi propaganda, contributing to an atmosphere in which genocidal ideology could fester. Due to the Tutsi insurgency and the Hutu government propaganda, the society was soon deeply divided along ethnic lines, with many Hutu blaming Tutsi for the violence, and in particular framing the Tutsi in the country as being intimately connected to, and acting as spies for, the RPA. This opened the gate to indiscriminate violence against civilian Tutsi across the country.

The genocide unfolded despite a considerable international presence in the country, including the United Nations Assistance Mission for Rwanda (UNAMIR), which had been tasked with overseeing the implementation of the Arusha Peace Accord. In the early days of the killings, many internationals left the country and the UN presence was subsequently reduced in number, in particular after Belgium decided to remove its troops following the assassination of ten of its soldiers who had attempted to protect the moderate Hutu prime minister, Agathe Uwilingiyimana (Reggers et al., 2022). Despite the fact that the killings were carried out under the gaze of the international community, the UN did not intervene due to its restricted mandate. Furthermore, as the use of the term genocide was avoided in Security Council meetings in early 1994, the UN was able to evade any mandate to intervene within the terms of the 1948 Genocide Convention. UN Security Council Resolution 918, which was intended to expand the mandate of UNAMIR in mid-May, received little support. In the end, therefore, the genocide was only stopped by the military victory of the RPA led by Kagame. Since the genocide had led many people – mainly Hutu – to flee, the UN Security Council in June authorised France to create a safe zone for humanitarian purposes, that is, to protect displaced persons and civilians at risk. Opération Turquoise was therefore established in the south-west of the country with this mandate, guarded by French and Senegalese troops. It is estimated that about 13,000–14,000 people, mainly Hutu, found refuge in the zone, yet they were not disarmed and continued the genocide even within the zone (Landgren, 1995).

After the genocide, low-intensity violence continued for several years between the RPF/A and Hutu rebel troops – mostly genocide perpetrators who had retreated and now sought to regain control – in the periphery of the country, as well as in the neighbouring Democratic Republic of Congo (Straus, 2019). Today, the country no longer experiences armed conflict, but its peace remains shallow. A deeply divided society and lingering mistrust indicate that the legacy of the genocide is still very prevalent today (see McDoom, 2022). Kagame and the RPF continue to rule the country, and while the Kagame government receives broad international praise for Rwanda's strong economic development, the political climate remains illiberal and the government rules with an iron fist. Little room for dissent remains on any political issues, least of all on the topic of the genocide – for which the official version is key to the government's legitimacy. Memory politics is profoundly affected by this and is utilised to strengthen the government's position.

The Rwandan memoryscape

In Rwanda, as in most post-violence societies, collective memory is highly diverse and politicised. It is situated in the wider contestation of the country's history going back to colonialism, including the questioning of whether Tutsi are 'autochthonous' (i.e. indigenous to Rwanda) and thus truly Rwandan (Eltringham, 2004; Pottier, 2002). Memory, or history, was at the very heart of the genocide and remains an area of intense dispute.

It is important to note that the memory of the Rwandan genocide varies considerably depending on individuals' experiences during the violence. It is estimated that between 300,000 and 400,000 Tutsi survived the genocide, about a quarter of whom were left suffering from symptoms of trauma (Rieder et al., 2013), affecting how they see the past. Survivors' organisations have been established to guard the memory of the genocide, organise memorial events, contribute to national memorialisation and take care of some of the memorials (Ibreck, 2010; Viebach, 2020). Often this is guided by the maxim never again – as reflected in the motive of the umbrella survivors' organisation Ibuka, which translates as 'remember' – which is likewise indicative of one of the essential objectives or aspirations behind remembrance: memory shall serve to prevent future violence. For many, it is thus imperative to remember. Remembrance is also a response to genocide denial amongst Rwandans inside the country and in the diaspora, and also to any tendency to relativise the atrocities through comparison with the killings of Hutu during and after the civil war.[3] And yet, many survivors are dissatisfied with the space that is made available to them for remembering, as well as with how they, as survivors, are instrumentalised for political purposes by the government (Fox, 2021; King, 2010).

Regarding people who were not targeted by the genocide, that is, mainly the Hutu population, many also lost loved ones in the war or in post-genocide-related violence, while others experienced displacement or imprisonment. For them, memory often takes a different, private form. Since it is not part of the national commemoration, and may run contrary to official narratives, some feel that their suffering is not recognised. This leads to resentment and, at times, to contestation of genocide memory itself. In some cases, this goes as far as genocide denial or what has been termed the double genocide thesis, according to which the genocide against the Tutsi is put on the same level as the killings of Hutu (Jessee, 2017b). Many, mainly Hutu, argue that their memory of the events and how it affects their lives at present is excluded from the official memory, that they do not have memorials to go to, that their agony is – and by implication they as a social group are – less important. As a consequence, alternative and, most importantly, private and unofficial forms of remembrance have emerged, which sometimes collide with and contradict the national and official versions of memory (Mwambari, 2021).

It is also instructive to look at the gendered nature of remembrance. Gender-based and sexual violence against mainly women was key to the Rwandan genocide. This is something widely acknowledged in Rwanda and affects how women are portrayed in memory narratives, in that they are portrayed almost exclusively as victims. That women were also rescuers, bystanders or perpetrators is often overlooked in current memory practices (Brown, 2017; Mannergren Selimovic, 2020a).

In addition to the people who were already present during the genocide, the many Tutsi who went into exile during the so-called Social Revolution of 1959 and who have returned to Rwanda since the genocide now constitute a new demographic group with new perspectives on the genocide and its aftermath. Referred to as returnees, many tend to support the government's line on history and subsequent politics (Jessee, 2017a) and frequently benefit from the economic and political development pursued by the RPF government.

As a consequence, even though the genocide appears rather dichotomous along the dividing line of ethnicity, there are significant differences within these groups, as well as a range of views on what and how to remember. In spite of the strong, top-down memory discourse of the government, Rwandans still have their own interpretation of the past (Jessee, 2017a: 237). Almost thirty later, the event is today transmitted intergenerationally through the way the genocide and its aftermaths are reflected upon in families and in society. Memory of the genocide is not just transmitted through memorials, commemorative events or educational initiatives, but also indirectly through socio-economic consequences that people still suffer today, such as torn family structures, the illness of parents, poverty or troubled community relations (Eichelsheim et al., 2017).

On the level of the state, memory is a top-down venture linked to the RPF-led government's project of national unity and reconciliation based on Rwandan citizenship (Buckley-Zistel, 2006a). A discourse of national unity is promoted to reshape the identity of the parties to the conflict by referring to a common past and future. National commemorations, the rewriting of history and the revision of its teaching, as well as museums and memorials, circulate this narrative (McDoom, 2021). The function of memory politics is well expressed by the researcher and NGO activist Odeth Kantengwa (2013: 111): 'The motive behind this remembrance has nothing to do with perpetuating feelings of hatred and vengeance. The purpose is rather to educate Rwandans and whoever might be interested in designing the better future of Rwanda.' For the government and some memory activists, memory is thus a political project to unite and reconcile the country. As will be explored, however, this view is not shared by all.

In the national memory discourse, 'only some civilian memories of violence are acknowledged while others are repressed' (King, 2010) and there are a number of government institutions such as the Commission Nationale de Lutte contre le Génocide (National Commission for the Fight against Genocide, CNLG) which serve as gatekeepers. Memory law, moreover, is increasingly politicised and any transgressions reprimanded (Jessee and Mwambari, 2022).

The government has furthermore sought to deconstruct ethnic belonging by passing legislation that criminalises all mention of ethnic identity. Nonetheless, in 2007, the Constitution was amended and the word genocide replaced with 'the 1994 Tutsi genocide' (King, 2010). In 2014, it was changed again to 'the 1994 Genocide against the Tutsi' (Baldwin, 2019: 356). While it seems ironic that the criminalisation of ethnic terminology that might abet divisionism does not extend to the official nomenclature given to the violent past, this dialectic is actually quite productive in the maintenance of power for the Tutsi minority leadership, without their ethnicity being overt (Baldwin, 2019). As ideology that can be alleged to promote genocide faces possible legal penalties (Russell, 2019: 15), it is impossible to tell a different story about the genocide or to challenge the government's official narrative. 'Never again' as a political maxim has thus become Rwanda's 'narrative of redemption, renewal, self-reliance and dignity' (Thomson, 2018: 242), rendering the ruling party the only arbiter of the country's non-violent future.

Mnemonic formation: the internationals

Internationals – in the form of colonisers, missionaries, foreign governments, the UN or the international community more generally – form a central component of the Rwandan memory narrative, and of the one deployed by its government in particular. In this narrative, the internationals serve the function of having an outside enemy on whom some of the responsibility for violence against the Tutsi population can be placed, thus highlighting an additional facet of victimisation for the victims of genocide while not absolving the direct perpetrators of culpability.

Our focus on the internationals as a mnemonic formation serves to examine critically their deployment as a trope in memory politics. It should be noted that beyond this academic investigation, we do recognise that (neo-)colonial legacies are still prevalent all over the world, including in Rwanda. We therefore do not critically engage with the fact *that* Rwandan memory politics focuses on the internationals, but we are interested in *how* this mnemonic formation is constructed and encouraged, and to what end.

According to the government's history discourse – as displayed in the memorial sites discussed in the next section – colonialism introduced the since-discredited 'Hamitic hypothesis', which argued that the Tutsi originate from northern and eastern Africa while Hutu belong to the Bantu people and constitute the indigenous population of the country. Allegedly physically resembling Europeans, Tutsi were portrayed as superior and were endowed with social and political functions, while Hutu were assigned the role of common farmers. As a consequence, over the course of history Tutsi came to be seen by Hutu not only as immigrants but rather as foreign occupants and oppressors. Importantly, the colonial administration issued identity cards which contained the ethnic identity of the carrier. As independence approached, and with the backing of Belgian missionaries, Hutu sought to overcome their political and social inferiority in the so-called Social Revolution of 1959. This brought a first pogrom against Tutsi, with repeated outbreaks of violence in 1962 and 1973. In foregrounding these developments, internationals – in the form of colonial powers and missionaries – are held accountable for having invented and polarised ethnicity in Rwanda, as well as for having instigated the first violence against Tutsi (Office of the President, 1999).

The most significant reference to internationals, however, is concerning their failure to stop the genocide while it was unfolding before their eyes. In the words of President Kagame, '[t]he UN and the international community as a whole abandoned Rwanda in 1994. … The UN's failure to intervene in Rwanda in 1994 shook my faith, and that of most Rwandans, in the UN system and the international community generally' (Kagame, 2008: xxi–xxii). As a consequence, a number of heads of states as well as a UN General Secretary have apologised. These apologies are often delivered at memorial sites or during memorial week in April, and shall be discussed below.

The government's version of history is systematically and pervasively propagated across the country through history teaching and civil education programmes, and seems to have a significant impact on the way Rwandans narrate the past today. For instance, in 2000, interviewees from diverse social backgrounds did not relate the country's past – including colonialism – to the genocide (Buckley-Zistel, 2006b; Longman and Rutagengwa, 2004); yet by 2016 individuals being interviewed mirrored the government's version of the colonisers' role in the construction and fixation of ethnicity. Brehm and Fox (2017) illustrate how their interviewees often held colonialists responsible for having instigated division in Rwanda, which ultimately led to genocidal violence. They conclude that '[b]y blaming colonialism, these survivors locate blame outside of Rwanda and suggest that the genocide finds its roots in a foreign institution rather than in Rwandan society itself, refuting ideas that deep-rooted hatred or long-standing problems within Rwandan society caused the violence' (Brehm and Fox, 2017: 121).

Sites: displaying international responsibility

In Rwanda, there are around 263 memorials.[4] National memorial culture is very active and strongly influences political and social developments by calling on people to participate in small and national commemorative events. Memory thus serves as a vehicle for forging the post-genocide nation. Reflecting the tight grip the government has on the history of the genocide, memorial sites are all similar in orientation; there are no visible counter-memorials that deviate from the national narrative about causes and consequences of the mass killing. In Rwanda there is no spontaneous, bottom-up memory movement expressed in plural and diverse sites. Instead, one finds a uniform memorial style, with a structured, top-down management and increasingly professionalised curation.

We can differentiate between local and national memorials, however. Most memorials are small, local and managed by local authorities and survivors' groups; they often emerged at mass graves containing human remains. In contrast, national memorials are under the management of the Commission Nationale de Lutte contre le Génocide (CNLG). Each national memorial includes mass graves that contain countless coffins holding the bodies of tens of thousands of victims, mostly in underground spaces that can be visited. They all include some form of exhibition, with the simple presentation of human bones, skulls and victims' clothes, as well as locally relevant weapons or other items (as in the sites at Nyamata, Ntarama, Nyarubuye, Nyange and Bisesero, for example). Other national memorials include full exhibitions with text, audio and video, produced in a highly professionalised manner and with a wealth of information (such as in Kigali and Murambi).[5] All national memorials have CNLG-trained guides to show visitors around, and to provide deeper explanations about the genocide and history in general and the dynamics of the genocide in that particular region, as well as explanations on specificities of the site and the exhibition.[6]

It would go beyond the scope of this chapter to introduce all the sites in detail, so we shall zoom in on the two most prominent national memorials – the Kigali Genocide Memorial (KGM) and the Murambi Genocide Memorial – as two places where the role of the international community is discussed in considerable depth. We further discuss the memorial to the fallen Belgian soldiers and an exhibition on the RPF/A, which both take a slightly different approach while continuing to be in line with the government's overall commemoration strategy.

The Kigali Genocide Memorial and the Murambi Genocide Memorial

In contrast to other memorials the two largest national memorials, in the capital Kigali and near the small town of Murambi in the south-west, dedicate considerable effort to explaining the causes of the genocide (Wolfe, 2020: 29) and in doing so focus on the internationals. Their exhibitions are well designed and are in line with a globalised style of sites memorialising atrocities (Björkdahl and Kappler, 2019; Sodaro, 2018: 105). Visitors are guided around the highly professional and modern exhibition space, clearly curated with both a national and particularly also an international audience in mind. At the KGM displays, objects, film, pictures and a catalogue are backed up by an audio guide available in various languages.[7]

The main national memorial centre is the KGM, located in Gisozi, Kigali, where expansive gardens alongside the centre contain the mass graves of some 250,000 victims of genocide. Its exhibition recounts the history of Rwanda leading up to the genocide and gives many details on the dynamics of the genocide and its aftermath. Besides the main exhibition space, there is also a comparative exhibition on other twentieth-century genocides and an exhibition on child victims. Archives, educational and conference facilities, a large amphitheatre used for events and a café are further features of the site.

The KGM attracts many visitors. Given its prominent position, including during commemorative events, it is unsurprising that the exhibitions' narratives are very much in line with the official narrative of the government (Jessee, 2017a: 46–57; Mannergren Selimovic, 2013: 345). Educating visitors on the genocide is one of the central objectives of the memorial: '[i]t is through education that we can prevent mass atrocities from occurring in our communities' (Kigali Genocide Memorial, n.d.). The KGM thus strongly invokes the notion of never again.

The largest exhibition, entitled *The 1994 Genocide Against the Tutsi*, is dedicated to explaining the history, development and scope of the genocide, and features the mnemonic formation regarding the role of internationals. Unsurprisingly, the section on colonialism is particularly prominent here. One display, for instance, shows a historic black-and-white photo of a Belgian general with the Rwandan King Mutara III Rudahigwa. The king is wearing his traditional royal costume as he engages in what appears to be a friendly, respectful conversation with the colonial administrators. The photo thus refers to the Belgian strategy of indirect rule through Tutsi leaders, and other pictures depict similar scenes. These images are stuck to a large poster wall with a group shot of five Belgian missionaries in the midst of a large group of Rwandan students, depicting the education by the Catholic Church and thus the Church's influence on ethnic relations. We also find an identity card in the display, on the top-left corner of which is printed '*Origine: People – Race – Muhutu*', as evidence of how the colonial authorities introduced identity cards fixing ethnic categories to individuals.[8] Through these images, the internationals are assigned a prominent role in Rwanda's history. By employing a colonial divide-and-rule strategy that favoured Tutsi, by mobilising Hutu against this Tutsi rule in missionary schools and by inscribing ethnicity in identity cards, the role and responsibility of internationals for creating and politicising ethnic identity is foregrounded.

Another section addresses the role of the UN: the resistance of the UN Security Council to having the killings referred to as genocide and the UN's failure to intervene and stop the violence (see also Ibreck, 2013). We see a photo of General Roméo Dallaire, who headed the UNAMIR peacekeeping mission, in front of a group of stern-looking peacekeepers. Dallaire's mouth is open, he is probably speaking and he looks agitated. Next to it, we see a copy of a document, a code cable, sent by Dallaire to UN Headquarters in January 1994, alerting New York that the situation in Rwanda was growing increasingly tense and that Hutu militias were being trained to carry out massacres. Visitors also see a photo of a white woman who looks as if she is fleeing the country; she is physically supported by Belgian peacekeepers while frightened Tutsi watch. A shot of French soldiers in front of a massive group of displaced persons (most likely Hutu) in the buffer zone created under Opération Turquoise adds to the depiction of the internationals as either abandoning Rwanda or aiding *génocidaires*.[9] The failure of the internationals to stop the genocide, their failure to save Tutsi when at the same time they were evacuating their own people, is strongly communicated by these pictures.

The Murambi Genocide Memorial is another national site that features internationals prominently. It employs a similar strategy but focuses on the role of the French government and military instead of that of colonialism and the UN. Opened on 21 April 1995 near Murambi in the south-west of the country, it stands on the hilly grounds of a former technical college. It contains the remains of 50,000 victims who were killed at the school and in the surrounding area, still buried in mass graves.[10] The exhibition is located on the ground floor of the main school building and has two separate rooms displaying some of the human remains behind smoked glass.

The French army and its Opération Turquoise based itself at Murambi Technical School from June 1994 onwards. The exhibition zooms in on the fact that as a result of this, many Tutsi were killed in the vicinity. It explains that Hutu pulling back into the area were protected by the French soldiers and continued killing with their full knowledge. Furthermore, the display mentions that there were considerable French arms sales to the extremist government in the lead up to and during the genocide, violating an arms embargo and stoking the genocidal violence (Cameron, 2015: 104). The memorial site includes a space at the top of a hill where, according to the guide, French troops placed a volleyball field next to mass graves, demonstrating their absolute lack of respect for the victims.[11] In this way the exhibition presents visitors not only with a strong narrative of international failure in responding to the genocide, but even with a construction of French complicity. At times, guides go as far as to suggest that French troops had 'internalized the Hutu extremists' genocide ideology' (Jessee, 2017a: 70).

The Murambi Genocide Memorial is the only other national memorial with a full educational exhibition and follows 'the same emotional template [as the KGM] with carefully designed display boards and presentations of personal stories' (Mannergren Selimovic, 2020a: 139).[12] Some of the pictures of the internationals are the same as in Kigali but there is an additional section on Opération Turquoise. One striking, colourful image in this section is a photo of a French soldier in uniform amid a group of very poorly dressed Rwandans, including children. The shot is taken from a low position so that the people seem fairly large. The soldier is talking to the group as if he is explaining something. There is also a picture of a French military vehicle driving down a tarmac road with a group of *Interahamwe* militia members, armed with sticks and clubs, running alongside the vehicles in a way that could be construed as part of a military drill. This is a well-known photo, the date of which is unknown. Most likely it was not shot at Murambi, but it has acquired an iconicity within Rwanda as evidence of French complicity in the genocide and their support for the Hutu *génocidaires*.

The most remarkable thing about the site is the display of hundreds of victims' bodies that have been conserved with lime, a presentation that most visitors will find visually and olfactorily disturbing. Regular treatment is necessary to preserve these mummified bodies (Viebach, 2014: 81). They lie on wooden racks, in close proximity to each other and frozen in bizarre poses; some still have rosaries or other jewellery around their necks. Some are organised by age and there is a room containing the remains of small children. Similarly to the memorials in Bosnia described in Chapter 3 and the displays of victims' bones in Cambodia discussed in Chapter 6, the display at Murambi holds very strong affective power due to its authenticity. For visitors, both Rwandans and non-Rwandans, it is a very emotional moment (Buckley-Zistel, 2007).

This deeply disturbing display renders Murambi, as a site, a symbol for the guilt of the internationals; the bones are displayed as a material representation of their moral and political failure. The combination of pictures of international actors alongside the emotionally charged display of human remains constitutes an unmistakably strong accusation. For Longman (2017: 8):

> Murambi memorial site shows a level of disrespect and deception that is indicative of a wider problem with efforts by the post-genocide government to confront Rwanda's past. Rather than honestly presenting what happened at Murambi, bodies are used for their shock effect. The fact that the bodies currently on display in Murambi did not even come from this site is not made evident … The truth of the tragedy at Murambi is secondary to the need for a political symbol.

For many survivors of the genocide, meanwhile, the display of human remains in Murambi and other memorials goes against their sense of ethics and dignity. Similarly to the KGM exhibition, there is no attribution of responsibility to Rwandans, nor is there any detailed explanation about the events that occurred in Murambi, in which 50,000 Tutsi were killed (Lisch, 2019).

Figure 4.1 Murambi Genocide Memorial (anonymous photographer, August 2018)

In sum, the two memorials dedicate considerable attention to internationals (not all displays and examples can be represented here). While some sections intentionally work with affect, the sections explaining the historical development from colonialism up until the genocide are analytical in style – even though some of the images are of course very painful to look at. The images are explained in the audio guide, in texts written on panels as well as in the exhibition catalogue.

Both memorials convey ambivalent messages regarding the culpability of Hutu. On the one hand, as Amy Sodaro states, 'there is a noticeable lack of blame ascribed to the Hutu – even extremists – or anyone else of Rwanda. Rather, the exhibit depicts a collective victimization of a Rwandan people that were torn apart by colonial forces. This is deliberate; in the effort to make sure that the museum does not threaten the fragile peace and tenuous unity among the Rwandan population' (Sodaro, 2018: 99). Producing unity and reconciliation was the government's strategy after the genocide, in an attempt to minimise divisions within Rwandan society and prevent new outbreaks of violence. This policy continues to some extent today. Instead of focusing inwards, which would involve blaming Hutu (individually or collectively) for the killings, the strategy was to externalise guilt and to construct an outside enemy. This was seen as carrying the best promise of internal unity.

On the other hand, though, visitors are directed by memorial staff and by posters exhibited at the sites to consider the matter of criminal accountability and complicity in the genocide. The disgrace is not only placed upon the Hutu Power extremists who orchestrated and executed the genocide, or the Hutu civilians directly involved in acts of violence. It is also placed upon the entire Hutu majority for their failure to intervene and protect their Tutsi fellow citizens. With the exception of a few commendable Hutu civilians highlighted in the KGM exhibit for their role as rescuers during the genocide, the Hutu population is condemned for allowing themselves to be manipulated by the genocidal ideology. They are criticised for their involvement in attacks or for turning a blind eye to the suffering of their Tutsi neighbours, thus aiding the killings (Jessee, 2017a: 53).

The Campaign Against Genocide Museum

Another site with similar messaging regarding the role of the internationals is the Campaign Against Genocide Museum located inside the Rwandan National Parliament. Opened in 2017, it serves to explain the RPF/A's military campaign to liberate the country (see Kimonyo, 2019). Framed in its self-presentation online, the museum

> depicts in details how the Campaign Against Genocide Plan was executed by RPF/A following the withdrawal of UN troops leaving the targeted Tutsi under the mercy of the Genocidaires and how only the RPF/A forces who were in the war of liberation took the unilateral decision to stop Genocide, Rescue victims of Genocide and defeat the Genocidal forces [sic].[13]

Consisting of nine rooms, the museum uses a mix of pictures, text, wax figures and simulations to showcase the RPF/A military strategy in great detail. A picture wall with the title 'UN abandoning genocide victims, APR [sic] rescuing them' displays some of the same photos as are on display at the KGM, such as the one from the early days of the genocide of a white woman being rescued by the Belgian soldier, as described above. The title of the wall adjacent to it reads, 'The role of Rwandan civilians and foreigners in the campaign against genocide', so that those held culpable and those considered as heroes are placed right next to each other. Against the backdrop of international failures, the museum with its prominent location within parliament highlights in no uncertain terms the heroic deeds of the RPF/A. As argued by Mannergren Selimovic: 'The militaristic theme is expressive, focusing on the heroic depiction of the military defenders, which resonates with the elevation of the Tutsi in exile who returned as saviours' (Mannergren Selimovic, 2020a: 136).

The Belgian Peacekeepers Memorial

There is, however, one memorial in the capital's city centre that focuses on a different group of victims. It was constructed by an international actor and is in contrast to the national museums: the Belgian Peacekeepers Memorial. This memorial was inaugurated in 2004, at a site bought by the Belgian embassy, to honour the ten Belgian soldiers who were killed under circumstances that are portrayed in the memorial as heroic. The incident took place in the first hours of the genocide while the soldiers were attempting to protect then prime minister, Agathe Uwilingiyimana. The memorial is situated at an authentic site as it centres on the single-storey, bullet-sprayed building in which the soldiers died. The central room of the building has been left with the bullet and grenade holes as they were following the shooting, and two adjacent rooms house a small exhibition explaining the genocide. This features explanations about the event, as well as a diverse mix of panels on human rights, humanitarian aid, pathways into and out of genocide, and various other aspects. On a plot of land beside the building stand ten individual stone pillars, one for each of those killed. The stone is rough and uneven, dotted with dimples (possibly a reference to the bullet holes at the buildings) and each has as many slits on one side as the age of the individual soldier it is dedicated to. Even though the bodies of the soldiers were returned to Belgium, annual commemorative events take place at the memorial, attended by relatives of the killed men and dignitaries.[14]

This site is of particular interest in the context of the internationals in the Rwandan memoryscape as it presents a decidedly different reading of events to the other sites discussed here. It foregrounds the loss of life – the sacrifices – of individual soldiers (naming the ten victims and honouring them), but more importantly it seeks to highlight the efforts made by UN troops stationed in the country to counter the genocide, as far as they were permitted to do so by their mandate (see also Reggers et al., 2022). It thus presents a more heroic counter-narrative of UN involvement, contrasting with the version that prevails nationally – of complete international failure – as depicted at the Kigali and Murambi museums. That Belgium withdrew all troops from UNAMIR after the deaths of the ten soldiers, thus undermining the peacekeeping mission, is not presented as any kind of moral dilemma in this memorial.

To conclude, while the national memorial sites installed following the genocide differ to some extent, they all – to varying degrees yet in very

Figure 4.2 Belgian Peacekeeper Memorial (photograph by Timothy Williams, August 2018)

similar ways – address the aspect of responsibility of the internationals for the genocide. In contrast, the Belgian memorial is the only one that portrays Belgian soldiers as heroes and saviours. As argued above, blaming outsiders for the genocidal violence carries with it the promise of uniting Hutu and Tutsi under the guise of a joint victimhood – all Rwandans, it seems, were victims of external influence from the time of colonialism to the UN missions. This discourse, however, elides any social cleavages and conflict lines within Rwandan society itself.

Agents: national memory agents structuring international involvement

As in all conflict-affected societies, Rwandan memory politics is driven by various agents who pursue their particular views and interests. The various narratives presented are very much coloured by agents' experience of and/or role in the genocide, which varies according to their presence in the country at the time or their absence, their gender, group identity, age and so on. Some of these agents are more powerful than others and thus more successful in determining memory politics. Some of these agents are more likely to effect or stifle change. Yet, despite the powerful role of government institutions, national memory is not monolithic. Moreover, international actors also play a role in shaping the Rwandan memoryscape, although it has been argued that they are for the most part willingly or unwittingly co-opted into the official narratives provided by the state (Straus and Waldorf, 2011: 12).

Rwandan organisations

Two Rwandan memory agents stand out: the governmental CNLG and the non-governmental Ibuka. The CNLG was created under Law 09/2007 of 16 February 2007 and was officially active by 21 April 2008. Its aim is to honour memory, tell peoples' stories and to rebuild Rwanda (Gahongayire, 2015: 113). The CNLG coordinates all state commemoration efforts and plays a key role in shaping the state narrative and its manifestation at 263 memorial sites and during commemorative events. It is mandated to suggest the annual commemoration theme during Kwibuka, the memorial phase that starts on 7 April. The theme is then officially decided upon by the Cabinet, chaired by the president of Rwanda. It is printed on banners displayed around the country, and artists and memory entrepreneurs include it in their work (Gahongayire, 2015: 116). Selecting the topic and preparing speeches that are rolled out at local events across the country ensures a coherent narrative nationwide.[15]

National memorials in Kigali and beyond the capital are administered by the CNLG, which also curated the exhibitions. This is a change, since for several years after the genocide memorials were staffed by local survivors; these have now been replaced by professionally trained CNLG staff, who often have no personal connection to the site (Viebach, 2014). The rationale behind this change is to ensure that there is a coherent official narrative at each memorial site, rather than a narrative shaped mainly by the individual and personal stories of survivors.

The creation of the CNLG to oversee memorial politics and practices testifies to the importance the government attributes to memory discourses. The Commission's mission is specifically to preserve the memory of the genocide, to promote research on the prevention of genocide and to fight against genocidal ideology. According to a CNLG officer, 'memorials should primarily serve as clear physical evidence of the genocide for future generations, especially to prevent a diminishment or denial of the genocide' (cited in Kantengwa, 2013: 112). As Kantengwa notes, the mandate to bring survivors and more generally Rwandans – whose 'social relationships [were] destroyed during genocide' – back together is also key to the CNLG's work: 'The philosophy behind CNLG's interest in promoting supportive networks where every Rwandan would participate is to combat ethnic divisions that characterized the past regimes. This interest also is based on national unity built on an implicit discourse of "Rwandanness" as an identity field' (Kantengwa, 2013: 113). In 2021, the CNLG was succeeded by a newly founded Ministry of National Unity and Civic Engagement (MINUBUMWE) and CNLG director Jean-Damascène Bizimana was appointed as the relevant minister, continuing the work of the CNLG in a more prominent political position and taking the political control of memory one step further.[16]

A second important organisation is Ibuka, which means to remember in Kinyarwanda, the language spoken across Rwanda. Ibuka is an umbrella organisation for various survivors' associations, and was founded soon after the genocide to advocate for, and support, survivors. It acts as an umbrella group for the work of survivor groups such as AERG (a student genocide survivor group), GAERG (a genocide survivors' group made up of college graduates) and AVEGA (widows of the genocide), among many others. Advocacy for social justice and activities around memorialisation processes feature as its key objectives.[17] It supports survivors in a variety of ways and has an important voice in Kigali and local representation throughout the country. While heavily dependent on international or government funding, it has taken a leading role in supporting local survivors in the construction and maintenance of memorials, the organisation of local commemorative events and advocacy (Ibreck, 2010: 333). In giving a voice to survivors it has at times even backed positions that go against government policy, for example, advocating against the centralisation of memorials and the exhumation of bodies from smaller, locally administered memorials.[18]

Ibuka's gaze is firmly fixed on survivors as its main constituency. Their voices and well-being are paramount in its activities, rather than national unity and reconciliation. As a consequence, while it does not actively counter government policies nor does it actively promote them. This constitutes some form of alternative memory politics, although in a very closed political environment. More broadly, memory agents can set their own agendas and push specific topics, as long as these do not stray beyond the (narrowly) defined confines of government-sanctioned memory politics.

International agents

In addition to Rwandan agents, internationals have an impact on the Rwandan memoryscape. The financial contributions made by international donors to support reconciliation have been considerable; there has been funding for memorial construction, justice processes and various projects for and with survivors, as well as technical advice on preservation, archiving and other aspects of the memorialisation process. Foreign approaches to memorialisation have shaped some of the approaches to dealing with the genocide at a local level. As is often the case in aid politics, shifts in donor priorities can impact the work of individual organisations; in this case, for example, mandating new focuses on education instead of on archiving.[19] Such international support suggests involvement in reimagining Rwanda after the genocide: 'International engagement is penetrating the very fabric of national identity, encroaching on territory normally reserved for the most profound domestic political agendas' (Ibreck, 2013: 149). Equally, however, this international engagement takes place within limited bounds set by a proactive government agenda in which international donors have no fundamental say in how memory is shaped, given that the government maintains a strong hold over memory politics.

Even without the possibility of influencing memorialisation, funding genocide-related activity is important to international donors. According to Ibreck, '[f]unding memorialization was a means to express regret for the failure of the international community to halt the genocide in 1994' (Ibreck, 2013: 155). The strong degree of international financial support and the presence of international dignitaries at commemorative events is suggestive of a strong degree of guilt regarding the problematic (lack of) international engagement during the genocide. The financial support is – to our knowledge – not discursively connected in any explicit way to apologies offered by the international community, particularly as this could signal some form of legal responsibility in terms of reparations. However, the financial engagement is framed as part of a project of restoration and the idea of never again, that acknowledges the shortcomings of the international community in 1994. While international responsibility for the genocide is indeed acknowledged by international actors, the topic of colonialism is diligently skirted around in order not to raise larger questions that could challenge the legitimacy of neo-colonial global politics. Even with their financial support, some donors realise that the way the Rwandan government shapes memory is problematic regarding ethnic relations in the country today, and foreign observers and academics continue to criticise the Rwandan government for using the memory of the genocide for political ends (Korman, 2015: 61).

One international organisation is particularly active in the Rwandan memoryscape: the Aegis Trust. It was founded by two British brothers, James and Stephen Smith, who had previously founded the National Holocaust Centre in the United Kingdom. The Aegis Trust designed and constructed the KGM on land provided by the city, and today continues to manage the site in close cooperation with the CNLG. Thus, the KGM is strongly tied into internationalised aesthetics and symbolism, as well as a globalised perspective on remembering. At the same time, its close partnership with, and oversight by, the CNLG ensures that the official narrative is embedded in a way that does not run counter to government intent. The involvement of the Aegis Trust does not appear to result in criticism levied against internationals at this memorial being downplayed in any way. Also, in partnership with the CNLG, the Aegis Trust has built up the Genocide Archive of Rwanda and is active in promoting research projects with international researchers and interns, as well as with Rwandan scholars. Again, the close partnership with the CNLG on all these projects ensures that the official narrative of the government regarding the genocide is not undermined by this international actor. While the Aegis Trust is an important agent in the memoryscape of Rwanda, there have been no reports of conflict with the CNLG or other government offices, and changes to official policies on how to remember the genocide are reflected in all of the Aegis Trust's work.

Narratives: international responsibility for genocide

When studying the narratives surrounding internationalism at these various sites, and between the relevant actors, three dominant narratives emerge, as well as some relevant sub-narratives. The three narratives are: international responsibility in terms of the passivity of international actors in the face of the unfolding genocide; international support for the perpetrators then and now; and the colonial roots of the genocide. All serve to construct a dichotomy between us (the Rwandans) and them (the internationals) as central to the government's 'unity and reconciliation' discourse. Creating an outside enemy serves the function of forging a coherent identity in a country still divided by the experience of the genocide (Buckley-Zistel, 2006c).

International responsibility for the genocide

The dominant narrative regarding the role of the internationals deals with the international community's failure to act during the genocide and its consequent responsibility for the massacres. This is evident in the following statement, for instance, where a range of international actors are held accountable: 'The failure of humanity in Rwanda can be attributed to the then Rwandan government which executed the genocide, the UN, the five permanent members of the Security Council and Belgium' (Rutikanga, 2013: 6). The state has an unmatched capacity to shape narratives of the past; it has the power to institutionalise collective narratives, to determine the content of textbooks and school curricula, and of course to implement its preferred policies regarding memorials and the events held there. During memorial events in Rwanda, narratives about the internationals are reinforced in events at which historians and officials give talks to the entire community on the history of the country, allocating co-responsibility for the genocide with the international community, as discussed above (Baldwin, 2019).[20]

Let us look again at the exhibition at the KGM, which seeks to a large extent to demonstrate the incompetence and indifference of the international community. This is evidenced, for instance, in the picture of the January 1994 code cable sent to the UN in New York (described earlier in the chapter), and also by captions which provide the context and conclude: 'No action was taken in response to the fax.'[21] The UN is portrayed as refusing to go beyond its mandate, even though Dallaire estimated that their small contingent could have de-escalated the situation. Dallaire is quoted as saying, 'Give me the means and I can do more'.[22] That the international community refrained from intervening to stop the genocide even as various nations' own citizens were being evacuated from Rwanda is represented in the photo of the white woman being rescued by a Belgian soldier discussed earlier in the chapter. The text accompanying that photo reads:

> Diplomatic staff and foreign workers left the country. Many left their colleagues, employees and friends to the mercy of the killers. Dignitaries of the Habyarimana regime, authors of the genocide, were evacuated. The number of foreign troops used in the evacuation would have been sufficient to stop the genocide.[23]

The narrative asserts that in the face of international indifference the RPF was the only actor able and willing to stop the genocide and to rescue the population, affording the army the moral high ground in post-genocide Rwanda (see King, 2010: 298).

A glimpse of how these narratives about the internationals affect visitors is captured by Liberta Gahongayire and Anne Marie Nyiracumi's (2014) study on entries in the KGM's visitors' book. The entries were addressed particularly strongly towards the international community: 31 per cent of women and 40 per cent of men who left comments chose to focus on the topic of international involvement. The authors explain:

> The focus of the international community messages is often recommendations in various forms of 'never again', lessons of what happened and remorse. There are two kinds of remorse in this book. One is addressed to the French government of the time (1994) and another to the international community. For example a visitor is not proud of being French because the French government did not protect people (Tutsi) and prefers to be a citizen of the world working for a better future. (Gahongayire and Nyiracumi, 2014: 1454)

This shows that the way the responsibility of international actors is portrayed in the KGM has been rather effective. Part of the importance of highlighting international culpability is to deflect attention from how the RPF invasion in 1990 and the subsequent civil war played a significant role in radicalising extremist Hutu. The exhibition at the KGM and other memorials is, unsurprisingly, silent on this issue (Jessee, 2017a: 55). Furthermore, one guide at a national memorial implicitly legitimised RPF atrocities during and after the genocide by verbally posing a question for visitors: if the international community did nothing, how could the genocide against the Tutsi be stopped without using force? This question was used to highlight that the 'double genocide' idea was wrong and even amounted to genocide denial.[24]

There is one memorial with an international focus in which the failings of the international community are not foregrounded: the Belgian Peacekeepers Memorial. This memorial, instead, portrays the UN peacekeeping troops' proactive action in their mission to protect Uwilingiyimana, as well as narrating a story about the Belgian soldiers' brave, albeit unsuccessful fight to stay alive once captured by Hutu extremists. The memorial is funded and run by the Belgian state,[25] so this alternative and less critical perspective regarding the Belgian involvement is perhaps unsurprising; however, the memorial nonetheless stands out in the broader memoryscape given its very different message on international responsibility. Belgian politicians regularly attend annual commemoration events here,[26] tying the memorial into broader diplomatic relations (McKinney, 2011: 167).

Support for perpetrators

The second narrative goes beyond the moral shock concerning the international community's non-intervention during the genocide, as international actors are constructed as actively supporting the perpetrators. This is most prominently found in discussions of French complicity. At the KGM, the exhibition frames the French as a trainer of the Interahamwe militias and the Rwandan army, and also as the source of weapons sold to the extremists, thus being driven by 'capitalist greed and related interests' (Jessee, 2017a: 54). This is tied to the accusation of anti-Tutsi racism. A guide showed us a picture of a French soldier who was pointing at a man and apparently claiming that he was not Hutu but Tutsi, thus – according to the guide – demonstrating how the French were trained to identify Tutsi. Next in the exhibition comes a horrific picture of bodies, which the guide causally connected to the racist French attribution of ethnicity.[27] This reinforces the impression that the French are accused of having directly supported the perpetrators.

In this vein, internationals are also held responsible for having armed militias in the run-up to the genocide. Due to its proximity to the pre-genocide, Hutu-led government, France is singled out as a country that supported the training and militarisation of military and paramilitary troops that were initially fighting in the civil war trigged by the RPF/A invasion of 1990.[28] Kagame explicitly 'hold[s] the French government … responsible for helping to arm and train the militias that dispersed throughout the country to wipe out the Tutsi population' (Kagame, 2008: xxii), as well as for having subsequently provided a safe haven for genocide suspects.

French complicity is seen as exemplified in Opération Turquoise, the French military operation that created a 'safe haven' that was then actually used by Hutu extremists to escalate the genocide in that region without being impeded by the approaching RPF troops. In the KGM, one text accompanying the exhibit reads: 'The only soldiers to arrive in Rwanda before the genocide ended were French military during Opération Turquoise, ostensibly to create a "safe haven" in the south of the country between the "conflicting" sides.'[29] This is repeated in the Campaign Against Genocide Museum, which furthermore explains that in the area designated the Zone Turquoise it was safe for Hutu extremists to carry on killing Tutsi under French supervision.[30] In one commemorative event in Huye, this French involvement was described as very direct, in that 'French soldiers accompanied Interahamwe and protected them'.[31] This aspect of internationals' culpability is given great prominence in the Bisesero and Murambi memorials, as both places were directly impacted by Opération Turquoise. In Bisesero, Tutsi had successfully resisted Hutu extremists for two weeks before being gathered in one area by the French and promised protection. They disarmed themselves, before subsequently being handed over, unarmed, by the French to Hutu extremists, who massacred them (see Jessee, 2017a: 70). In Murambi, the terrible and fatal impact of Opération Turquoise is also discussed in general terms, along with allegations that French troops gang-raped survivors who had come to their military base for protection. The perceived lack of respect for the dead on the part of the French troops is also mentioned; their placing of a volleyball court directly next to a mass grave at Murambi (see above) is cited as a demonstration of this. It is also interpreted as demonstrating they were inspired by genocidal ideology.[32]

Colonialism

The third narrative focuses on the attribution of historical responsibility to international actors, both under formal colonialism and in the post-colonialist era. President Kagame used the occasion of the twentieth anniversary of the genocide to point to the colonial origin of ethnic divisions by stating:

> Historical clarity is a duty of memory that we cannot escape. Behind the words 'Never Again', there is a story whose truth must be told in full, no matter how uncomfortable. The people who planned and carried out the Genocide were Rwandans, but the history and root causes go beyond this country.[33]

Kagame's statement is based on the narrative that Rwandans lived in unity and harmony until the arrival of colonialists, who introduced and politicised ethnic divisions as part of their strategy of indirect rule (Buckley-Zistel, 2006a; Purdeková and Mwambari, 2022; Shyaka, 2003). How ethnicity 'became the weapon of the colonial master'[34] is discussed by exhibitions and guides at memorials, in education, during commemorative events and more broadly in the public discourse.[35]

A closer look at the KGM is instructive. The exhibition clearly communicates how ethnic divisions were introduced by the colonial powers and how these eroded unity, paving the way for future violence. It highlights 'the catastrophic impact of European theories of race and the Catholic Church on relations between Hutu, Tutsi, and Twa' (Jessee, 2017a: 54; see also Ibreck, 2013). A guide at the KGM explained that prior to colonisation, the identity groups Tutsi, Hutu and Twa were structured socio-economically but that the eighteen clans within the country, each of which had members in all three socio-economic groups, were more important. Pushing this further, he argued that the Belgian colonial power aimed to implement a genocidal ideology so they started promoting Tutsi and giving them preferential treatment, as they believed them to be better.[36] During a commemorative event in 2019 one of the participants posed the question: if divide and rule in colonial Rwanda was so key, why did genocide only take place in Rwanda and not in all the colonies that had experienced similar divide and rule strategies? Panel members and individuals in the audience gave various responses, but one trajectory in the responses was to highlight that divide and rule as a colonial strategy needed to be stronger in Rwanda because its people speak the same language and have the same culture. The country's unusually strong pre-colonial unity called for more strongly divisive measures on the part of the colonial powers, it was argued.[37]

Beyond memorials and museums, commemorative events offer further occasions for this narrative to be communicated. This statement during a commemorative event explains how the colonial power transferred its own ethnic difficulties onto its new subjects. It delineates a Rwanda before colonialism where unity prevailed and a Rwanda after colonialism where division prevailed:

> When the colonialists came in our country, they found us as a united front. First came the German but they didn't stay for long. They didn't do anything that destroyed the unity of the Rwandans. Then came the Belgian. Back in their country, there are two parts that don't agree with each other but act civil towards each other because they know the law. There are those that are called the Flemish people and the Walloons. They don't speak the same languages. They even don't live in the same areas to this point. Those are the kind of division that they brought and planted in the minds of Rwandans. That was based on the division they already had in their country. They came to Rwanda and decided to change the other social classes into ethnicities. They then said, these are Tutsi, those are Hutu and those are Twa. They also documented it. That is where the division among Rwandans started.[38]

No matter how the divisive policies of colonial powers are explained, the narratives all emphasise that these policies represented the origin of genocidal ideology in Rwanda: a once peaceful and united country was led into interethnic hostilities, laying the foundation for the 1994 genocide.

We generally do not disagree with the historical analysis of the destructive impact of colonialism and its complex legacy in the context of Rwanda and beyond. In our analysis of the mnemonic formation concerning the role of internationals, however, we are interested in illustrating how references to the colonial past are central to present-day memory politics. The recurring theme of colonialism legitimates the government's policy on what is officially referred to as 'unity and reconciliation', according to which the categories of Hutu and Tutsi were mere colonial inventions. This is enhanced by the legislation on divisionism, referred to above, that prohibits references to Hutu and Tutsi in public and political discourses. To produce unity and reconciliation, the national strategy requires the political importance of these ethnic markers to be diminished and seeks to abolish them altogether.

Events: international engagement through apologies and visits to memorial sites

As meaning-making performative mnemonic practices, events potentially have a strong impact on collective identities. The memoryscape of Rwanda is dotted with a variety of events, often in planned and regular intervals, particularly around the commemoration period Kwibuka, which starts on 7 April every year. Kwibuka translates as 'to remember' and often involves 'a walk to remember, night vigils, prayers, testimonies, poems, remembrance and healing songs, decent burial when new remains are discovered, speeches of the official guests' (Gahongayire, 2015: 113). International agents are also involved in commemoration, albeit to a relatively limited degree. Many events take place at the site of a memorial, but some are held at larger venues such as stadiums. As Wagner-Pacifici (2015) suggests, these events form a significant aspect of, yet also constantly reproduce, wider memory politics.

Apologies

Some of the most striking events in which internationals feature in Rwanda's memoryscape are those at which public apologies are offered by leading international politicians or senior representatives of foreign countries or organisations. These dignitaries formally admit guilt, either on behalf of themselves or the international actors they represent, for a failure to intervene in the genocide, often at memorial sites and/or during Kwibuka.[39] This is because, McMillan argues, in the international consciousness, the genocide is 'a source of "bitter regret" ... and "shame" ... for those who failed to prevent it' (McMillan, 2016: 170). Apologies are considered a powerful gesture towards the victims because they acknowledge that victims have been harmed. Apologies recognise wrongdoing on the part of the apologiser (Tirrell, 2013) and they reduce shame and guilt on the part of the actors responsible. Thus far, however, the public apologies by international dignitaries remain unmatched by any expressions of forgiveness on the part either of the victims or the Rwandan state. This is significant because it is in sharp contrast to national reconciliation programmes elsewhere which may have victim–perpetrator encounters as a central component, that is, genocide survivors in arranged meetings with individuals who carried out the genocide; in such programmes elsewhere, perpetrators are strongly encouraged to apologise, and victims are strongly encouraged to act in a spirit of reconciliation and to express forgiveness.

There is a long list of non-Rwandan figures who have offered their apologies. One of the first was Bill Clinton, who visited Rwanda in 1998 as US president to apologise for the actions – or rather inactions – that fell under his personal responsibility. During the genocide, it was the United States in particular that kept the UN from using the term genocide since it feared that sending foreign troops into Rwanda would repeat the debacle that had occurred in Somalia five years earlier, when US troops were publicly lynched. Clinton is reported to have said in his apology: 'We did not act quickly enough after the killings began. We should not have allowed the refugee camps to become safe havens for the killers. We did not immediately call the crimes by their rightful name: genocide' (cited in Tirrell, 2013: 174) Strikingly, though, Clinton only stayed for a few hours in Rwanda and did not even leave the airport. In preparation for his visit the Rwandan government had constructed a temporary memorial at the airport and had brought in human remains and mummified bodies from other sites (Korman, 2015: 61). In the end, Clinton did not lay a wreath at the airport memorial, very much to the disappointment of the Rwandan government. Its handling of Clinton's visit meanwhile had caused resentment among genocide survivors, who reportedly saw it as a pointless gimmick.[40] Given the function of apologies in acknowledging the harm done to the victim, such poorly executed events, which exacerbate the humiliation or anger of victims, will likely serve to reinforce the feeling of having been terribly wronged rather than mend any relationships.

Further apologies were offered by the then prime minister of Belgium, Guy Verhofstadt, in 2000, by Kofi Annan as UN secretary general in 1998, and by his successor at the UN, Ban Ki Moon in 2014. In 2017, Pope Francis asked for forgiveness for the Catholic Church's role in the massacres.[41] During his visit to the KGM in 2010, then French president Nicolas Sarkozy did not apologise as such, but delivered a broader message: 'What happened here is unacceptable, but what happened here compels the international community, including France, to reflect on the mistakes that stopped it from preventing and halting this abominable crime'.[42] Throughout these apologies we thus find narratives that correspond to the Rwandan government's perspective, as explained above.

It is key *who* apologises, that is, the apology must come from an agent who is considered to be responsible, so that the shame, guilt and remorse that the apologiser expresses can be deemed as direct and relevant. As such, these apologies are highly political events performed publicly by the highest statesmen and stateswomen. *Where* the apologies occur, the sites themselves, are usually chosen to be symbolic; the site selected most often, as we have seen, is the KGM, a space created for the memory of the entire genocide. The controversial nature of Clinton's airport apology reinforces this point: the location chosen contributes a potentially important symbolic weight. In Rwanda's memory politics, apologies as mnemonic practices thus have clear symbolic importance.

Visits to memorial sites

When internationals visit memorial sites (mainly the KGM) to apologise their visit is also an opportunity to perform regular diplomatic duties. According to Giblin, this required diplomatic engagement includes:

> a visit to the KMC [alternative acronym for Kigali Genocide Memorial Centre] shortly after arriving in the country, the laying of a wreath on the mass graves in front of the memorial wall, the touring of the exhibition inside the memorial-museum, the signing of the guest book, a speech in which an explicit or implicit apology is made for the failure to stop the genocide, and photographing by the media throughout the visit, especially the laying of the wreath and the viewing of the memorial exhibition. (Giblin, 2017: 60)

To name a few prominent visitors to the KGM: then UK prime minister Tony Blair visited in 2006, retired president Bill Clinton again in 2005 and George W. Bush while in office as US president travelled there in 2008. The KGM is thus a must-see for every high-profile visitor to Rwanda, not least due to the lingering feeling of guilt among members of the international community for having failed to intervene in the genocide. On 7 April, the first day of the annual commemorative events, international dignitaries show up for the official ceremonies, as happened in 2019, for example, at a high-profile gathering at the Kigali Convention Centre, followed by an event at the Amahoro Stadium in the same city. For the Rwandan government, in turn, this is a welcome opportunity to reinforce its own legitimacy, to create conditions that might encourage foreign investment and to put pressure on countries in which genocidal killers are still at large (Giblin, 2017). Against this backdrop, participation in commemoration events is not for all internationals. In 2014, the French ambassador to Rwanda was disinvited from the main ceremony in the Amahoro Stadium by President Kagame. When the ambassador asked if he could at least lay a wreath at the KGM, this too was denied. The diplomatic incident followed tensions between Paris and Kigali after Kagame stated prior to the commemoration that France had played a direct role in the genocide and had even participated in carrying it out on the ground.[43] Ten years earlier, the French vice-minister of foreign affairs had been present during the main commemorative event, and had found himself being directly accused by Kagame, who explained in his speech that the French had knowingly trained and armed the militias and army units who had carried out the genocide, and had criticised the audacity shown by the French when they participated in the event without having apologised (Reyntjens, 2011: 23).

The SANE analysis: memory and the quality of peace

Thirty years after the genocide, peace in Rwanda remains shallow. By exploring memory politics through sites, agents, narratives and events, this chapter has illustrated how the monolithic character of remembrance in Rwanda stands in the way of a memoryscape that allows alternative and plural accounts of the past. The mnemonic formation of the role of internationals serves as a diagnostic site for analysing present entanglement and peace.

We chose to look at memory politics through the prism of the role of the internationals – including the colonial administration, the UN, the French and Belgian military, the international community, international organisations and dignitaries – because they are a very visible topic in current memory discourse in Rwanda. The detrimental role of internationals is explained in today's memory politics as a continuity: from the era of colonialism up until today, internationals (in various forms and guises) have had a negative effect on the country. What is surprising, though, is that prior to the genocide there was no strong anti-Western or anti-colonial sentiment in Rwanda. Colonialism had been brought to an end there without violence against the colonial master, as Belgium simply granted full independence in 1962 (Mamdani, 2001: 106). While in other former colonies the struggle for, and the moment of, independence is highly constitutive for national identity, in Rwanda Independence Day on July 1 is a public holiday but is not a day when official celebrations are held. In contrast, three days later Liberation Day – the day the RPF/A liberated the country from *génocidaires* – is an important celebration because it preaches unity, as a Rwandan journalist explains.[44] Prior to the memory politics around the genocide, the international actors were thus not seen as the outside force responsible for suffering in the country. Yet, as Longman (2017: 265) stresses: 'The shift after 1994 to depicting the colonizers as a source of division and violence relieved Rwandans from their responsibility for what ultimately happened, allowing Hutu to feel less guilty and Tutsi to feel less threatened by their compatriots.'

Shaming internationals through narratives concerning their culpability also has the effect of silencing criticism of the current authoritarian government; this in turn allows an extremely hegemonic power structure to persist, suppressing any dissenting voices both with regard to how the past should be remembered as well as how the 'now' should be lived and the future imagined. 'Domesticating the world' (Reyntjens, 2011), that is, telling the world what to do and not to do, is used as a strategy to fend off criticism regarding Rwanda's illiberal democracy, poor human rights record and involvement in violence in neighbouring countries. This strategy is often accompanied by accusations from outside (and inside) the country that international actors are threatening the unity of the country or are supporting genocidal ideology.

What might be described as a historic shame prevents the international community and its institutions from pushing too far in terms of dealing with crimes carried out by the RPF during and after the 1990–1994 civil war and the genocide. The international community is therefore participating in silencing claims to victimhood that might emanate from communities or individuals that are not Tutsi. For Ibreck (2013: 152): 'Central to the Rwandese strategy for maintaining political autonomy was deploying the memory of the genocide, exploiting the guilt felt by development partners to fend off criticism.' So, while international donor money is expected for memorials, history teaching and other ways of spreading memory politics, it is expected to be used exclusively in line with government narratives. Events such as apologies, or participation in commemoration events by international actors, serve to bolster the government's legitimacy internationally. Agents such as the CNLG are in a very strong position to control memory discourses both in-country and beyond, and in doing so increasingly to silence alternative narratives. Ultimately, this will lead to an ever more pervasive muting of other actors.

Crucially, the hegemonic narratives about the past that clearly define good and bad (as illustrated with reference to our mnemonic formation of the internationals) lead to certain groups and individuals being excluded from being able to claim victimhood. As delineated in the first part of this chapter, remembering the genocide is strongly affected by individuals' experiences during the genocide. These experiences differ depending on age, whether a person was in the country in 1994, gender, and of course whether a person identifies as Hutu or Tutsi. By enforcing a top-down discourse around national unity and reconciliation – a discourse that does not allow anyone to identify as either Hutu or Tutsi and which until 2007 even precluded discussion of the genocide of the Tutsi – differences in grievances are eliminated.

There is just one exception: the memorial to the Belgian peacekeepers is tolerated even though the soldiers were non-Tutsi victims. This is a glaring exception to the otherwise ever stronger reticence about non-Tutsi victims. In fact, both Hutu and Twa were among those killed by Hutu extremists, sometimes for refusing to participate in the genocide, sometimes when mistaken for Tutsi or for other reasons.

Conclusions

Based on our analysis of internationals as mnemonic formations, our conclusions regarding Rwanda are sobering: the hegemonic memory politics of the Rwandan government has a strong, negative impact on political and social relations. Creating this enemy beyond the borders of Rwanda carries the promise of forging a coherent identity that will be neither Hutu nor Tutsi but Rwandan. Yet the way this has been orchestrated in a top-down manner, through a style of memory politics that does not leave room for alternative accounts, is detrimental. Peace remains shallow. Our look at the interplay of sites, agents, narratives and events does not reveal any entanglement of various ways of remembering the genocide, but rather finds a discourse that has been static – for thirty years – and continues to be hegemonic and exclusive. While memorials are often sites where diverse perspectives about a violent past are debated and discussed, in Rwanda memorials have 'constrained rather than encouraged democratic discourse' (Longman, 2017: 318). Instead of opening up a space for public participation they close it down and limit engagement of agents who conform with the general memory politics of the country. In Rwanda, therefore, memory politics leaves little space for plural voices about the past and instead reproduces the tenets of Rwanda's current illiberal regime.

As demonstrated in the other empirical chapters of this book, in societies emerging from violence there is usually not one hegemonic memory that dominates all interpretations of the past. Rather, we can observe various entangled strands that at times share the public space without friction and at times conflict and collide. In the case of Rwanda, we do not want to argue that a diversity of memories does not exist, but rather that this diversity is not given any space or recognition in public discourse. There are, of course, groups who remember the country's recent history differently, but they have to do so in private.

Regarding the role of the internationals, we agree with Pottier (2002: 203) that the RPF 'as Rwanda's post-genocide spiritual guardian, displays exceptional skill at converting international feelings of guilt and ineptitude into admissions that the [Rwandan Patriotic] Front deserves to have the monopoly on knowledge construction'. We conclude, therefore, that the prevailing mnemonic formations around the role of the internationals have a negative effect on peace. In Rwanda, the lack of plurality regarding memory sites, agents, narratives and events can be seen as an indicator of a closed political space where deeply entrenched conflict lines are difficult to challenge. While we agree that it is paramount to take issue with a toxic colonial legacy and to address the failures of the internationals during the genocide, in Rwanda this has been done in a way that does not allow for pluralism and alternative Rwandan voices. What results is a reckoning with the country's recent past that is deeply flawed.

Notes

1 The genocide has since 2014 officially been labelled the '1994 genocide against the Tutsi' (Baldwin, 2019: 356), a phrasing that is problematic in its redaction of any non-Tutsi suffering, but one that the government has been forceful in implementing in order to not allow any moral equivalency of violence against other groups.

2 Most recent academic studies estimate the number to be around half a million, while the Rwandan government estimate is much higher, at 1,074,017 (Ministère de l'Administration Locale, du Développement Communautaire et des Affaires Sociales, 2004).

3 Attempting to put a number to, respectively, Tutsi casualties of the genocide and Hutu casualties of war, as well as victims of crimes against humanity committed by the RPF/A after the genocide, is a highly sensitive task. For a multimethod discussion see Guichaoua (2020).

4 Conversation with an NGO staff member who was associated with a memorial research project. The precise number is hard to ascertain, particularly because it changes regularly, sometimes as new memorials are opened but more often as local memorials are closed and the mass graves moved to larger memorials.

5 The memorial in Gisenyi in the country's outer north-west was under renovation during data collection in mid-2018. It was scheduled to reopen in February 2019, but is not currently listed as a national memorial. It had been planned to include a detailed exhibition, similar to those at the KGM and Murambi sites.

6 At the Kigali Genocide Memorial an audio guide replaces a personal guide for most visitors.

7 Memorial visit in August 2018; notes from field journal.

8 Memorial visit in August 2018; notes from field journal.

9 Memorial visit in August 2018; notes from field journal.

10 Memorial visit in August 2018; notes from field journal.

11 Memorial visit in August 2018; notes from field journal.

12 At the time of fieldwork, the memorial in Gisenyi was under construction and was planned to include a full exhibition, similar to that at the KGM.

13 https://rcb.rw/Rwandan-Museums.html (19 January 2024).

14 Memorial visit in July 2018; notes from field journal.

15 Participant observation and informal conversations during commemorative events in April 2019; notes from field journal.

16 www.minubumwe.gov.rw/ (14 April 2023).

17 https://ibuka.rw/#about (27 March 2023).
18 Notes in field journal from informal conversations at local memorial sites in August 2018.
19 Informal conversation with an anonymous employee of an NGO in August 2019; notes from field journal.
20 Field notes from participant observation of various national and local commemorative events in April 2019.
21 Exhibition catalogue, p. 18.
22 Exhibition catalogue, p. 27.
23 Exhibition catalogue, p. 27.
24 Memorial visit in July 2018; notes from field journal.
25 Museum visit in August 2018; notes from field journal.
26 www.newtimes.co.rw/news/kwibuka25-belgian-peacekeepers-honoured (19 January 2024).
27 Memorial visit in August 2018; notes from field journal.
28 www.nytimes.com/2017/12/13/world/africa/rwanda-france-genocide.html (3 June 2020).
29 Exhibition catalogue, p. 27.
30 Memorial visit in August 2018; notes from field journal.
31 Researcher Augustine Nshimiyimana, speaking during commemorative event on 9 April 2019 at a sector-level memorial in Huye District.
32 Memorial visit in August 2018; notes from field journal.
33 http://paulkagame.com/?p=3339 (19 January 2024).
34 Researcher Augustine Nshimiyimana, speaking during commemoration event on 9 April 2019 at a sector-level memorial in Huye District.
35 For example, visits to Bisesero and the KGM in August 2018 and commemorative events in April 2019; notes from field journal.
36 Visit to memorial in August 2018; notes from field journal.
37 Field notes from participant observation of a commemorative event in April 2019 in a sector of Kicukiro, Kigali.
38 Field notes from participant observation of a commemorative event in April 2019 at a Pentecostal church in Karongi.
39 Kwibuka is 100 days long, but most national-level events are focused in the first week, while the remaining period sees commemorative events held in locales around the country, usually on the dates associated with killings in those specific communities.
40 http://news.bbc.co.uk/2/hi/special_report/1998/03/98/africa/69487.stm (10 June 2020).
41 www.theguardian.com/world/2017/mar/20/pope-francis-asks-for-forgiveness-for-churchs-role-in-rwanda-genocide (9 June 2020).
42 http://news.bbc.co.uk/2/hi/africa/8535803.stm (10 June 2020).
43 www.tdg.ch/l-ambassadeur-de-france-persona-non-grata-au-rwanda-140246574798 (30 March 2023).
44 www.dw.com/en/why-rwanda-doesnt-celebrate-independence-day/a-62318399 (30 March 2023).

5

South Africa: the legacies of colonialism

Although the colonial period of South Africa's history has clearly had considerable influence in shaping its contemporary political system, that influence is often downplayed in favour of a shorter-term focus on apartheid as a stand-alone phenomenon. In this chapter, therefore, we shall examine the mnemonic formation of South Africa's colonial era, investigating how this focus makes visible longer-established dynamics of marginalisation and a continuity of unequal governance that favours the colonial powers' descendants at the expense of those subject to the violent structures left by colonialism. We will show that the memory landscape as it pertains to colonialism is starkly divided between those who take that landscape for granted or even feel nostalgic about it and those who are seeking to challenge and transform it from different perspectives. Mutual entanglement between those two approaches is rare. The chapter will therefore illustrate the ways in which the South African memoryscape is fragmented between those mnemonic forces, which show considerable variation and diversity in and of themselves, and perhaps more so than in the case of Cyprus (analysed in Chapter 2). The various manifestations of colonialism, and of resistance against it, produce a much more complex picture of the South African post-colonial memoryscape than the commonly assumed binary distinction between black and white South African experiences.[1] Instead, articulations of resistance against colonial legacies in both material and symbolic forms have recently been gaining more traction. We will therefore show that the search for peace in South Africa will need to reflect this complexity and fluidity. An inclusive peace implies rectifying and repairing the persisting political, social and economic injustices created by colonial history. It also means that the diversity of interests, needs and positions on all the different sides needs to be adequately represented in any process that aims to restore justice to those who are disadvantaged and discriminated against by the legacy of colonial structures. To demonstrate this, the chapter will investigate a diversity of sites, agents, narratives and events that deal with the past of colonialism as well as the legacy of colonial violence. Their interplay will cast light on a segmented memoryscape that is shaped by mnemonic variations and dissonance in the ways in which European colonial presence is remembered today. We shall thus seek to understand why South Africa has struggled to achieve a peace that is considered just by most of its population and to illustrate how different forms of resistance are being mobilised to challenge the lingering power of colonialism in mnemonic terms. An exploration of the ways in which colonial memory is being countered is therefore an intrinsic element of the search for a just peace.

Colonial rule in South Africa

As in many other post-colonial societies, the history of colonial rule in South Africa as it affects the present is not a straightforward story. European efforts to colonise South Africa can be viewed in successive stages, starting with Portuguese explorers' attempts to establish trade relations on the Cape Peninsula on the south-western tip of South Africa. This was followed by a period of Dutch colonisation there (officially launched in 1652), and then British colonial armed intervention from the late eighteenth century was aimed at securing control of what was to become South Africa. Colonial rule had manifold manifestations and included the introduction of the slave trade by the Dutch East India Company (the Verenigde Oostindische Compagnie, or VOC), with enslaved workers being shipped in from Dutch colonies in Asia. The VOC shipped approximately 4,300 enslaved people to the Cape between 1652 and 1795 – when the territory formally came into the possession of the British Empire (Armstrong and Worden, 1989: 112). While the VOC had initially only been interested in using the Cape as an intermediate station for ships bound for Asia, their presence soon meant the loss of land by the indigenous population, not only to the Dutch but eventually also to British settlers. At the Cape, those affected were primarily the KhoiSan (that is, non-Bantu-speaking indigenous groups, many of whom were enslaved (Abrahams, 1996)). As a legacy of that period, the great bulk of land in South Africa is still today in the hands of white South Africans, who constitute less than 10 per cent of the population (see Department of Rural Development and Land Reform, 2017).

Colonial rule also led to the introduction of the migrant labour system. Sections of the local population were expelled from areas being industrialised and consigned to so-called 'homelands' in remote, less fertile parts of the country; the consequent decline of African agriculture would contribute to the availability of cheap, migrant labour. By the late nineteenth century, the discovery of diamonds in Kimberley and of gold near Johannesburg meant that British settlers and descendants of the original Dutch settlers (known as Boers and today referred to as Afrikaners) engaged in a race for wealth. Eventually the British army would engage with the Boers in the conflict now referred to as the South African War. The British and the Boers eventually concluded a peace accord that led to the creation in 1910 of the Union of South Africa as a self-governing dominion of the British Empire. This laid the foundations for the further formalisation of white rule and ultimately, from 1948, the apartheid state – even as much of the rest of Africa was beginning to move towards independence from white rule. When South Africa became a republic in 1961, therefore, its non-white population effectively achieved independence from Britain but without decolonisation. Many of the laws that the apartheid state would employ to segregate people based on their race had been introduced under colonial rule, including the Native Land Act (1913) and the Urban Areas Act (1923). Such legislation was aimed at ensuring the forced removal of non-white people from the centres of profit and was situated in a wider landscape of spatial inequalities (see Beinart and Delius, 2014; Parnell, 2002).

Colonialism can be seen, therefore, as an overarching phenomenon that inevitably involved diverse forms of violence. These were both direct (physical violence, forced movements of communities, land grabs) and structural-symbolic (the privileging of settlers' needs over indigenous needs, setting up structures of inequality) (see Maddison, 2013). What all these forms of violence have in common, though, is a clear social stratification between white people and 'others' (including black, 'coloured', Asian and indigenous people),[2] with the white people creating hierarchies that would necessarily elevate them over the other categories they had assigned. The dehumanisation of the other through discriminatory tools of governance is part and parcel of such approaches (Kebede, 2001: 540). If we then move to understand apartheid as a continuation of, rather than a break with, colonial practices, we understand that many policies that the apartheid state exploited – such as the Land Act of 1913 which effectively dispossessed 'natives' – reach back to the era before apartheid. As Ramutsindela (2001: 60) demonstrates, the structures in which the South African nation has taken shape are built on the foundations of a colonial state. As a result, the ways in which cultural heritage is celebrated, that is, whether in an inclusive or exclusive manner, is a dynamic that emerges out of the post-colonial state (Ramutsindela, 2001: 79) and is therefore deeply structured by the power relations established during the course of colonial rule. Memory is the negotiating agent between the colonial past and its legacies, which continue to shape the present.

The South African memoryscape

Various local, regional and global histories intersect across South Africa's history. However, what the country is most known for in mnemonic terms, both locally and internationally, is the period of apartheid, which shaped South African society in the twentieth century. There is a richness of academic writing on the ways in which the apartheid past is being dealt with and commemorated, from studies on the long-term implications of the Truth and Reconciliation Commission (TRC) (Vora and Vora, 2004) to the memorialisation (Marschall, 2010) and artistic processing (Miller and Schmahmann, 2017) of this violent episode of history. Museums and monuments dedicated to apartheid oppression can be found all over the country: Johannesburg's Apartheid Museum and the Hector Pieterson Museum, Cape Town's Robben Island prison and the site of Mandela's capture in KwaZulu-Natal are just a few of the many manifestations of the effort to deal with the legacy of apartheid through memory work. It is therefore hardly surprising that the memorialisation of apartheid has become the prime marker of the country's tourist engagement (see Björkdahl and Kappler, 2019), representing a key incentive for many visitors, especially those from Europe.

Certainly, the visibility of apartheid in South Africa's physical heritage landscape has to be seen as intimately linked to that of the African National Congress (ANC) (Cawfood and Fisher, 2022). In a way, the liberation struggle led by prominent figures within the ANC – including Steve Biko, Winnie and Nelson Mandela and Oliver Tambo – is a central factor in understanding the continued popular legitimacy of the ANC, despite the numerous challenges that South Africa is currently facing. These challenges range from questions of inequality and poverty to poor housing and infrastructure, with fear and crime remaining visible markers, particularly in urban zones. A mnemonic narrative that is heavily scripted by on-going political contestations is tangible in the ways in which the nation understands both its recent past and its transition to a new, more democratic state from 1994. Nonetheless, first-hand memories of apartheid continue to be contested, incorporating a number of tensions between different social forces that have not been resolved to this day.

At the same time, we suggest that the focus on apartheid as an isolated episode that originated in 1948, rather than as a continued phenomenon of colonialism, has tended to compartmentalise and contain guilt within South Africa's national realm. The fact that apartheid represents an institutionalisation of colonial practices in the realm of the South African state cannot be ignored, so that a clear distinction between *before* and *during* apartheid makes only limited sense. Instead, along the lines of what

Gregory (2004) calls 'the colonial present', we could argue that colonialism successfully found ways of infiltrating the state, with the result that its influence endured beyond its formal life-cycle and was clearly seen in the governance techniques employed by the apartheid government. Therefore, while the effects of colonialism spilled into what then became known as the apartheid regime, responsibility for continuing forms of violence came to be shifted towards South African actors rather than the colonial powers. Internationally, this has naturally served the post-colonial powers, which are thus able to avoid engaging with how they are historically implicated in South African politics. Domestically, this avoidance has also meant that the topic of reparations (land return, most prominently) has partly shifted off the political agenda (Forde et al., 2021). This was possible because apartheid was, at least for a certain amount of time, considered as dealt with, and a closure achieved through the mechanisms of the TRC, which prioritised forgiveness and amnesty at the expense of redistribution and reparation (see Walters, 2009). An engagement with the colonial roots of apartheid would have required more profound, controversial and contested questions to be addressed, and would risk mobilising forces that might threaten the fragile status quo. Such an engagement has consequently often been avoided in contemporary political and academic discourses. Any interrogation of why the TRC's mandate was limited to the apartheid, rather than being broadened out to include the longer-term legacies of colonialism, questions the extent to which the changes in South Africa in the 1990s in fact signal the rebirth of the nation (Witz et al., 2017: 2). There has indeed been a critique voiced vis-à-vis the TRC for failing to reach back into the colonial period (see Walters, 2009: 47). This is perhaps particularly surprising in a context in which it has been argued that even the mechanisms of the TRC itself can partly be traced to colonial origins (Sitze, 2013). Having said that, it is noticeable that in recent years increasing attention has been paid to the legacies of colonialism, including the status of indigenous groups, as well as to slavery and colonial resource exploitation. The higher visibility of indigenous identities in public spaces or the presence of the Iziko Slave Lodge (Cape Town), as we will outline, are indicators of these higher levels of mobilisation around the longer-term legacies of violence, illuminating historical processes beyond the immediate legacies of apartheid. Colonial legacies are not immune to emerging resistance.

This is certainly not to dichotomise apartheid and colonialism as competing memory discourses from which one has to be chosen as more salient than the other. Instead, it is to suggest that apartheid can be seen as the extension and continuation of longer-standing global patterns of oppression. Herwitz (2011: 235) suggests that without the South African War (between the British army and the Boer settlers), the apartheid state would not have come into existence – something which suggests the pathway dependencies of different historical episodes. An approach that instead considers the continuities of violence in turn allows us to view South African politics as part of a global, historical pattern and no longer absolves the colonial power from its implication in the various manifestations of violence that were introduced through colonial rule, some of which we will outline. This is particularly relevant in a context in which heritage has often been seen as inherently therapeutic (Meskell and Scheermeyer, 2008) rather than transformative. Therefore, the reduction of apartheid into a twentieth-century phenomenon may not be sufficient in addressing the traumas and socio-economic inequalities that have their origins in South Africa's colonial past, and which continue to haunt the poorest of the poor particularly. What is more, the field of heritage continues to be marked by 'complexity, controversy and contestation' (Rassool, 2000: 1). History in this respect continues to be subject to social contestation (Stanley and Dampier, 2005: 110) and post-colonial questions such as land return or the continued disparities in resource distribution are at the heart of such struggles. The mnemonic representations of colonial violence are often scripted in subtle, unofficial transcripts. Witz et al. (2017: 27 ff.), for instance, stress the importance of investigating oral histories in order to gain deeper access to such marginalised voices, beyond the discourses represented in the formalities of post-colonial public spaces.

Mnemonic formation: colonialism

A notable chain of events in terms of challenging South Africa's colonial legacies was the student protests in the context of the #RhodesMustFall campaign. The protests began in 2015 when a student at the University of Cape Town (UCT) put human excrement on the statue of Cecil Rhodes which powerfully overlooks the university campus. The figure of Rhodes, a leading British colonialist in southern Africa in the 1890s, is across the region and beyond a strong signifier of the colonial period, and the campaign quickly gained local, national and global momentum (Holmes and Loehwing, 2016: 1207). Students went to protest against the colonial legacies in the design, curricula and staffing of their universities and in Cape Town were eventually successful in having the statue removed from its central position on campus; today, only the pedestal remains as a reminder of its formerly prominent position. Certainly, the removal of the statue can only be seen as the tip of the iceberg: protests continued thereafter, linking the colonial legacies of higher education to questions of social justice in the form of the #FeesMustFall campaign. The extent to which the protests affected discussions around higher education must not be underestimated (although tuition fees were, at least initially, not raised as a grievance). The protests were received with both praise and scepticism among the wider public. However, their longer-term legacy remains to be seen. For instance, there is still an equestrian statue of Rhodes behind the UCT campus, one of the streets at UCT is still named Rhodes Avenue and very close to the campus we can still find a Rhodes High School. Similar tensions have emerged at other universities around the country as well: the University of Pretoria continues to have a reputation as a 'white' university, while Stellenbosch University is working, through its Transformation Office, to deal with its strong colonial and apartheid legacies.

It is particularly striking that the post-apartheid government has adopted an approach that means leaving colonial and apartheid-era monuments untouched (Marschall, 2006: 177). As a result, we can still find plenty of physical reminders of colonialism, and even glorifications of that phenomenon, throughout South Africa. With numerous statues of Rhodes still prominently in situ in public spaces, there is still a flavour of heroism around the colonial legacies as well as notions of progress, reflecting a certain romanticising of the colonial past. The government has broadly decided to not remove such physical reminders of colonialism and apartheid and has instead been funding new, modern memorials signalling the transition to a new South Africa. This decision can be read as an attempt to reconcile the colonial past with the transition to democracy – an approach that has certainly been controversial as it continues to grant perpetrators of violence public space (Herwitz, 2011: 238), coupled with a risk of further alienating local communities from the heritage that surrounds them (Ndoro and Pwiti, 2001). What this means is that there is a bifurcation in South Africa's mnemonic landscape: on the one hand, the reminders of a violent past are still publicly visible; on the other hand, there are attempts to counter those with new memorials that signal the birth of a new nation. Yet, as this chapter will show, much of the resistance against colonial legacies does not emerge from formal, government-led processes, but is instead a result of hard work at the grassroots and the engagement of activists who have been fighting for transformation for a long time.

In terms of mnemonic stratification, it certainly has to be said that colonialism as a mnemonic formation is not divided only along the lines of race. Partly reflective of the wider mnemonic landscape of South Africa, it can be said to be primarily male dominated (Coombes, 2003: 107 ff.; Marschall, 2006: 180; Witz et al., 2017: 47), with limited change taking place in terms of how such representations are challenged. Divisions in society that are mirrored in the colonial mnemonic formation can thus be said to be intersectional, split along the lines of race, gender and class – to name but a few lines of segregation. This fragmentation is clearly reflected in the mnemonic formation around colonialism, which is shaped by competing centrifugal forces, as our analysis of sites, agents, narratives and events will show.

Sites: holding nostalgia and resistance in place

Mnemonic sites hold memory in place and give it material presence in the public sphere. In that sense, the physical landscape upon which the materials of South African heritage rest is shaped by the bifurcation between colonial and post-colonial artefacts. In fact, 'the physical landscape remains riddled with colonial architecture and monuments that recall histories of exclusion and violent oppression' (Autry, 2012: 147). As outlined above, while this was a deliberate strategy by the ANC government in terms of its approach to heritage, the fact that Cecil Rhodes continues to be present all over Cape Town in the form of statues can be seen as alienating to many (Holmes and Loehwing, 2016: 1212) and therefore produces a range of powerful activist responses, some of which we will outline. The sites we discuss in this chapter are only a small selection from a vast memoryscape. They have been chosen for their iconic character and their influence on the debates around South Africa's colonial legacies.

Colonial nostalgia at the Voortrekker Monument and the Rand Club

Perhaps one of the most well-known and most contested monuments reminiscent of colonial South Africa is the Voortrekker Monument, a gigantic stone-based monument that stands on a hill outside the country's administrative capital, Tshwane/Pretoria.[3] Inaugurated in 1949, it strongly evokes the apartheid government, which erected it 'to commemorate the Day of the Covenant, an Afrikaner holiday marking the occasion when fewer than 500 Voortrekkers, led by Andries Pretorius, defeated 10,000 Zulu fighters in retaliation for a Zulu attack in the Battle of Blood River in 1838, according to Afrikaner mythology' (Autry, 2012: 149). Certainly, given the historical reference point that is being commemorated as the nineteenth-century Great Trek of Afrikaner settlers towards Pretoria, it can be considered a colonial monument, dating back to the period preceding the formal establishment of the apartheid system. The site itself has a rather powerful aura about it: situated on top of a hill overlooking the city and built in an imposing, monolithic style, from the outside it signals power and sturdiness. On the inside, it comes across as myth-laden, featuring romantic depictions of pilgrimage in both its carved murals as well as through the artefacts exhibited on its lower floor. There is little text accompanying the displays to contextualise the story for visitors. Instead, the space plays with imagery,

Figure 5.1 Voortrekker Monument (photograph by Stefanie Kappler, November 2017)

visual representations and mythical depictions of colonial battles. In that vein, the eternal flame that forms part of the monument can be interpreted as the Afrikaners' symbol of bringing 'civilisation' (Holmes and Loehwing, 2016: 1213), in a metaphor deeply rooted in the colonial imagination. The Voortrekker Monument sits somewhat uncomfortably in South Africa's mnemonic landscape, acting as 'a repository for Afrikaner material culture, which no longer fits easily into the exhibitions of national culture and history at mainstream museums' (Autry, 2012: 155). There had been discussions about the future of the monument, which largely finances itself from visitors' contributions, but the ANC eventually decided it should remain as a reminder of apartheid (Coombes, 2003: 20). Including a Garden of Remembrance and the South African Defence Force Wall of Remembrance, the Voortrekker has elevated itself to the status of primary mnemonic site for the Afrikaner community and continues to represent memory from the romanticised perspective of the Great Trek.

To a certain extent, what the Voortrekker is to the nostalgic Afrikaner community is what the Rand Club in Johannesburg is for the nostalgic white, English-speaking community, descended from British settlers. Situated in downtown Johannesburg, in a rather impoverished area, the Rand Club building stands out as a symbol of past imperial glory and resource wealth. Rhodes had it built in 1887 at the height of the area's gold rush – which was essentially the reason why the city of Johannesburg came into existence. The Rand Club was established as a private club, exclusive by nature and design, and built for white business entrepreneurs. Today it retains this policy of exclusiveness, with no random visitors allowed in. Women have only been admitted since 1993. Although it is not a museum, nor is it intended as formal memorial to an era, the club still projects a spirit of colonialism through the ways in which its interior is set out. Munro (2018) describes this as follows: 'Rhodes' spirit is still right there, as you move towards the bar. He stands as a custodian to the colonial past as a small bronze figure, in iconic pose pointing to a British hinterland in Africa.' Much of the interior is indeed, if not maintained in the original material, rebuilt with material imported from the United Kingdom to retain a notion of authenticity (as a bartender pointed out during a personal visit to the club). There may be a small degree of transformation taking place at this site: there is a statue of Paul Kruger, Rhodes' Afrikaner opponent, which could be read as a sign of atonement in respect of the Afrikaner community, as well as images of Nelson Mandela and Thabo Mbeki (Munro, 2018). This, however, does not detract from the feeling that this is still a place of the 1900s (Munro, 2018; and personal research diary, 2017). Colonialism, classism and racism are tangible within this space. They are articulated not only through the artefacts on casual display in the club and an interior design bursting with

Figure 5.2 Entrance door to the Rand Club with reflection in mirror (photograph by Stefanie Kappler, November 2017)

icons of wealth, but also through its closed-door policy. Despite current ambitions to revamp the space in terms of modernising it (as of 2019), it still stands as a mnemonic space, frozen in time and reminiscent of an enduring colonial mind-set that still tends to exclude non-white people, women and those living in poverty.

ANC-led heritage: Freedom Park

Rather than dismantling such colonial-era monuments or sites as the Voortrekker and the Rand Club, the ANC government has moved proactively to fund and support more inclusive memories through its National Legacy Projects, which aim to address a wider section of the population. Those projects are selected and officially identified as heritage sites deemed particularly worthy of preservation, enjoying legislative and financial support from the government.

One of the most important sites among the government's National Legacy Projects is Freedom Park, a memorial site outside Tshwane/Pretoria, which opened in 2007 and covers a vast area of land. Freedom Park is to be seen as part of a larger collection of Legacy Projects, which all speak to the emergence of a rainbow nation and are intended to underline an appreciation of diversity as the country moves on from the years of apartheid. They famously include the former prison site on Robben Island and Constitution Hill in Johannesburg, which, according to the Department of Arts and Culture, 'create visible reminders of, and commemorate, the many aspects of South Africa's past' (Department of Sport, Arts and Culture, 2020).

Unlike the Rand Club with its spirit of wealth and its recent moves to espouse inclusion, Freedom Park is pervaded with symbols of poverty and the experience of being excluded. It curates histories of slavery and colonialism and presents artefacts from this violent history. Spread across a hill adjacent to that of the Voortrekker Monument, Freedom Park can be viewed as a counter-monument to the former (Autry, 2012: 148) and was deliberately set up to form a different perspective to the Voortrekker's romanticised approach to colonialism. To a certain extent, there are parallels: like the Voortrekker, the Freedom Park in a claim to inclusivity likewise commemorates the South African War of 1899 to 1902, and features a memorial wall including the names of around 75,000 fallen fighters from the different sides of fighting, both white and black South Africans. However, Freedom Park does not take the 'white experience' as its point of departure, and its strong focus on colonial history is done in an attempt to present the points of view of those oppressed by colonial violence and to feature more traditional African and indigenous world views. Particularly the objects on display in its main exhibition building suggest a focus on a pre-colonial genealogy

Figure 5.3 Part of the memorial wall at Freedom Park (photograph by Stefanie Kappler, November 2017)

and a pan-African approach to South African heritage. Nevertheless, the objects that visitors can view in the open air, and specifically the Garden of Remembrance, do deal more directly with some of the on-going tensions in the South African memoryscape. The Wall of Names, for instance, commemorates South African victims of various wars (including the two world wars along with the South African War) in an attempt to speak to a range of groups in the country.

In-betweenness at hybrid sites: the Castle of Good Hope and the Iziko Slave Lodge

In line with the government's policy of juxtaposing rather oppressive sites, such as the Voortrekker Monument, with a set of newly curated sites, such as the National Legacy Projects, there are also attempts to redesign colonial-era memorial sites through a rescripting of their messages (see Forde, 2019). Although originally a colonial site, the castle in Cape Town is being rescripted to provide a perspective that is somewhat challenging to its colonial past. It certainly cannot be denied that the Castle of Good Hope – as it was called in Dutch and Afrikaans when built by the Dutch East India Company in the seventeenth century – has a history clearly associated with colonial violence and continues to serve as a marker of colonial power (Witz et al., 2017: 106). On the other hand, there are now attempts to use the space to feature indigenous histories, as well as some artwork that can be read as problematising colonial violence. The personification of the attempted hybridisation of colonial and indigenous histories at the castle is the historically verified figure of Krotoa (also known as Eva),[4] an indigenous woman who worked under Jan Van Riebeeck, the colonial administrator of the Dutch East India Company, and who acted as a translator between the Khoi people and the Dutch. While she can be said to have long been a somewhat contested figure, first in terms of potentially having acted as a traitor to her own community by working with the Dutch and second in relation to her being banished to the prison on Robben Island for alleged alcohol problems, she has nevertheless been claimed as an ancestor by some indigenous as well as Afrikaner groups. She represents an in-between character. To her memory, a bench was dedicated on the grounds of the castle in 2016. The bench inscription reads:

> This bench, produced from a beam of ironwood from the Castle of Good Hope, honours the memory of Krotoa, a Khoi woman, a servant, interpreter, mother and widow who was burried [sic] here on the 30th of September 1674.
>
> We honour the memory of Krotoa, as hers is a story of endurance, fortitude, hope and triumph of the human spirit over adversity. We see in her the convergence of prejudice and humiliation based on race and gender.

> Krotoa's life epitomises the very struggles that many women in our society are still faced with today.
>
> This bench was unveiled by the Honourable Minister of Defence and Military Veterans,
>
> Nosiviwe Noluthando Mapisa-Nqakula
>
> on the 19th of August 2016.

The gesture by those administering the site to dedicate a bench to Krotoa's memory can be seen as a powerful one in terms of acknowledging indigenous histories alongside dominant colonial memories, as they are presented at the castle. Yet it is certainly remarkable that the name that is marked in bold on the bench is not Krotoa's but that of the minister who unveiled the bench. This choice can certainly be read as a marker for the ways in which the history of Krotoa is only partly about her as a woman and a historically significant actor; at least as importantly it is an opportunity for the current ANC government to present itself as the legitimate curator of her legacy. Indeed, some of that kind of tension is tangible at the castle throughout. A source speaking under condition of anonymity pointed out that, although the site does host much that is relevant to the indigenous histories of the Western Cape, some people still feel hesitant to visit it due to its colonial and military connotations.[5] Indeed, the castle is still army property and comes across as such to visitors as well through the presence of military personnel and arms exhibitions. Any transformative ambitions with respect to the

Figure 5.4 Memorial bench for Krotoa at the Castle of Good Hope (photograph by Stefanie Kappler, July 2018)

Castle of Good Hope have therefore so far been somewhat limited in their application.

Certainly, the figure of Krotoa implicitly stands for a very particular type of 'coloured' heritage, in how her story relates to the encounter between the KhoiSan and the Afrikaner communities, although the question of the VOC's involvement in the slave trade is usually elided. This history can primarily be found curated in the Iziko Slave Lodge in Cape Town. One of the city's oldest buildings, it was once where enslaved people, mainly from Asia, were held by the VOC. The museum now offers visitors a permanent exhibition on the history of slavery in Cape Town. This is complemented with a number of temporary exhibitions speaking to contemporary socio-political issues, such as gender-based violence or the question of the repatriation of human remains as they relate to colonialism. The fact that the museum oscillates between its focus on history and on contemporary issues is illustrated by its very structure: while the ground floor is dedicated to its historical and political exhibitions, the upper galleries continue to house objects that are largely unrelated to slavery (such as silverware and pottery items). The museum website suggests that those latter exhibition spaces are in the process of being updated and transformed (Iziko, 2020a), while their very existence is a testimony to the wider curatorial debates that history museums are undergoing in terms of whether they focus on an activist as opposed to a conservative approach. It also reflects the limitations that larger, formal institutions face when critically engaging with troubled histories. Much of the substantial resistance against colonialist perspectives, and efforts to recast the memory of colonialism, emerges not from such large institutions but from informal, activist spaces, such as the Lwandle Migrant Labour Museum.

Community-based museums: the Lwandle Migrant Labour Museum

While the mnemonic sites outlined above tend to benefit from access to funding and institutional power, it is much more difficult for those in poorer and politically marginalised communities to create sites in which their interpretations of colonialism are curated and heard. Yet community initiatives situated outside the urban centres are reclaiming community heritage as their own. The Lwandle Migrant Labour Museum (LMLM), for instance, was established in the Lwandle township outside Cape Town in an attempt to institutionalise memories of the migrant labour system that originated under colonialism, from the perspective of those whose movement was controlled by the colonial and then the apartheid administrations (Mgijima and Buthelezi, 2006). It was set up in collaboration – as well as amid a degree of friction – with the inhabitants of Lwandle. The museum's aim is to

Figure 5.5 Courtyard of Slave Lodge (photograph by Stefanie Kappler, June 2018)

Figure 5.6 Lwandle Migrant Labour Museum (photograph by Stefanie Kappler, July 2018)

commemorate the harsh conditions under which the black labour force was exploited in the past. In its main exhibition space the visitor is confronted with objects relating to segregation under apartheid, as well as life stories from Lwandle community members, testifying to how they were affected by the migrant labour system. Elements of the exhibition space also flag up on-going issues of eviction in the Lwandle neighbourhood, thus weaving together elements of past and present injustices. Next to the exhibition space is Hostel 33, a space in which the museum visitor can contemplate what the crowded accommodation endured by migrant workers in Lwandle might have looked like and felt like. The furniture in the space, as well as its rudimentary sanitary facilities, indicate the dire conditions in which the workers would have been housed at the time. This experience is reinforced by the location of the museum in one of the poorer communities outside Cape Town, so that the museum visitor is confronted not only with the historical message of the museum, but also, in passing through the neighbourhood where it stands, with some of the long-term legacies of colonial-era inequality.

As the sites discussed in this section have shown, there are a variety of ways in which the memory of colonialism can be curated, both in romantic and transformative terms. While the funding situation and access to political power differs from site to site, it is notable that many of the sites resort to a mechanism of formal museum communication to emplace their mnemonic messages. Curatorial differences can clearly be found between the different sites – the LMLM, for instance, places much more emphasis on oral histories than do the exhibits found in the Rand Club or the Voortrekker Monument – but there seems to be a deliberate choice of the museum format as a way of articulating, editing and presenting contested histories (Kappler and McKane, 2022). However, community museums such as the LMLM are situated within the community they seek to represent and stand in a more direct position of accountability to that same community. The memories generated at that site are therefore in direct correspondence with those who provide, shape and curate it locally.

Agents: engaging colonial memory

Actors involved in South African memory-making are manifold and can be found at local, national and international levels. They range from smaller grassroots organisations to major government initiatives promoting the curation of memories as they relate to contemporary political goals. Identifying the primary locations of agency in the field is further complicated by the fact that many of the memory artefacts are to be found in private hands and are thus not accessible to the public or are only partially accessible. This is one reason why, we would suggest, the fragmentation of memory also extends to the ways in which mnemonic agency is shaped. Quite a few smaller heritage organisations and groups tend to align themselves with particular stakeholder interests, as this ensures at least a degree of visibility and funding from their own target audience. At the same time, it also prevents any denser entanglement or cross-overs between the various agents in society and thus contributes to the development of parallel narratives, not unlike the case of Cyprus.

Curating and funding colonial nostalgia

Colonial nostalgia is curated in private and public spaces. Specifically connected with the Voortrekker Monument and its management is the Heritage Foundation (Erfenisstigting), located at the foot of the monument. The foundation primarily caters to an Afrikaner audience and sustains itself solely through donations. The kinds of memory it features (as presented in the exhibition space) certainly relay a particular version of history, with the Anglo-Boer War (elsewhere now generally referred to as the South African War) playing a central role and a memorial to fallen soldiers just outside the foundation headquarters only featuring those South Africans who died up until 1993 – the year when apartheid formally ended. The foundation thus works within a community that more or less identifies with the Voortrekker version of history and generates its income that way. Their role is to be seen as promoting the historical version of the Great Trek, both within the Afrikaner community itself and to its national and international visitors alike.

While the Voortrekker Monument is dependent on donations and ticket sales, including from tourists, the Rand Club is dependent on its own fundraising model. As a private club, it is largely run by its membership and funded by membership fees as well as by hosting events (weddings, parties etc.). The management changed recently, but the fundamental structures have remained in place, in that the membership is the main decision-making body of the club. Certainly, the figure of Rhodes, as a white, British colonialist, is crucial in articulating the kinds of actors who will typically engage in and with the club. Despite now being open to all genders and races, members can be said to be mainly drawn from the wealthier sections of Johannesburg and to be largely uncritical of the colonial legacies that are at the origin of the club. The Rand Club specifically emphasises the closed and exclusive nature of its operations, as non-member visitors were, until very recently, not allowed inside the club. In 2019, in an attempt to generate income to sustain the club's financial situation, it became possible for non-members to dine inside the club. The management and membership are thus no longer exclusively about protecting a narrative of British colonialism; the main concern is to generate the revenues that help the club stay afloat. A degree of modernisation and an influx of new users of the space come with this decision. Such new users may be less explicitly prone to colonial nostalgia, yet still pursuing that feelings of glamour and exclusivity that the club sought to symbolise through its implicit connection with the British Empire. Such new forms of agency, in terms of who uses the space, ensure that the club takes into account its role in a changed political landscape, now reinventing itself as a commercially accessible heritage venue for events (Rand Club, n.d.).

Apart from such high-profile, larger institutions maintaining heritage from a colonial past, there are quite a large number of smaller heritage organisations, some with subtly stated group affiliations, some with the primary goal of preserving heritage at the national, South African, level. Examples would be the Johannesburg Heritage Foundation, the Gauteng Heritage Action Group, the Heritage Portal, the Heritage Monitoring Project, the Tshwane Building Heritage Organisation, the Cape Town Heritage Trust, among many others. They tend to share a focus on the built environment, that is, tangible heritage, and are often operated by volunteers. It is noticeable that not all, but the majority, of the smaller organisations focusing on tangible heritage are run by white South African communities and often the heritage that is to be protected attracts mainly white tourists (see Snowball and Courtney, 2010: 567). As a result, the bifurcation of heritage activism is, perhaps inadvertently, mirrored in the kinds of areas and heritage that are deemed worthy of preservation by such organisations. Their concerns tend to reflect a more privatised agenda in terms of representing small sub-sectors of the population and stand somewhat in contrast to the more inclusive ambitions implied in the ANC government's declared agenda. It also means that their agency is considerable vis-à-vis their own host communities, yet is limited with respect to an engagement that reaches across the already interested and involved volunteers.

ANC-led agency: memory and the state

From the government's point of view, and in response to the strong presence of colonial nostalgia in the South African memoryscape, the Department of Arts and Culture has established National Legacy Projects that receive government support in their heritage work. These are primarily focused on, although not limited to, the heritage of the apartheid period and represent important reference points for domestic politics and also for being placed on the tourist map. Particularly with respect to obtaining donations from

European donors or tourist income, a focus on apartheid history has of course been a more common approach than a focus on colonial oppression, locally and globally (see Rassool, 2000). However in terms of visitors to those sites, it is somewhat striking that, despite the curatorial efforts at Freedom Park, the Voortrekker Monument has around fifteen times as many visitors (Jethro, 2016: 456). Indeed, during a personal visit to both monuments in 2017, on two subsequent days, the Voortrekker Monument was overcrowded, particularly with tourists arriving by tour buses, whereas we seemed to be the only visitors at Freedom Park. In that sense, the two adjacent memorial sites serve very different audiences and are used very differently. The road connecting them has, with powerful symbolism, been named Reconciliation Road but does not seem to be regularly used by pedestrians or cars.

Freedom Park is less financially dependent on visitor numbers than is the Voortrekker Monument, given that it enjoys considerable government support and funding. It is a flagship project that symbolises what the ANC government seeks to embody, namely the notion of a 'rainbow nation', shaped by the struggle against an oppressive past and going forward through a pan-African prism. Like some of the other government-supported heritage sites (Robben Island being a particularly prominent example), such sites generate a degree of income through sales of entrance tickets and also fulfil the role of narrating a history from the perspective of the ANC. This agenda can be read as a way of diplomatically mitigating the more exclusive aspects of heritage that romanticise colonial rule in South Africa, without necessarily explicitly condemning it. And while Freedom Park may enjoy its status as part of the government's Legacy programme, its outreach into wider society is hampered by the lack of visitors, and perhaps by the fact that potential local and national visitors may feel this site is not in a strong position to address questions of inequality and the continuing influence of the colonial era.

Curating in-betweenness

Another formal memory institution, the Castle of Good Hope, is connected to the government's overall approach to heritage in terms of recontextualising some of its problematic colonial heritage. Certainly, some agency has to be ascribed to the curators of the actual sites that speak from positions of in-betweenness. The castle, a site with historical authenticity, is administered by the Castle Control Board, which has oversight of the museum's curatorial activities and continues to house the Cape Town Highlanders Regiment, thus maintaining a link to its military history. At the same time, the ways in which the narratives of the KhoiSan (in this chapter explored through the symbolic role of Krotoa) are advocated have to be seen from beyond the walls of the museum, including the work of memory activists, among others. For instance, the activism of the KhoiSan groups and descendants of Krotoa have been important in understanding the ways in which the castle has approached its historically problematic role, in the life of Krotoa and beyond. Jethro (2017: 350) outlines the protests mounted by those groups in 2015 over the fact that Krotoa was memorialised through a bench, an item that is used to sit on or, unfortunately, to urinate against. This protest is linked to the KhoiSan's return of Krotoa's spirit to the castle the following year, a process through which the agency of the past curators and that of the KhoiSan became intertwined, in an attempt to find ways of commemorating Krotoa in a dignified way. It has to be seen as part of a larger picture in which Krotoa is discussed as a key mnemonic character in terms of understanding her role as an in-betweener between the KhoiSan and the Dutch colonisers, whether that be through literature (see Conradie, 1998) or a controversial film, *Krotoa*, made in 2017.

In comparison, one could argue that the slave narrative is somewhat more centrally controlled by the curators of the Iziko Slave Lodge. The museum at the Slave Lodge, however, also maintains links to the KhoiSan communities and involves them in a number of its projects. In addition, while the permanent exhibitions of the Slave Lodge are directly ascribed to the museum's curatorial agency, and highlight the Cape Carnival as a marker of the rich cultural heritage introduced to the area by enslaved people, the site also hosts a number of temporary exhibitions that transcend the immediate original focus of the Slave Lodge, instead drawing links with contemporary agendas linked to oppression and inequality. One such temporary exhibition on show in 2018 was entitled *I am What I am*, and was curated collaboratively with photographer Irene Grobbelaar-Lenoble and SWEAT (the Feminist Collective at the Sex Workers Education and Advocacy Taskforce) (Iziko, 2020b). Such collaborations highlight the intersectionality of the issue of oppression and marginalisation, and are thus addressed by a diverse set of actors inside and beyond the space of the Slave Lodge. The Iziko Slave Lodge also receives frequent school visits and entertains strong links to schools in the area. Museum education specialists, therefore, have to be seen as important actors in terms of scripting the Slave Lodge's narratives for a younger audience as well.

Community-based heritage activism

In addition to the work that larger-scale institutions such as the Iziko Museums group do, an increasing number of smaller initiatives are challenging the dominance of white and government activism in the heritage field. The LMLM is certainly not the only community-based museum; it vaguely follows a similar path to that of the District Six Museum in Cape Town, which builds its curatorial effort on its origins in, and links with, its immediate surrounding community. Some community regeneration initiatives pursue this same aim, including working with marginalised voices in the emergence of memories. This is particularly important, as McEwan (2003) has suggested that the voices of black women had largely been excluded from the narration of the truth and reconciliation process. This process of exclusion can certainly be extended beyond the scripting of apartheid, as it represents a colonial hierarchisation of memory actors and narratives alike (McEwan, 2003). However, undoing the hegemonic and deeply engrained scripting of colonialism from the perspective of the most powerful and wealthy stakeholders in society remains a difficult challenge for those engaged in a rather fragmented and privatised public space. The dominance of only a few well-funded and politically supported initiatives may not be very surprising in a context in which alternative voices and archives struggle for institutional survival on a daily basis. Specifically, what the LMLM has achieved is to have secured the involvement of the politically, geographically and economically marginalised Lwandle community, as well as a new set of curators, thus enhancing the diversity of actors engaged in the memory and heritage landscape. Despite some tensions in the relationship with the local community (see Mgijima and Buthelezi, 2006), the museum now draws on a different set of actors in its curatorial activities. The fact that the museum is situated in the heart of the community it seeks to represent, alongside its wider, national focus on migrant labour, means that it is, at least to a degree, accountable to this community. The museum has to have dialogue with its community to survive. It also acts as a source of income for some members of the community, albeit on a small scale, which means that the Lwandle community is directly affected by the museum, its visitors and its economic activities.

Overall, the analysis of agents in the colonial memoryscape has shown that there is some intense competition over the shaping of the colonial memory discourse, ranging from a certain glorification of the era to a more explicit statement of the long-term negative effects that colonialism has had, particularly on indigenous and other politically marginalised communities. It becomes clear that the curators of the different mnemonic sites play a key role in articulating different social and political positions, thus shaping a kaleidoscope of narratives, as we will now attempt to show.

Narratives: a segregated memoryscape

It is understood that in a spatially and temporally segmented mnemonic formation, the fragmentation of agency also translates into the narratives that are being deployed to script the past. Witz et al. (2017: 223) point out that a characteristic of South African memory narratives is that they tend to be highly directed:

> The narrative of South Africa's national heritage is inventoried and rendered through typologies of region and province: the Western Cape as that of 'slavery'; the Eastern Cape as that of ethnic 'homeland'; Gauteng as 'mining Soweto' (the urban); Kwazulu-Natal as 'royal tradition'; the Free State as 'the battlefields'; Limpopo and the north as 'sorcery and nature'; Kimberley as 'the diamond'; and the Northern Cape as the 'genesis of the indigenous'.

Following this line of argument, narratives of heritage follow the mnemonic physical infrastructure of the country, with specific narratives ascribed to specific parts of the country. This can certainly be considered colonial in nature, in that colonial governance itself sought to subdivide the country into different zones of profitable labour, 'homelands' and zones of transition (see Kappler, 2020). Such divisions in turn produce narratives that ascribe particular qualities to spatial entities. However, the scripting of narratives is not only geographically determined; it is also ideologically bound. As with the lines of divisions within sites and agents, so can mnemonic narratives be broadly categorised into those that romanticise and whitewash colonial governance on the one hand and those that take a critical stance vis-à-vis colonial practices on the other. The latter tend to raise debates about land distribution, museum returns and reparations, and are particularly vocal in activist and grassroots circles. This, again, echoes some of our findings from Cyprus, as well as from Bosnia and Herzegovina, where much of the resistance against nationalistic discourses emerges from a community of activists.

Colonial nostalgia narrated

As far as colonial nostalgia is concerned, some of the nuance can be found in the debates around white-on-white violence, for instance. One of the key reference points, specifically in the Afrikaner community's narratives, are the concentration camps set up by the British (see Stanley and Dampier, 2005). The conditions under which specifically Afrikaner women and children found themselves in those camps are therefore well communicated within that community. This narrative is promoted at the Voortrekker Monument and portrays the British as enemies of the Afrikaner people (Witz et al., 2017: 57), rupturing the notion of colonial glory to an extent. However, it has to be added that this narrative of white-on-white violence is somewhat detached from its colonial underpinnings as, for instance, black and other non-Afrikaner victims have long been edited out in the official commemorations of the concentration camps (Stanley and Dampier, 2005: 101–2). There are now attempts to rectify this narrative so as to increasingly acknowledge the numerous black victims of the camps (Stanley and Dampier, 2005: 108), marked, for instance, by the more prominent relabelling of the Anglo-Boer War as the South African War, as both white and black South Africans died in it. The complex hierarchies of forgetting come to the fore in this debate.

As a result, contestations around the ways in which different victim groups of the past should be commemorated, and how, continue to feed into political debates in the present, not just between the different ethnicities but also within them. This is a question of acknowledgement and dignity for many. For example, such contestations fed into political tensions around two competing commemoration events held at the Voortrekker Monument in 1988. During those events, South Africa's Conservative Party accused the ruling National Party of having sold out the national cause to the British during the ceasefire after the South African War (Autry, 2012: 152). The fact that the contestations about the right narrative of the war came at a time when the apartheid government was at a weak and vulnerable point was no coincidence. The political tensions of the 1980s provoked the emergence of competing notions of nationalism and whiteness. The different political notions of white South African identity and its place in history served to channel on-going political tensions faced by the apartheid state. Yet again, the issue of the black victims of the South African War was relegated to the background, something that reflected the hierarchy of victims that is constructed in those mnemonic narratives.

In sharp contrast to the Afrikaner narrative of being the victims of the British, the kinds of narratives promoted around the Rand Club centre on the wealth generated by the mines (not least due to the club's physical proximity to the banking district of Johannesburg), the figure of Cecil Rhodes and the British royals' connection to the club. A city tour guide unrelated to the Rand Club emphasised the visit to the club made by then British monarch Queen Elizabeth II as reinforcing its identity, while remarking in passing on the contested reception she had received in a city that is marked by the exploitation on the part of the British Empire.[6] The legacies of the empire, those who support it and those who continue to be its victims thus link to vastly different accounts, not only of the past but also of the present relationship of South Africans to the era of British dominance.

At the same time, many of the narratives spun in terms of South African memory have to be seen as directed to an economically important stream of incoming tourists. It certainly has to be acknowledged that many tourists, particularly ones from Europe, show only limited interest in terms of exploring the complicity of their own countries in South Africa's complex colonial legacies. A more nuanced picture, as opposed to the black-versus-white narrative of apartheid, is rarely presented to tourists. As a result, the dominant narrative marketed to tourists is that of apartheid or a rather romanticised version of colonial history. Witz et al. (see 2017: 83 ff.), for instance, explain how the narrative of the tourist experience in South Africa is largely guided by romantic depictions of colonial-era villages. Instead of questioning colonial violence, tourists experience a narrative of colonial Africa in which 'civilisation' meets indigenous villages. Given that much of the national economy hinges on tourism, it is not surprising that representations that play down colonial violence have become deeply engrained in local and national mnemonic narratives as well. The associated need to market, professionalise and commercialise memory narratives to make them attractive to a transnational audience is part and parcel of this process (Björkdahl and Kappler, 2019). In the debates about how the centenary of the South African War should be commemorated (which we will outline in further detail later in the chapter), it was rather obvious that the tourist gaze was an important factor shaping the design of the various commemorative events (Grundlingh, 2004: 369). The ways in which the celebrations were presented were substantially designed in the light of how appealing they would be to potential international audiences, and this set the tone for the mnemonic narratives that were created domestically as well.

ANC-led narratives of the rainbow nation

The main narrative recalling the recent past promoted by the ANC is that of apartheid, Nelson Mandela's legacy and post-apartheid reconciliation. Of course, this does not represent how the past is remembered nor is it a coherent narrative among black South Africans, as the legitimacy of the reconciliation-based narrative is increasingly facing resistance, not least from the party of the Economic Freedom Fighters (EFF); they emphasise the need for land redistribution and call for more drastic decolonisation measures generally. In that context, much of the (somewhat waning) acceptance of the ANC among the broader public is grounded on the liberation struggle, which the party uses as its main currency for the consolidation of power, along with notions of pan-Africanism. The Legacy Projects therefore first and foremost aim to highlight this struggle and to support projects that emphasise the notion of a rainbow nation, in a spirit of inter-racial reconciliation. Freedom Park's above-mentioned memorial wall, for instance, deliberately includes non-white victims of the South African War – a clear counter-narrative to that of the Voortrekker Monument. Interestingly, certain Afrikaner groups opposed this wall on the grounds that the soldiers of the South African Defence Force were not included in it, although they can be found in the Freedom Park's archives (Autry, 2012: 159). Eventually, this criticism was somewhat appeased by including on the wall the Afrikaner victims who fell in the South African War (Autry, 2012: 159). In that sense, mnemonic contestation has been a key feature of this site as well, despite its more inclusive ambitions.

It is worth noting, though, that the museum belonging to Freedom Park consists of different elements, with the permanent exhibition referring to colonial injustices and oppressions, whereas the outdoor spaces of the museum primarily pursue a discourse of inclusion and reconciliation. The tension between these two narratives has not been resolved by the curators. Instead, it is up to the visitors to make sense of the friction between these two different narratives in the same museum. A degree of romanticisation and nostalgia for the pre-colonial era seems almost unavoidable in this context: the image of a peaceful pre-colonial African continent juxtaposed with symbols of post-apartheid reconciliation provides a language that suggests an overall political consensus that has been merely interrupted by a period of inequality and segregation.

Narratives of in-betweenness

The curation of colonial narratives is notably different with respect to the question of slavery, which was widely used within the area that is now South Africa as a colonial tool for procuring unpaid labour, but which has long only enjoyed limited mnemonic attention outside the confines of the Iziko Slave Lodge. Indeed, the discourse on slavery and the associated identity groups was somewhat submerged by apartheid politics during the era of apartheid (Worden, 2009: 26). It is only in recent years that slavery as a phenomenon worth remembering and talking about is gaining more prominence, particularly in the Western Cape, where European colonialists brought in many enslaved people from Asia, roughly from the seventeenth to the nineteenth century (see Worden, 2009), while some enslaved people were also brought in from elsewhere in Africa. The Slave Lodge in its displays is increasingly trying to link Cape Town's slavery history to on-going political challenges, not only in terms of the legacies of slavery on the Western Cape, but also pointing to techniques of modern slavery that represent a continuation with, rather than a rupture from, a legacy of oppression and forced labour. At the same time, despite a growing interest in enslaved people's heritage and ancestry, a curator suggested that there continues to be a high degree of denial about the histories of enslaved people in South Africa.[7] This tendency raises some of the challenges that arise when dealing with difficult and violent histories: how can justice be done to such violent histories while finding adequate, aesthetic ways of commemoration? This question sparked particular debate when Cape Town mayor Helen Zille facilitated the erection of a new monument dedicated to slavery in Cape Town, very close to the Slave Lodge. This monument is situated next to the slave tree site, where memorial inscriptions on the ground note that a tree once stood under the shade of which auctions of enslaved people would take place. The newer monument consists of a number of black memorial stones, each engraved with attributes linked to Cape Town's history and legacies of enslaved people. The inscriptions range from place names to religion and languages, yet without a formal explanation for the possibly uninformed visitor. Worden (2009: 39) points to the controversies around this monument, specifically noting that its content is rather obscure and lacking historical context. Certainly, the attempt not to script the narrative or direct the spectator clearly in terms of the messages communicated can be upsetting for those who would like their violent histories narrated explicitly rather than suggested or vaguely alluded to. It can therefore be said that the narratives presented at the Iziko Slave Lodge aim to provide a detailed, mainly fact-based, historical narrative of slavery, tied to the physical space of the Slave Lodge, whereas this more recent monument attempts to play with abstraction and subjectivity. It deliberately refrains from a specific scripting as to how the memory of colonial slavery should be commemorated.

In contrast, finding markers that draw attention to the suffering of the KhoiSan are rather rare, and only in 2020 did the government agree to a heritage route dedicated to highlighting KhoiSan heritage. The abovementioned film centring around the historical figure of Krotoa may be read as an effort to put the role of the indigenous population in the spotlight, but it has been accused of romanticising colonialism. In general, many of the narratives that relate to the history and violence suffered by the KhoiSan are limited in their visibility in the public sphere and need to be actively sought out. For instance, the Castle of Good Hope has an exhibition of historical paintings, grouped as the William Fehr Collection. The paintings in this collection are not explicitly narrated but are presented to an interested audience. The exhibition does not form part of the official visitors' tour of the castle. In our personal experience, it was by coincidence that a museum guard pointed out a painting by Thomas Baines, entitled *Victoria Falls with Stampeding Buffalo*, which depicts a group of colonialists as hunters chasing buffaloes off a cliff. Hidden from direct view are indigenous hunters, withdrawing into the bushes, threatened by the weapons of the colonialist hunters as well as witnessing the loss of their prey in an act of brutality. It is certainly unlikely that the nineteenth-century British painter Baines had intended to make a statement about the brutality of colonial hunting; picking up on this narrative therefore remains a challenge for an interested audience or those deliberately looking for signs of suffering as experienced by the indigenous populations in and around South Africa. This is, however, changing. The Iziko Museum group (2020c), acting as curators of the William Fehr Collection, offers critical thoughts on the collection on their website, outlining a critique of the colonial structures represented through it. In that sense, the multi-media presence of Iziko helps present a more dynamic narrative to an online audience, although it is one that can be ignored by those who prefer to stick with a quick, and most likely uncritical, visit to the castle.

Community-based narratives and their wider significance

The LMLM's move to memorialise the migrant labour system – which was a typical colonial strategy of maximising profitability – from the perspective of those exploited by it certainly presents a very different kind of narrative to the one usually presented in urban centres, which is primarily directed at a tourist audience. Located outside the main urban areas, the narratives at the LMLM have limited reach outside the museum's immediate geographical location. Nonetheless, the aim remains to attract a tourist audience here as well, which may be one of the reasons why the museum largely scripts migrant labour as an apartheid legacy rather than a colonial one, with a focus on artefacts such as the infamous passbook (*dompas*) and signboards preserved from the apartheid era. In addition, the move from oral histories to museum practice can be read as a sign that Lwandle's narratives are being framed for an audience beyond its immediate locality, given that museum practice has often been seen as a Western practice (Minkley et al., 2017). In addition, the museum represents migrant labour not only as a localised issue for the Lwandle community but as a national question as well (Murray and Witz, 2014: 139). Indeed, migrant labour has been used throughout South Africa and is particularly prominent among the workforce working on the mines around Johannesburg. The LMLM's framing of migrant labour as a national question can therefore be read as an attempt to move out of a space of liminality vis-à-vis the tourist sector in Cape Town and, by connecting to narratives from other parts of the country, to claim a more central space in the mnemonic landscape of South Africa.

What this analysis of mnemonic narratives in relation to colonialism has shown is that they are shaped by factors such as how accessible they are (location) and by whom they are promoted (agents). These factors in turn determine, not exclusively but to a large extent, what degree of nuance and resistance can be introduced. In a way, the need to speak to a global tourist audience must not be overlooked, especially in terms of how the complexity of domestic debate is reduced, translated and curated in the mnemonic spaces discussed in this chapter. The physical spaces and their scripted narratives are thus restricted in their flexibility to shape more complex storytelling. We therefore find very limited degrees of entanglement between the narratives glorifying colonialism and those that memorialise the violence colonial rule has been based upon. They may relate to the same reference point – colonialism – but they differ so much in their language, audiences, reach and ambitions that they reach out in different directions.

We will now turn to an analysis of associated mnemonic events, in order to investigate the extent to which those allow for a more dynamic representation of mnemonic trends.

Events: commemoration in a post-colonial setting

Commemorative events can be very diverse in nature: they can be politically heated or merely routinised practices embedded in the everyday. Often, either of those have a connotation of nostalgia in terms of an attempt to time-travel into a different time in history, whether that be in relation to celebrating colonialism itself or pointing to the multi-faceted nature of resistance against it. They come in different shapes and forms, ranging from bigger movements (such as the above-mentioned #RhodesMustFall campaign) to local community events, from informal activities to formal public holidays. And while the reach of those different events may differ, they represent performances of memory, which have affective and persistent effects on people's relationships with the past as they experience and live it in the present.

Celebrating colonial nostalgia

In the South African calendar of mnemonic events, the centenary of the South African War has received particular attention as a 'cult of centenary' (Grundlingh, 2004: 359), not least with respect to the different ways in which the country's different constituencies relate to it. This is facilitated by the fact that the war does not have a specific site for its commemorations, as the relevant mnemonic sites are spread throughout the country. The mnemonic fragmentation is thus spatial in nature but not exclusively so. Dominy and Callinicos (1999), for instance, point to a number of controversies that emerged around the centenary planning process throughout the 1990s, in terms of whether it would be done in a controversial or conciliatory manner, who would host the main festivities, and how and where those would be held. Certainly, the most hotly debated question was around which kinds of actors in the conflict would be remembered at the event. In the end it was decided that all participants and victims of the war were to be commemorated, whether Boers, indigenous Africans or British. This was a conciliatory step, although many controversies remained around what a just way of marking this historical event would look like (Grundlingh, 2004: 363–4;

Witz et al., 2017: 164). According to Dominy and Callinicos (1999: 396), this constituted a particular challenge for museums as there was no clear consensus about how many black South Africans had actually been involved in the war. One important step, after all, was the government's decision to label the war officially as the Anglo-Boer South African War (Grundlingh, 2004: 361) rather than just the Anglo-Boer War, as a symbol of honouring the many black victims whose destiny had largely been neglected before. That was perhaps one of the key achievements of the centenary commemorations, despite an otherwise high degree of marginalisation of African perspectives and actors from these events. This is the background against which we illustrate in the following section the post-apartheid decision to rebrand the majority of public holidays to include African events in the commemorative calendar.

Institutionalising ANC-led commemorative days

The tensions around the commemorative events related to the legacy of apartheid translate into the wider commemorative calendar in South Africa, particularly with respect to the ANC's decision to turn the old, often colonial, national holidays into a new set of holidays, renaming them and giving them a new purpose. For instance, Van Riebeeck Day, Kruger Day or Day of the Vow were abolished and replaced with alternative holidays, such as Mandela Day (Nelson Mandela's birthday, a day South Africans are encouraged to dedicate to working for charitable purposes), Youth Day and Reconciliation Day. As part of the South African post-apartheid nation- and state-building exercise, it became important to rebrand national holidays accordingly (see Becker and Lentz, 2013: 2). This sent powerful messages about what kinds of history would be celebrated and commemorated, as well as signalling a reassignment of the weightings in victim hierarchies. In this context Becker and Lentz (2013: 4) argue as follows: 'national holidays per se do not necessarily reinforce national unity and integration; they can just as well intensify debates and conflicts about what vision of the nation and which future course in respect of the rights of minorities should prevail'.

Certainly, the manner in which such national holidays are endowed with meaning depends on how they are aesthetically performed by different actors (Becker and Lentz, 2013: 5). The government may have set the framework for a new set of national holidays, but has only limited control over which groups of the population engage in, or resist, the celebrations. The erection of the Voortrekker Monument in 1949, for instance, on what was until then Dingaan's Day, symbolising the defeat of the Zulu warriors, and was also known as Day of the Vow and Day of the Covenant, is clearly a legacy that is hard to rebrand as an initiative for reconciliation, although the date, 16 December, is now called Reconciliation Day as part of the renaming of national holidays that took place at the end of the apartheid era. Most South Africans are aware of these changes, although engagement with this new South African holiday remains uneven. The Voortrekker Monument continues to host a celebration on that day that ties in with its colonial histories, gathering a community of nostalgic Afrikaners when the light hits the empty tomb at its base – somewhat defeating the notion of reconciliation as the ANC aims to define it. And while the government's renaming initiative may not have put an end to the colonial nostalgia of some, it still symbolises a mnemonic turning point in the ways in which uncritical evocations of the colonial era are deemed acceptable in the public sphere. The initiative has had the effect of confining colonial nostalgia to specific, clearly delimited commemorative spaces.

Events: the ambivalence of in-betweenness

Apart from the more nationally directed and government-led national holidays, we can also observe some shifts in the ways in which indigenous histories are rescripted through selected events at a more local level. In the context of the legacy of Krotoa, the Khoi woman who worked for Van Riebeeck, a number of mainly KhoiSan groups organised events to reinstate her somewhat compromised reputation. Just as with the unveiling of the bench at the castle outlined earlier in the chapter, it was important for a group of KhoiSan followers to organise a spiritual event during the course of which Krotoa's spirit was taken to a new burial site, away from the castle where she had been brutally tortured. However, the memorialisation of Krotoa is certainly not without contestation within the indigenous communities either. On the one hand, placing the bench to commemorate Krotoa as a gesture was appreciated by some of the indigenous communities who attended its unveiling ceremony and performed a ritual to mark the event spiritually. On the other hand, the protests against the commemoration of Krotoa with a bench that people can sit on, as we outlined earlier, point to the competing narratives as to how she should be commemorated and in what historical role. The protests are particularly indicative of the competing narratives relating to Krotoa, as either a revered ancestor of the KhoiSan population or as a traitor for collaborating with Van Riebeeck (see Samuelson, 2007). Events around the indigenous heritage of the Western Cape specifically tend, however, to be rather small in size.

In sharp contrast to this, and connected with the Iziko Slave Lodge's focus on the cultural diversity introduced by the slave trade, the annual celebrations of the Cape Town Carnival are rather large. Speaking to local, national and international audiences alike, the carnival represents a celebration of diversity and is organised with the collaboration of a number of community groups. It dates back to colonial times, when enslaved people were given a day off work to celebrate alongside the European colonisers. Today, it represents an important factor for tourism in Cape Town as the carnival lends itself very well to marketing purposes in terms of South Africa's new identity as the rainbow nation. The status of the carnival as an officially approved celebration certainly supports its efforts to project a diversity branding – something that community-based heritage associations find harder to do.

Community-based heritage celebrations

Events speaking to community-based heritage are often (though not necessarily) locally contained, as they each relate to a particular contextual setting. This may involve community high tea or lunch meetings (as happens in Cape Town's Homecoming Centre, which belongs to the District Six Museum) or community-based celebrations. The LMLM website (www.lwandle.com), for instance, announces events including a Christmas party, a book launch and anniversary celebrations. Events in the museum may not take the form of highly institutionalised and generously funded events; they are more likely to focus on immediate community needs and engagement activities. School visits are one way of establishing educational events that eventually become routine, while at the same time highlighting the narratives promoted at the museum. This does not mean that high-profile events do not take place: the LMLM proudly talks about its opening event in 2000 by the famous 'poet and ex-Lwandle resident, Sandile Dikeni' (Lwandle Migrant Labour Museum, 2020). Such occasional highlights in the museum's calendar place it in a socio-political context and endow the museum with authority, both vis-à-vis its own community and the wider national and international sphere.

What can generally be said about the ways in which events specifically have challenged colonial legacies is that they have been the most flexible of our four categories of analysis, namely sites, agency, narratives and events. Events have been able to mobilise at least parts of society more quickly and have shown some real transformation in the texture of the mnemonic landscape in South Africa. This is partly due to their ephemeral nature, which resists institutionalisation and control. At the same time, the fragmentation of memory does remain, too; most events are not shared in a cross-ethnic way by various sectors of the population, as the organisation of, and participation in, events is still split along the lines of colonial-racial identities.

The SANE analysis: memory and the quality of peace

As the interaction of colonialism-nostalgic and colonialism-resistant sites, agents, narratives and events has shown, South Africa's colonial legacies are still very much present in the contemporary political sphere, despite the attempts and efforts of a variety of memory entrepreneurs to move beyond colonial frames. Often, the continued presence of colonial structures is couched in the language of apartheid, as the two phenomena are closely linked historically, with the latter building on the foundations of the former. Apartheid, as a strongly visible mnemonic formation, can therefore not be seen as isolated from colonialism, but as a continuum.

In relation to the mnemonic formation of colonial violence, this chapter has shown that sites, actors, narratives and events are fragmented and compartmentalised in nature, in the sense that there are some elements that romanticise colonial violence, whereas there are other elements that resist and challenge the associated historical injustices. These elements tend to be mutually disentangled. Both camps are fragmented within themselves, so a complex, segmented mnemonic landscape emerges. As those elements are hardly in dialogue with each other and mutual entanglement is limited, the ways in which resistance against colonial legacies is debated struggle to reach into those spheres in which they most urgently need to be heard. This then means that the legacies of the colonial past, with the associated structural inequalities, tend to be discussed in rather contained spaces and their expressions tend to fail to reach across different memory strands. This is comparable to the mnemonic divisions of the two museums of national struggle in Cyprus.

Questions of historical accountability, including issues of reparations and land return, do not tend to be popular discussion themes among the white South African community. The silence around those questions is quite tangible in those circles. If we understand peace as inclusive and dialogical, then the disentangled nature of sites, agents, narratives and events in South Africa is hardly promising. And while such fragmentation of the mnemonic landscape might be expected to lead to a nuanced engagement with the meaning of peace in a mnemonically divided society, dichotomous representations of South African histories continue to dominate. As a result, we can observe the emergence of a plurality of parallel peace(s), each internally homogenous but limited in its entanglement with other views of history beyond its own. The acknowledgement of what colonial violence has meant, and continues to mean, for its victims is therefore limited in nature, and the dignity of those victimised by the colonial system is continuously jeopardised.

This does not mean that all is doom and gloom, however. There are certainly mnemonic elements that aim to promote inclusiveness and dialogue as well as an in-depth engagement with colonial legacies. In terms of sites, Freedom Park is an example in which the curators attempt to script an inclusive history that restores dignity to the victims of colonialism. It is therefore surprising that it does not receive higher numbers of visitors, as the colonial Voortrekker Monument does. Similarly, the introduction of new national holidays or attempts to decolonise educational structures have pointed in a similar direction. They were meant to present a way of signalling, at least to a degree, a new beginning for a history ridden with inequalities and violence. However, it remains to be seen to what extent such processes will be able to achieve a more substantial transformation, in terms of stirring a discussion across different sectors of society. Certainly, the transformation of the mnemonic landscape is a dynamic process in which the power balance keeps shifting, and the fact that issues of injustice and marginalisation are being raised publicly is a promising first step. For instance, we could argue that the mnemonic marking of the suffering of South Africa's indigenous people, through the activities around the legacies of Krotoa for example, is a first step of acknowledgement towards granting this community more political, social and economic rights. We can also see a higher degree of representation of indigenous heritage in museum collections now (see Bredekamp, 2006). This trend is no guarantee of a real, political transformation, as there is still a risk of such marginalised histories being romanticised or used instrumentally for political gain. However, as we have seen with the #RhodesMustFall campaign, bringing contested issues into the public sphere does have the potential to gain societal traction that can transcend local and even national borders. From the perspectives of the victims of colonialism – to this day – the restoration of their dignity through the acknowledgement of on-going structural injustices is an important step towards dealing with a legacy of violence. The next step will be to raise questions around how such injustices can be politically and economically compensated for, in terms of making peace meaningful to those who have been silenced for so long. Peace, understood in mnemonic terms, thus has to signify more than a simplified version of society, shaped by binary views on the past. Instead, it has to actively undo mnemonic silences, disentanglements and amnesias on the one hand, and deal with material transformation on the other hand. Understanding the different layers of fragmentation and stratification in the memory landscape is a first step towards understanding the multidimensional nature of victimhood, the injustices of representation particularly for the poorest and less politically represented sectors of the population, as well as the need to talk about, and act on, questions of reparation and restitution as crucial factors for the restoration of mnemonic dignity.

Conclusions

As this chapter has shown, and as in our other case studies, South African contemporary political structures must not be viewed in isolation from a past in which society was starkly divided between the colonial power and those who were its victims. The continuity of such structures translates into a political system in which not only memories of the past but also visions of the future are starkly divided. Breaking up this century-old discursive pattern poses a considerable challenge to those who seek to transform it. However, with emerging discussions about land reform or other mechanisms of restitution in the higher education sector, there are encouraging signs that such engrained patterns are gradually being broken down. It remains to be seen to what extent such debates will translate into material redistribution and a more formal acknowledgement of the violence of the past – not only by powerful actors within South Africa, but also, importantly, by the former colonial powers in Europe. For a social peace that is inclusive of all races, as well as one in which those who are currently marginalised may find a political stake, this will be a difficult but necessary step, signalling a true commitment to peace in South Africa and beyond.

Notes

1 We have decided to avoid capitalisation for all racial categories for consistency and to reject the forms of racial categorisation promoted by the apartheid regime.
2 Racialised terms were used by the apartheid government as a form of classifying South Africans into different legal categories. Perhaps most strikingly to the reader, the term 'coloured' was used to denote people of mixed race and is still commonly used in South Africa today. We use it in speech marks ('…') to distance ourselves from its racist underpinnings.
3 The former Pretoria is now known as Tshwane.
4 Indigenous groups, such as the KhoiSan, were classified as 'coloured' under apartheid.
5 Interview, anonymous source, Cape Town, 6 July 2018.
6 City tour, Johannesburg, 2017.
7 Interview, anonymous curator, Cape Town, 3 July 2018.

6

Cambodia: the power of the dead

This chapter investigates a mnemonic formation in Cambodia that has an ephemeral and religious nature somewhat different to the other ones discussed in this book: namely, the power of the dead. In analysing how bones and spirits have been treated since the genocide carried out by the Khmer Rouge in the late 1970s, the hegemonic memory of the government and its inhibiting effect on the quality of peace becomes visible. The government's emphasis on preserving the bones of some of those killed by the Khmer Rouge as evidence of the regime's barbarity serves broader political purposes but ignores survivors' calls for the bones to be cremated. In Theravada Buddhism as followed in Cambodia, the cremation of a person's mortal remains in a context of traditional funeral rites is deemed necessary to release the spirit of that individual from the afterlife to be reborn. Consequently, as long as victims' remains have not been cremated survivors are haunted by the presence of these spirits and worry about their lost loved ones' cosmic well-being. This situation thus impinges on the dignity of both the dead and the survivors, undermining the quality of peace.

Analytically engaging with the dead as victims of past violence gives us insight into the struggles for political power today and the influence of memory on the prospects for peace in post-genocide Cambodia. This analysis renders visible various dynamics that transcend standard social and political interactions, and it incorporates spiritual dimensions that are important in understanding how many Cambodians perceive and interact with sites of memory. For most Cambodians, the presence of spirits is very real, which renders the spirits of the dead relevant to our investigation of memory and peace in this country. Thus, not only do 'stories of the dead provide a culturally acceptable mode of narrating history and suffering, [but also] the dead are as constitutive of contemporary social order and stability as the living' (Bennett, 2018b: 199–200). Spirits can therefore themselves be seen as agents, and studying the dead allows us also to think about forms of non-human agency. Of more central interest to the chapter, though, is an interrogation of how these spirits and the uncremated bones of the deceased are perceived by the living, how different actors talk about them in different ways and how these perceptions are instrumentalised in the politics of memory. We shall therefore analyse the power of the dead as a political issue that is actively negotiated and through which political interests become visible, impacting the prospects for peace.

In studying the dead and their place in Cambodia's memoryscape we draw on the excellent anthropological literature on the dead in Cambodia (among others, see Arensen, 2017; Bennett, 2015, 2018a, 2018b; Guillou, 2012, 2014, 2017; Tyner et al., 2014), and take these insights regarding the power of spirits, bodies and karma to be understood through the prism of our social scientific approach to understanding the politics of memory.

The genocide by the Khmer Rouge

Cambodia suffered decades of violence. The country also suffered from the war spilling over from neighbouring Vietnam, it fought not one but two civil wars and it experienced genocide. This genocide, carried out by the Khmer Rouge regime in 1975–1979, is the main reference point for remembering atrocities, violence and conflict in the country. Heading a state they called Democratic Kampuchea, the Khmer Rouge exercised full control throughout the country, pursuing their utopian vision of a peasant revolution that would make the country more self-sufficient through rice production, and thus independent from the capitalist and purportedly imperialist West. This peasant revolution saw the Khmer Rouge empty the cities and force the entire population to engage in agricultural labour, working the rice fields and building the necessary irrigation systems. Under this regime that lasted less than four years, between 1.7 million and 2.2 million people died or were killed, out of a pre-genocide population of around eight million (Tabeau/Kheam, 2009, 19). About half the dead fell victim to hunger, overwork and disease within a politically radical and terribly mismanaged Communist state that sought to implement a peasant revolution but failed to prioritise feeding its population. About one million more people were executed for various reasons: ethnic minority groups – the Cham, Vietnamese, Chinese, Lao and Thai – were targeted and some groups were almost entirely wiped out. All those associated with the previous regime's administration or military, as well as intellectuals and religious figures, became targets for the mass executions, in order to provide a clean political slate for the revolution (Chandler, 1999: 45, 2008a: 265; Tabeau and Kheam, 2009: 19). From late 1976, as the revolution appeared not to be flourishing as the leaders had expected, the regime began to suspect hundreds of thousands of individuals of being internal enemies seeking to sabotage its rule (Chandler, 1999: 45–76). There were massive purges, within the Khmer Rouge itself and among the broader population, of those suspected of being part of elaborate (but non-existent) networks of foreign agents (Chandler, 1999: 123–30, 2008a: 267). Further, the regime killed those deemed to be anti-revolutionary. This attribution could be bestowed upon an individual for the simplest of things: eating outside of collective meals; engaging in sexual intercourse outside of state-sanctioned marriage; or being too slow at one's assigned duties, to name just a few.

However, despite the prominent position that Democratic Kampuchea obviously occupies in recent Cambodian history, its violence is embedded in a broader *longue durée* of violence. In the wave of post-Second World War decolonisation across the world, Cambodia's monarch Norodom Sihanouk had in 1953 negotiated full independence, with Cambodia no longer a French protectorate in association with neighbouring Vietnam (see Chanda, 1986; Kiernan, 1985). Sihanouk remained in power in various political positions, enjoying immense popularity – particularly outside the cities where people were less affected by his mismanagement of the country's economy – and steering a politically neutral course regarding the escalating war in Vietnam (Chandler, 2008a: 233–54; Kiernan, 1996: 17). Sihanouk was toppled from power in 1970 by his prime minister, General Lon Nol, and subsequently the country became closely allied with the US administration. The new government then allowed massive aerial bombardment of the eastern parts of the country by American fighter planes in their vicious hunt for Viet Cong fighters, even though these incursions into Cambodian territory saw more than 100,000 tonnes of bombs released and at least 150,000 Cambodian civilians killed (Chandler, 2008a, 252; Kiernan, 1996: 24).

Excluded from power, Sihanouk entered into an unlikely alliance with a hitherto relatively small Communist rebel group, later known as the Khmer Rouge. The Khmer Rouge's restrained socialist propaganda combined with the former monarch's call to arms – publicised via radio and word of mouth – allowed the rebels to grow rapidly and to engage Lon Nol's regime in an intense civil war (Bultmann, 2017: 9). Five years of civil war and US war crimes left about half a million people dead by the time the Khmer Rouge entered the capital Phnom Penh on 17 April 1975 (Chandler, 2008a: 256). The Khmer Rouge's initial popularity as the war ended quickly evaporated as all aspects of life became subject to their totalitarian control: Sihanouk was put under house arrest, the cities were evacuated, all property and land was eventually collectivised, and money and religious observance abolished (Chandler, 2008a; Kiernan, 1996).

The next three years, eight months and twenty days – numbers etched into Cambodian collective memory – saw violence and the harshest kind of repression wreak devastation on the country, until defectors from the

Khmer Rouge, supported by the Vietnamese military, liberated the country by taking Phnom Penh in January 1979. As the Khmer Rouge retreated to the Thai border a new, second civil war emerged between the Vietnamese-backed government and complex constellations of rebel groups, including the Khmer Rouge. This violence continued to ravage much of the country until the Paris Peace Agreement of 1991, and more sporadic violence continued until the late 1990s, when peace was finally established (see Chandler, 1999: 157–88, 2008a: 277–95; Etcheson, 2005).

Democratic Kampuchea was clearly only one period in the country's longer continuum of violence, but the massive scale of killing during this period lends it prominence in transitional justice efforts and broader politics of memory. Hun Sen, who first took office as prime minister in 1984, remained in power until 2023 before handing over his position to his son Hun Manet.[1] Political violence and human rights violations have continued to occur, with repression bolstering the government's ability to maintain power (Un, 2019: 47, 59). This power is also underwritten by legitimation strategies that emphasise how Hun Sen and his comrades liberated the country from the Khmer Rouge, stoking (unrealistic) fears of their return should he ever lose power (Williams, 2022: 162).

The Cambodian memoryscape

Despite the broad array of violent events in the country's history, the Cambodian memoryscape is strongly focused on the period of Democratic Kampuchea. This temporal focus does reflect the time period of the worst horrors and the most violent phenomena, but the lesser visibility of other time periods of suffering is predominantly a political decision useful for prime minister Hun Sen and his government. As many in his government, including himself, were Khmer Rouge members in the first civil war before defecting and liberating the country, a focus on atrocities carried out after their defection is politically prudent. Nonetheless, the country has experienced phases of memory in which the government has remembered the violent past of Democratic Kampuchea in different ways at different times. Given the autocratic nature of governance in the country (Un, 2019), it is unsurprising that the Cambodian memoryscape is hegemonically structured according to the political interests of the incumbent government. Nevertheless, these political interests shift over time to highlight various ideas about culpability and victimhood that are politically useful in the moment (Williams, 2022).

Beginning with the fall of the Khmer Rouge regime and the outbreak of the second civil war, the government pursued a policy of highlighting the torturous and murderous legacy of the Khmer Rouge. This demonisation of the Khmer Rouge was politically expedient, both in terms of legitimising in the eyes of the world the invasion of the country by Vietnam (particularly given Vietnam's international status as a pariah state in the aftermath of the Vietnam War) and in mobilising the country's own population against the Khmer Rouge in the context of the on-going, second civil war (Brown and Millington, 2015: 32; Hinton, 2018: 47; Hughes, 2006: 272; Tyner et al., 2014: 286). The government opened the Tuol Sleng Genocide Museum in August 1979, just months after the fall of Democratic Kampuchea, displaying the horrors of the space in which it was constructed: the museum is housed in a complex that was known as S-21, the central detention centre operated by the regime. Thousands of prisoners were interrogated and tortured there (Brown and Millington, 2015; Williams, 2019). In the early 1980s, the government that had replaced the Khmer Rouge sought to mobilise support in the civil war and instructed that local memorials be constructed across the entire country; skulls and bones were gathered from mass graves and brought into around eighty officially approved memorial spaces (Hughes, 2006). Besides its political function in materialising the horror of the recent past, this centralisation of victims' bones and skulls was motivated by the fact that the remains were otherwise often being eaten by cows in cases where mass graves had been unearthed by looters.[2] The government then introduced the Day of Maintaining Anger in 1984 (Sion, 2014: 113), a national commemoration day to remember the horrors of the Khmer Rouge period and rally the population around the flag in the on-going civil war against their remaining forces. In 1988, the Choeung Ek Killing Fields site was opened as a further important national site of memory; many of the people who had been Interrogated at the S-21 detention centre had subsequently been transported to be killed there (Hughes, 2006).

In the 1990s and in the context of peace talks, the local memorials became less important and the state ceased to assume responsibility for their upkeep. Subsequently, religious figures were primarily tasked with maintaining them (Hughes, 2006: 279), although many fell into disrepair due to lack of funding. Government rhetoric towards the Khmer Rouge also became milder in an attempt to bring them into peace talks and successfully negotiate peace. Peace negotiations came to fruition and violent conflict ceased, even prompting Hun Sen, as prime minister in 1998, to call metaphorically for a hole to be dug in which to bury the past (Chandler, 2008a: 356).

The government has not actually buried the past in Cambodia. Since the cessation of the civil war and the advent of peace, it has not dismantled the memorials around the country, nor has it returned to its demonising rhetoric of civil war days, however. Instead, it still uses the past productively for its own ends by reminding people of the horrors of the previous regime, while confining responsibility to the Khmer Rouge's now-deposed top leadership (Williams, 2022; forthcoming). Although it offered amnesties to defecting Khmer Rouge cadres in the 1990s, the government has since allowed a very narrow transitional justice process to take place against a small number of former Khmer Rouge senior figures, with prosecutions by the Extraordinary Chambers in the Courts of Cambodia (ECCC), also known as the Khmer Rouge Tribunal (for an introduction, see Gidley, 2019; Hughes, 2015; Manning, 2017). The ECCC is a hybrid institution, with the participation of international staff through the United Nations as well as Cambodian, government-appointed staff. Its operations have been marked by political interference by the Cambodian government (Orentlicher, 2020; Ryan and McGrew, 2016: 72; Un, 2019). For example, the tribunal has witnessed international personnel repeatedly attempting to expand the remit of prosecutions, while Cambodian prosecutors and judges have systematically blocked any attempts to widen it beyond the five people originally indicted in the ECCC's first two cases, even though a majority of victims support further prosecutions (Williams et al., 2018: 62).

Beyond the ECCC, various civil society organisations contribute to the transitional justice process in judicial and non-judicial ways, although such projects are often thematically tied to the ECCC (Hinton, 2018: 43; Ryan and McGrew, 2016: 92; Sperfeldt, 2012). Most importantly in the context of this chapter, non-governmental organisations (NGOs) are key to providing reparations awarded through the ECCC (Sperfeldt, 2020), including, among many other things, the erection of memorials (Williams, 2019), therapy projects and cultural performances (Grey et al., 2019; Shapiro-Phim, 2020). Transitional justice efforts are, however, mostly structured by the government in ways that prioritise their political interests and thus do not necessarily contribute to societal resilience (Williams, 2021).

In this memoryscape the dead are only sometimes present, as for example when there are discussions over whether the remains of the dead should be displayed in memorials or cremated. At other times their presence is more tangential, as when they are discursively rendered as evidence for the ECCC, or when spirits influence whether people visit memorials or how stories are told in cultural projects. But this chapter demonstrates that the dead – through their spirits and bodies – are salient topics in the politics of memory, and that how Cambodian society deals with its dead has manifest consequences for the quality of its peace.

Mnemonic formation: the power of the dead

Within this broader memoryscape, we focus on how the dead are used in the politics of memory and on the power they exert over the living. Here two aspects play overlapping and interconnected roles: first, there are the material remains of the individuals who were killed or died under the Khmer Rouge, that is, their bones; and, second, their more intangible, although equally salient, spirits.

The vast majority of the Cambodian population – as in much of Southeast Asia – subscribes to Theravada Buddhism (Harris, 2015).[3] The pagoda is the primary social space in most villages and strong value is ascribed to Buddhist practices, such as merit-making to improve one's karma and to expedite rebirth for oneself and one's loved ones (Bennett, 2018a). Buddhist tenets are complemented and expanded by animist concepts that emphasise the importance of spirits and structure social interactions with the dead. In Cambodian culture, therefore, spirits play an important role in everyday life and can exert strong affective power over individuals. To understand the politics surrounding these spirits in the Cambodian memory of the Khmer Rouge, we need to understand the nature of spirits in this country and how these are intimately connected to the bones of the deceased.

Spirits are omnipresent in Cambodian culture and in the country's social, political and geographic landscapes (see e.g. Beban and Work, 2014; Work, 2017). They also play an important role in how victims engage with transitional justice when more secular, universal perceptions of justice and reconciliation are overlaid with Buddhist readings of these transitional justice processes (Gray, 2012; Williams et al., 2018; Zucker, 2009, 2013) and with understandings that focus more strongly on spirits (Hinton, 2018: 180, 208). Among the broad array of spirits in Cambodia, their emotions and malevolence vary (Bennett, 2018b: 189; Bertrand, 2001). Of particular importance are *neak ta* (local guardian spirits), which are tied to a certain location and can take on human attributes such as hunger (the *preta* spirit is known as the hungry ghost) or loneliness, communicating with humans directly or through dreams (see e.g. Guillou, 2012). While these spirits can also possess people (Bertrand, 2001), this has not been reported for the spirits of dead Khmer Rouge (Guillou, 2012: 225, 2017: 225). However, the dead in mass graves are more likely to become *neak ta*, given their association with the ground and the specific location (Guillou, 2014: 155).

The spirits of one's ancestors play an important role in many Cambodian traditions, in the context of a fundamental belief in the concept of rebirth after death. Funeral rites are important to release the spirit of the deceased from its connection to the individual's body so that rebirth can take place; otherwise, the spirit remains present and potentially haunts the space.[4] Karma, accumulated through merit-making, is influential in how soon someone is reborn. There is an 'understanding that the improper treatment of human remains prevents the transformation of a body's spirit, trapping it instead in this world as a ghost' (Arensen, 2017: 71). Cremation is the standard (although not the only) option for funeral rites, and it is widely believed that the cremation of the body necessitates the participation of family members (Arensen, 2017: 72; Bennett, 2018b: 190; Cougill, 2007).

In cases of unnatural or violent death, one speaks of 'bad dead' (*khmaoch tai hong*) and the spirit of the deceased is less likely to be reborn (Cougill, 2007) and more likely to 'transform into malevolent entities of various forms staying near the living' (Guillou, 2012: 216). While the funeral rites are not vastly different for bad dead and focus on dedicating merit to the dead (Guillou, 2012: 217), cremation is seen as more urgent in such cases (Hughes, 2006: 275). As with other cremations, these rites should be performed by families. It follows that when the bodies of Khmer Rouge victims have not been individually identified and the rites performed by their families, there is a higher likelihood that those individuals will not be reborn and will remain in the area of their death as (potentially malevolent) spirits.

During the Khmer Rouge period around two million people died or were killed, so survivors of course became accustomed both to the corpses and to the spirits around them (Bennett, 2018b: 191; Guillou, 2014). Subsequently, hauntings at mass graves were understood more as 'the result of the *kmoac's* [ghost of a recently deceased person] own confused emotional state, and although they frightened some people, and made others sick, they were not malevolent' (Bennett, 2018b: 191). While many spirits are of people unknown to the local population, due to the many population transfers under the Khmer Rouge, often the dead are broadly identifiable as having belonged to one set of victims or another, for example as Khmer Rouge cadres or as members of other warring factions from the 1980s. People make few distinctions between ghosts of civilians or soldiers, however (Arensen, 2017: 80).

During the 1980s Buddhism remained forbidden under the new socialist regime, meaning that the remains of the dead could not be cremated as religious tradition decreed. Many spirits therefore continued to inhabit the spaces in which they were killed, terrorising (or supporting) the local populations. Thus, spaces of memory are inhabited not only by the living but also by the dead, first in the form of spiritual beings and as a malevolent or benevolent presence, and second through their continued physical materialisation in the form of the uncremated bones.

In the immediate aftermath of the Khmer Rouge regime, the bones of the dead served an important political purpose as evidence of the terror that the former regime had wreaked on the country. In the context of the post-Vietnam War invasion and liberation of Cambodia by Vietnamese troops and Khmer Rouge defectors, bones became the cornerstone of the new government's legitimation strategy (Guillou, 2014: 151–2). As such, the bones fulfilled a key political role as evidence, even if this at the same time had direct consequences in hindering the liberation of the spirits and their rebirth. While most bones remained untouched in mass graves, some were gathered together to be placed in the local memorials described above. The local population participated in this, in part also to preserve the bones from being stolen or eaten by cattle, as mentioned above; there are also reports that some individuals took fragments of bone as talismans to bring luck and to incorporate into their homes (Bennett, 2018b: 195).

While Buddhist practices were gradually reintroduced in the late 1980s and early 1990s (Hughes, 2006: 274), the bones of the deceased remained uncremated, mostly because the government still wanted to maintain the bones as evidence of the cruelty of the former regime. They were later also framed as judicial evidence in the context of the hybrid tribunal (see above). Furthermore, given that bones are not individually identified (with the exception of people who were recognised in the immediate aftermath of violence before decomposition set in or who were identifiable by their clothing)[5] there was and still is a hesitancy to perform funeral rituals, as these should be conducted by family members.

In this context, then, the dead as spirits are co-constitutive of social order and stability in post-genocide Cambodia, and they unfold subtle forms of agency. Spirits in Cambodia can have emotions, feel hunger and take on many characteristics of human beings, as well as interacting with humans who are still alive. It is this interaction that makes them important as subjects in the analysis of the politics of memory. Interactions with spirits are not always negative, but in the case of those who died during the Khmer Rouge regime they tend to be driven by fear on the part of the living. This is because the spirits of those killed in unnatural, violent deaths are more likely to be malevolent. It is this fear of the spirits that precludes interaction with some memorial sites for many people, with parents not wanting their children to visit or work at such places. The area around the Tuol Sleng Genocide Museum was more or less deserted for many years as people refused to live in the vicinity due to the many malevolent spirits, despite its prime location near the centre of Phnom Penh.

Sites: emplacing the dead

In the politics of remembering the genocidal past in Cambodia, two sites stand out in terms of their national and international significance: the Tuol Sleng Genocide Museum in the capital Phnom Penh and the Choeung Ek Killing Fields, about 17 kilometres away. Around eighty other memorials are peppered across the entire country, each enshrining the bones of the deceased, which in most cases are on public display, as well as hundreds of unmarked mass graves. Each of these sites is a gateway into understanding how the dead are instrumentalised in negotiating the meaning of the past in the present.

Tuol Sleng Genocide Museum

The Tuol Sleng Genocide Museum is Cambodia's most prominent genocide memorial site (for overviews, see Brown and Millington, 2015; Hinton, 2016; Hughes, 2003, 2008). It occupies part of the space previously taken up by S-21, the leading detention centre in an intricate network of security centres across the country (Ea, 2005). Here more than 15,000 people were brought to be interrogated and tortured (Chandler, 2020), although most were not killed in this location but were transported to the nearby killing fields at Choeung Ek. Both sites have been turned into memorials that today are major Phnom Penh tourist destinations that shock and horrify many visitors due to their disturbing histories and the material evidence with which visitors are confronted (Bickford, 2009; Brown and Millington, 2015; Buckley-Zistel and Williams, 2022). In both places, these horrific impressions are enhanced by informative but emotional audio guides available to visitors (Buckley-Zistel and Williams, 2022).

The Tuol Sleng Genocide Museum is housed in a complex that was a secondary school before it was converted into the S-21 detention centre, with four three-storey buildings surrounding a leafy garden area and an administrative block in the centre. On some of the buildings that have walkways facing the garden area one can still see the barbed-wire installed to prevent prisoners from escaping or committing suicide.[6] On Building A's ground floor one finds rooms with beds and shackles as they were discovered after the end of Democratic Kampuchea, with photos on the wall showing scenes that include tortured and dead prisoners. The core of the exhibition is in Building B, where photos with relatively short captions are displayed alongside other exhibits, such as a large pile of clothes that belonged to victims of S-21, as well as some costumes and a sample of Khmer Rouge cadre clothing. Building C has been left as it was found in 1979, to give an idea of what some of the prison cells and rooms looked like. In Building D on the ground floor, one can see a measuring stick and the box camera for taking photos of newly arrived prisoners. There are thousands of prints of these photos on display, as well as instruments of torture and graphic paintings by one of the survivors of S-21, the artist Vann Nath. At the end of the exhibition there is a small memorial space where people may place incense (part of religious practice) or write a note.

Physical remnants of victims are also on display at the Tuol Sleng Genocide Museum. First, there are cases containing skulls in Building D; a member of staff reports some visitors taking selfies in front of them.[7] And second, there

Figure 6.1 Building with holding cells at Tuol Sleng Genocide Museum (photograph by Timothy Williams, June 2018)

is a photograph of a previous installation that consisted of over 300 exhumed skulls and bones in the shape of a map of Cambodia, with the main rivers and the Tonle Sap lake painted in red to signify the spilled blood. This particularly shocking element of the exhibition was removed and replaced by this photo in 2002, as will be discussed in more depth later in the chapter.

Choeung Ek Killing Fields

Almost without exception, people interned at detention centre S-21 (where the Tuol Sleng Genocide Museum is located today) were subsequently killed, most often after being transported outside of Phnom Penh to a site near the village of Choeung Ek, to the south of the city. The site is now notorious as the Choeung Ek Killing Fields. Visitors today encounter a relatively open space, with many trees and located next to a lake; at first sight it is not clear that 129 mass graves roll out across the space. As visitors follow an audio guide provided at the entrance they are guided through the site, listening to background information on the space itself and the broader history of the genocide. Walking around the site, visitors often see fragments of bones on the ground, particularly during the rainy season when soil gets washed

Figure 6.2 Stupa at Choeung Ek Killing Fields (photograph by Susanne Buckley-Zistel, June 2013)

away; staff members only collect up these fragments every few months.[8] These fragments and the more curated displays of bones and clothes – as in the Tuol Sleng Genocide Museum – are framed as 'evidence' in the audio guide and interviews with staff conducted by the fifth author.

The site contains few buildings, but towering above the green spaces that predominate one finds a strikingly ornate example of a carved stupa (the domelike structure usually containing Buddhist relics). It is reminiscent, for visitors, of Cambodian religious architecture across the country, albeit considerably more monumental in scale. Constructed in 1988, this stupa houses around 9,000 skulls and bones; it was built during a period in the late 1980s when a government policy shift tentatively allowed a revival of Buddhist practices (Hughes, 2006). The memorial is designed to conform with Buddhist tradition. Rachel Hughes evocatively summarises the site's architectural impact: 'The memorial does not attempt to symbolically redeem the dead, as in other memorial traditions. It instead preserves the injustice and impropriety of the victims' deaths in its architectural form' (Hughes, 2006: 276).

Importantly, an additional layer of disturbance haunts Cambodian visitors to both the Tuol Sleng Genocide Museum and the Choeung Ek Killing Fields, beyond the already horrific nature of these sites: the spiritual realm. Cambodian visitors speak of being afraid of the spirits of the deceased who – due to the violent nature of their deaths, their bad karma or the lack of cremation – have not been released for rebirth. Staff members have reported that their parents were very uneasy with their working at such a site or even tried to forbid them from taking up their posts.[9] Furthermore, for many years there was a noticeable absence of school groups visiting these sites, particularly compared with other post-genocide countries. This may be partly due to economic constraints and the government's lack of interest in integrating the violent past into state-school curricula, but it also appears to be deeply rooted in parents' fears of having their children visit such haunted spaces – which could bring their offspring bad luck – as well as the children's own fear of this bad luck.[10]

Local memorials

As described above, the 1980s saw the government build dozens of smaller memorials around the entire country. There are around eighty such memorials that demonstrate 'significant uniformity in the age, form and commemorative function', suggesting that ministerial directives were carefully adhered to (Hughes, 2006: 278) – although other analysts suggest that the processes were more locally driven.[11] The structures are built as traditional stupas with ornate carvings, although they are often only a few metres high and thus not much larger than some family graves. As with the two national-level memorials and in stark contrast to other graves in the country, these sites also display human remains, especially skulls and long bones that are laid inside, in the memorial structure, and visible through windows.

Where the sites include inscriptions, these are very much in the language of the 1980s, emphasising hatred of the Khmer Rouge and highlighting the horrific nature of Democratic Kampuchea.

These local memorials are often close to religious sites and were often constructed within pagoda complexes, both because of the 'auspicious nature of temple grounds' and because they had often previously contained mass graves due to the fact that as the Khmer Rouge often used such sites for incarcerations and executions (Hughes, 2006: 279). Despite their prominent locations, many have fallen into disrepair and do not play an important role for most of the year, with certain festivities, whether religious or more politically oriented, being an exception (see the 'Events' section). The sites are not particularly controversial today, having lost the negative political role that made them key to mobilisation against the Khmer Rouge and legitimation of the incumbent government during the civil war of the 1980s.

Unmarked mass graves

The national and local memorials discussed in this chapter were created by, and served the political agenda of, the national government. Their impact on the daily lives of the local population has varied; they received significantly more attention from Cambodians in the 1980s than they do today. Beyond these sites, and out of sight of all tourists and most researchers, there are other unofficial sites of key importance that are locally known but remain unmarked, uncommemorated and often untouched (Guillou, 2012; Tyner et al., 2014). For example, mass graves were regularly discovered in the first years after the fall of the Khmer Rouge regime, particularly by farmers ploughing fields. While these were then sometimes looted for any valuables, or cattle would eat the bones of the deceased at these mass graves, the sites remained otherwise untouched unless the remains were exhumed to be put in the local memorials described in the previous section. Most mass graves remain unnoticeable and unmarked by any building or even signs, although they are nowadays known to the local communities. Often the presence of human remains at such sites only became known about after the end of Democratic Kampuchea, as the Khmer Rouge regime laid a veil of secrecy and silence over much of what happened during this time. The locations of killings were seldom visible to the broader population (even though it was known that large numbers of people were disappearing and many were being eliminated).

These sites have not become part of any wider political recognition or remembrance of the past violence, but they have been highly significant to the people living around them, particularly as they were haunted by the spirits of the uncremated dead (Bennett, 2015, 2018b). There has been no political will to mark these sites or deal with bodies at most such mass graves, even as these sites have acquired a strong negative significance among the local population. Moreover, there are reports of women becoming pregnant from the mass graves as they looted them in the 1980s, with spirits thus being rebirthed (Bennett, 2018a, 75), and the lives of survivors becoming directly interlocked with the spirits of the deceased, rendering the sites in some cases even more significant to local populations.

In conclusion, various national and local sites are salient in Cambodia's memoryscape. The increasingly familiar tourist sites of the Tuol Sleng Genocide Museum and the Choeung Ek Killing Fields are the most prominent, and beyond those high-profile sites there are the dozens of local memorial spaces constructed by the government in the 1980s. These official and recognised sites are complemented by many more informal sites that are spaces of horrific memory due to the killings that occurred there and the bodies that remain buried in mass graves. These sites – recognised or not, official or not – include bones and skulls as human remains on display, and thus have strong implications for the spiritual realm. Here, spirits of those unable to be reborn shape Cambodian people's perceptions of the sites and their interactions with them.

Agents: the government and its critics

Within the Cambodian memoryscape the government occupies a central position, given its strong hold on power (Un, 2019). But other actors are also important; they may be politically less influential but their understandings are nonetheless co-constitutive of the more diverse memoryscape. Here, we will home in on the late King Sihanouk as a political actor with a provocative role, as well as some of the men and women who are involved in memory work through the positions they hold at memorial sites.

The government as dominant memory agent

Since the Khmer Rouge were overthrown by forces including the Vietnamese, the same party has continued in power albeit renamed and rebranded over time; Hun Sen first became prime minister in December 1984 and remained in power until 2023, albeit sharing the position during some moments of political instability in the 1990s. The government has clearly held a dominant position in the Cambodian political landscape and in the past few years has reneged on many of its democratising moves, dissolving the key opposition party and limiting press and civil society freedoms (Un, 2019). The government has used its dominant political position to pursue its strategic interests in activities that impact collective memory and its meaning for today. The politics of memory in Cambodia is therefore structured in a way that strongly reflects the governing elites' interests, even as these have changed over the decades since the end of Democratic Kampuchea (Williams, 2022).

The government influences the politics of memory directly. For example, the Tuol Sleng Genocide Museum is a national museum that comes under the jurisdiction of the Ministry of Culture and Fine Arts; any changes to the museum, its exhibition or the narratives provided at the site need ministerial approval. While the Tuol Sleng Genocide Museum has witnessed many additional programmes, temporary exhibitions and changes over the past few years that certainly serve to change the character of the space, these must all adhere to government policy and the fundamental tenets of the space remain unchanged. On the judicial level, meanwhile, the government has attempted to influence decision-making by the ECCC, as mentioned above. Cambodian members of staff at the institution are appointed by the government and are often individuals with close links to government circles. The government can be confident that ECCC staff members will act in accordance with their political interests, for example with Cambodian prosecutors and investigating judges preventing any further cases from proceeding at the tribunal, as the government has little interest in widening the scope of trials.

(Marginalised) memory entrepreneurs

While government policy undoubtedly holds significant sway over the politics of memory in Cambodia, there are, of course, other actors who are key to shaping the memoryscape, both in adherence with, but also in contradiction to, the government's interests. For example, at the Tuol Sleng Genocide Museum many of the staff members act in line with government interests when they use the bones of the dead as evidence in educating the next generation; at the same time, however, they share the more broadly felt uneasiness rooted in religious beliefs concerning the non-cremation of the bones and the lingering presence of spirits (see the 'Narratives' section). As memory agents, they are obviously important individuals as they shape the memorial site and engage in education programmes and outreach.

A more political agent with a very different role in the Cambodian memoryscape was the late King Sihanouk. Sihanouk was one of the country's most influential and charismatic, yet ambiguous, figures, from when he negotiated Cambodia's independence from the French protectorate until his death in 2012. He filled various roles beyond that of king at different times through his long career, including king-father, head of state and prime minister. His role in the country's history is complex, including an alliance with the Khmer Rouge that began with the campaign to bring down General Lon Nol, whose coup had removed Sihanouk from power. This alliance broke when the Khmer Rouge put the king under house arrest when they seized power. In 1981 Sihanouk founded the armed rebel and political movement Funcinpec, but would be a key figure in the peace negotiations of the early 1990s aimed at ending the country's second civil war. As a popular statesman, his word carried great weight regardless of what his formal political status was at any particular time. When in 2001 he addressed a letter to Prime Minister Hun Sen critiquing the display of skulls at the Tuol Sleng Genocide Museum, on the grounds of lack of respect for the dead, it was an important political event and one that the government felt obliged to react to. The government did not change its policy, as we will discuss, but did remove the skull map in 2002 (Brown and Millington, 2015: 33). The bodily remains were never cremated, however; they remain displayed on glass shelves (Tuol Sleng Genocide Museum, 2019: 90–1).

Narratives: how to treat the dead

Given the hegemonic nature of memory politics in Cambodia, we find little physical manifestation of any fragmentation of memory narratives – in contrast to other countries studied in this book. Nonetheless, concerning the role the bones of the dead should play today, and the consequences this has for the spirits, two narratives do compete within the spaces of memory. For some Cambodians, the fundamental question is: should bones be preserved as evidence of past violence or should they be cremated?

The hegemonic narrative advanced by the government of Prime Minister Hun Sen argues that the bones of the dead should be preserved, as they are needed as evidence of the horrific crimes carried out by the Khmer Rouge regime. A counter-narrative quietly adhered to by some memory actors, but which was more vocally advocated by Sihanouk, argues more along religious lines that the bones should be cremated to help set free the spirits of the deceased for rebirth. Interestingly, this debate relates not to all the uncremated bones in Cambodia, including the large numbers still lying in mass graves; it concerns itself primarily with the bones that are on public display in the various memorial sites around the country, including the Choeung Ek Killing Fields and at the Tuol Sleng Genocide Museum.

An especially intense debate has concerned a group of bones that were part of a controversial installation at the Tuol Sleng Genocide Museum. As outlined above, the installation showed a map of Cambodia made up of around 300 skulls that had been exhumed from mass graves in Svay Rieng province (Tuol Sleng Genocide Museum, 2019: 90); it showed the country's main rivers and its largest lake, Tonle Sap, highlighted in a blood-red colour (Brown and Millington, 2015: 33). According to an exhibition curated to mark the forty-year anniversary of the opening of the Tuol Sleng Genocide Museum, the 'purpose of creating a Cambodian map with skulls was to symbolize the loss of millions of Cambodian lives from all parts of the country under the reign of the Khmer Rouge' (Tuol Sleng Genocide Museum, 2019: 90). After the intervention by Sihanouk (detailed below), the museum dismantled the installation in 2002. It did not cremate the skulls, however, opting to continue to preserve them as evidence of the atrocities committed. The skulls were moved to be displayed in glass cases behind a small memorial stupa; a photograph of the map made up of skulls now adorns the wall where the installation once hung. The museum suggests that 'the new arrangement demonstrated the respect and good intentions of the museum towards the souls of the victims who died. It was assumed that Cambodians and foreigners would pay respect to the skulls when they saw them' (Tuol Sleng Genocide Museum, 2019: 91).

Preserving bones as evidence

First we will examine the narrative that construes the bones of Khmer Rouge victims as evidence of past atrocities, and therefore as an enduring symbol and reminder of the peace and stability provided by the current government, in contrast to that era. This is the hegemonic narrative advanced by the government, as it served and continues to serve the political purposes of the ruling elite. When the opponents of the Khmer Rouge liberated the country, the bones were necessary to demonstrate to the outside world (and to any remaining Khmer Rouge supporters in the population) the extreme cruelty of the ousted regime and the genocidal scope of its violence. By highlighting this genocidal violence, the new government in Phnom Penh strove to legitimise its invasion of the country with the help of Vietnamese forces, and also to rally support for its on-going military struggle against the Khmer Rouge in what became a second period of civil war. The bones were tangible and undeniable evidence of the atrocities, which were explicitly framed as the kind of system that would be reverted to if the Khmer Rouge took power again.

Later, when the fighting had ended, the bones took on an enhanced function: they still serve as a reminder of the violent past, but nowadays the emphasis lies especially on the on-going security that the government provides (and implicitly that only the government can provide). Interestingly, it is reported that even Buddhist clergy have declared that it is helpful to preserve the bones (Cougill, 2007: 40); while it is obviously difficult to know whether this support for government policy is wholly sincere when expressed in an authoritarian context, it is at least indicative that the bones-as-evidence debate has gained political currency and is not in diametric opposition to the interests of the Buddhist clergy.

With the advent of peace in the 1990s, the question of whether the bones still needed to be displayed did arise with more intensity. Given the continued political utility of displaying the bones to help bolster the government's legitimacy, the preservation of bones is now also framed in terms of legal evidence needed for the ECCC. Speaking at a rally in Kampong Chhnang in April 2001 – and in reaction to King Sihanouk's letter – Hun Sen offered to hold a referendum on whether remains should be cremated or preserved; he stipulated, however, that this could only take place after any trial of former Khmer Rouge had concluded. He thus drew on the original characterisation of bones as visual evidence and transformed this into a matter of legal evidence (Hughes, 2006: 285). Furthermore, forensic analysis of the bones (Fleischman, 2016) plays into these ideas of their evidentiary value – although only limited forensics have been carried out. The narrative that the bones need to be conserved as evidence thus has the political and legal function not only of legitimising the earlier Vietnamese-assisted invasion of the country to oust the Khmer Rouge, with an additional emphasis on on-going security; it has also been framed in terms of providing future justice for the victims of Khmer Rouge atrocities. Obviously, this intersection of security and justice is politically useful to the government and is seen as highly effective in underlining its claims to legitimacy.

Besides these political and legal functions, the hegemonic narrative also argues that it is important to preserve the bones for educational purposes (Sion, 2014: 109), and that they serve as a powerful form of communication with younger generations who have not experienced the violence of the Khmer Rouge themselves (Reinermann, 2020).[12] A connection of the materiality of the bones to postmemory has also been noted as significant in understanding the value of bones for the next generations (Henkin, 2018).

In interviews with various members of staff at the Tuol Sleng Genocide Museum, the debate as to whether the bones of the victims should be displayed as evidence, or whether they should be cremated out of respect for the dead, is strong.[13] One staff member, for example, highlighted how displaying skulls was important as 'proof of the way that the Khmer Rouge killed the people' and that the display of skulls corroborated some of the photos of killing and mass graves shown at the memorial.[14] Most staff members acknowledged the value of the bones and skulls as evidence, with potential for educating the next generation. As one museum employee, herself a survivor of the Khmer Rouge regime, expressed it: 'Keeping the bones is not useless for us, [for] the next generation to know what happened during the Pol

Pot regime. So that the young generation will know about it.' Interestingly, she then went on to highlight on a more personal note that preserving the bones was also good because it helped motivate her to celebrate religious ceremonies for the deceased, gaining merit for herself as well as for the dead.[15]

Cremating bones to set the spirits free

The second narrative in circulation regarding the display of victims' bones stresses that it goes against the cultural practice of cremation and is detrimental to those who have died, as their spirits cannot be released adequately for rebirth. This can be seen as a counter-narrative that seeks to undermine the hegemonic narrative that sees the bones as evidence; it instead highlights how not cremating the bones undermines the dignity of the dead and also negatively impacts the living, who are haunted by these restless spirits. This second narrative thus shifts the focus from a political rationale to a more dignity-focused approach towards the dead.

Given the government's firm grasp on power in Cambodia, opposition to the display of bones has not been widespread in the population, or at least not within public spaces. An exception is provided by Sihanouk, who sought to throw his political weight as monarch behind this cause in 2001. Sihanouk's open letter to Hun Sen asked for the skull map at the Tuol Sleng Genocide Museum to be removed and the 300 skulls to be 'cremated according to Buddhist practices so that the souls of the victims could be reincarnated' (Tuol Sleng Genocide Museum, 2019: 91). This demand was supported by the artist Vann Nath, who was a prominent survivor of the S-21 detention centre. While this debate did force the government to discuss the role of the victims' bones openly, in the end it led only to the map being dismantled without the bones being cremated, and more generally to a vague commitment to hold a referendum at some point in the future on how to deal with bones, and this only after the end of a judicial process. Given that this debate occurred in 2001, it is fair to say that the government has been relatively successful in entrenching its own favoured narrative in a solidly hegemonic position.

The intention of cremation suggested in the counter-narrative is two-fold. First, cremation would allow the spirits to be released from the state of limbo they have been in when tied to the bones; they can thus engage in reincarnation. Their cremation would play a part in restoring dignity to the victims who lost their lives under the Khmer Rouge (see Reinermann, 2020). One female staff member at the Tuol Sleng Genocide Museum, for example, said that she would personally prefer the bones to be cremated in order to respect the dead. Interestingly she added: 'Fortunately, we don't know who they are. If we were – you can imagine – if we were the family of them and we come here to see our relatives' … skulls inside here, it will be emotional to them.'[16] This suggests that although the anonymity of the dead (as the lack of DNA analysis means individuals have not been identified) does make it difficult or impossible to perform the required ceremonies for individual victims, it at least has the advantage that family members can hope it is not their own relatives' bones on display. This uncertainty may lessen the painful impact for grieving family members of a display featuring human skulls, which some perceive as denying the dead their dignity.

In addition, the consequence of this rebirth would be that the spirits would disappear and no longer haunt the living. This ties in, for example, with a strong unease about the presence of bones from a religious perspective among members of staff at the Tuol Sleng Genocide Museum. In interviews, some individuals first highlighted their fundamental support for preserving the bones as evidence, and particularly for educating generations to come, thus adhering to the hegemonic narrative; however, they then stressed that they are personally deeply uneasy with the preservation of the bones and the presence of spirits that it entails. Some staff members at the Tuol Sleng Genocide Museum, for example, reported that their parents were deeply opposed to their starting work there due to the spiritual danger they thought them to be in. Beyond the staff, it impacts how other people today interact with the memory of the past, and particularly whether people are prepared to visit sites they see as haunted. At the Tuol Sleng Genocide Museum, staff notice that students and also their parents are reluctant to visit, as they are deeply concerned about the ghosts bringing them bad luck. One senior staff member reported: 'We try to convince them the … museum is not a museum of ghosts.'[17] Another woman working at the Tuol Sleng Genocide Museum mentioned that some visitors whom she guided round the museum commented on the fact that showing the skulls was disrespectful to those killed; nonetheless, other visitors would pose in front of the display for selfies, in a way that is easily seen as lacking respect.[18] Thus, the display of skulls is not only problematic in itself, as a decision taken by those curating the display and by those with political oversight; it also enables visitors to engage with the human remains in ways that exacerbate this disrespect, even if such practices are in theory not allowed.

The presence of spirits, as well as the shocking nature of the bones at the memorials, is disturbing to surviving victims of Khmer Rouge rule. In a survey of 439 survivors, when asked what they thought about the fact that the bones and skulls of those who did not survive are sometimes kept in stupas (at memorials), 35.8 per cent of respondents indicated that it made them feel fearful, and 39.9 per cent found it upsetting because the people were not cremated. Only 26.2 per cent suggested that it was good because it reminded people of the past and was evidence of what happened, while 19.4 per cent responded with 'don't know'.[19] There are significantly more survivors, then, who are either fearful and/or disturbed by the presentation of bones in memorial sites than survivors who look positively on their being presented as evidence. This sentiment is echoed by a woman from Kampot province who as a victim of the Khmer Rouge participated in an NGO programme that included a visit to the memorial: 'I felt very shocked because after I visited the Tribunal, I also went to Tuol Sleng Genocide Museum. After I saw too many bones. ... Felt too shocked that when I got home, I became sick. Because there are piles of bones like a mountain, that I could only see the bones of the dead people.'[20] Furthermore, even people who did not experience the violence themselves are reported to advocate for cremation of the bones, experiencing their display as disrespectful, as Jan Reinermann (2020) found in his research with young Cambodians.

Events: spiritualism and politics

The final element of our analytical tetrad relates to the events held in the sites discussed above by the various memory agents salient to our analysis. In relation to bodies and spirits, the primary form that this takes are the religious ceremonies where offerings are given with the aim of gaining merit for oneself and for the spirits of the dead, aiding them in the journey to rebirth. Such ceremonies are the focal point of Cambodia's P'chum Ben festival (usually referred to in English as the 'Day of Ancestors'), but are sometimes also performed on other occasions. They are held within the religious space of the pagoda, meaning that memorials as spaces are merely incidentally linked to this festival, when the memorial happens to be located at a pagoda. When that is the case, offerings can be made at the memorials, too, but the memorials do not figure in any particular way in understandings of these ceremonies. Meanwhile, spontaneous forms of commemoration are untypical at memorial sites, where the bones and skulls are securely locked away, even when the sites are being used as part of an official religious ceremony.[21]

While spirits are constitutive of this type of event, the materiality of the bones is not, removing such purely religious events from most discussions on the politics of memory. Nonetheless, the ceremonies in which offerings are made to aid the spirits of the departed intersect with two important commemorative national holidays that are highly significant for the politics of remembering and for dealing with the genocide. They are the Day of Maintaining Anger (20 May) and Victory over Genocide Day (7 January).

P'chum Ben: the Day of Ancestors

Spirits can be, and are, appeased through offerings (Bennett, 2018b: 189; Guillou, 2014: 155), and as spirits can gain merit and improve their karma in an attempt to be reborn better or faster they can also engage in actions helpful to the people they interact with – they can bring them luck or offer guidance. Even in the commodification of the Choeung Ek Killing Fields site and its thirty-year lease to Japanese-Khmer business JC Royal Co., the company makes sure to take the well-being of the spirits seriously, reacting to dreams of employees and making offerings to 'hungry' spirits (Bennett, 2018b: 199). Furthermore, there is also a spirit house within the site, which is referred to in the audio guide as 'a dwelling place for spirits that have not found rest'.[22] At the Tuol Sleng Genocide Museum multiple ceremonies are also held every year to aid the spirits.[23]

As the most important holiday in the Cambodian calendar, P'chum Ben is a fifteen-day festival during which offerings are made to convey merit to the spirits of one's ancestors (see Holt, 2012). The offerings are made at the pagoda and feed the spirits in an attempt to appease them and help them on the path to rebirth; the making of offerings thus provides important opportunities for deceased loved ones, and also comes with the possibility of gaining karma for oneself by engaging in these practices.

The festival was outlawed under the Khmer Rouge, as were all other Buddhist practices in an attempt to eliminate religious observance. Despite the change in regime, this major festival remained forbidden through the late 1980s; the government, headed by Hun Sen from 1984, was initially hesitant to embrace Buddhist traditions. When the P'chum Ben festival was re-established in the early 1990s, Anne Guillou (2012: 218) describes a 'huge relief among the population in the days following the first festival, as if the atmosphere was suddenly lighter and quieter'. The festival is relevant to people because merit can be paid to the dead independent of their actual bodies – which are, in contrast, essential for funeral rites (Guillou, 2012: 218). It therefore allows family members to expedite rebirth for their deceased loved ones even without the knowledge of where they were killed or where their bodies are. In what Judy Ledgerwood (2012) describes as an 'act of "social resilience"' the festival can contribute to consolidating connections with individual spirits, in a context in which cremation is not allowed. The re-legalisation of this key spiritual holiday was thus a deeply political move due to its positive reception by ordinary Cambodians.

Political commemoration days: Day of Maintaining Anger and Victory over Genocide Day

Two major events relate more strongly to the politics of memory: the so-called Day of Maintaining Anger (*Tivea Chang Kamheng*)[24] and Victory over Genocide Day. The Day of Maintaining Anger, held on 20 May, was an important political event that the government introduced in the 1980s, in the context of the second civil war. It was aimed particularly against the Khmer

Rouge (Sion, 2014, 113). It was celebrated annually across the country with large events, rallies and speeches and was the most important political holiday related to the country's genocidal past. It did not draw on spiritual references but was a secular, political event, a rallying around the flag. In terms of sites, as well as being held primarily at memorial sites around the country, some of the day's events would be held in spaces suitable for large political rallies. In the early years of this day being observed, during the civil war, the events were used as an important moment of government propaganda to mobilise support for their fight against the Khmer Rouge by reminding the population of the horrendous past, as well as the danger that this could return should the government not prevail in the civil war. With the coming of peace in the 1990s, the day had served its purpose and was no longer a major event. However, the date of 20 May as an important political event was revived in 2001 as a 'Day of Remembrance' (Manning, 2017: 151). The ECCC has designated the Day of Remembrance an officially recognised symbolic 'reparation'. Reflecting the origin of this national day back in the 1980s, when Buddhist practices were still forbidden, it continues to be a secular event.

Victory over Genocide Day is marked on 7 January every year to commemorate the invasion of Cambodian and Vietnamese troops, who crossed the border to liberate the country in 1979. Given that the government that this invasion brought to power was essentially the origin of the current government, it is one of the most important political days of the year, with national and local-level events. One female victim of the Khmer Rouge who is a civil party seeking redress at the ECCC described this day as 'the second birthday of Khmer Rouge victims',[25] suggesting it gave them a new lease of life and highlighting the importance the day holds for her personally. For many people though, the day is perceived primarily in political terms. Hun Sen and various other government officials participate in events, give speeches and use the event to celebrate the government's part in liberating the country from the Khmer Rouge, and to bolster its on-going legitimacy. While there was previously a strong onus on surviving victims to participate in these ceremonies, most report they have not taken part in events organised on this day for several years now, most often explaining that they have not been invited and there is no pressure to participate.[26] While these political events are predominantly held at government administrative offices, most surviving victims of the Khmer Rouge use the opportunity to engage in religious ceremonies also at their local pagodas, in practices similar to those performed for P'chum Ben. One woman, a victim of the Khmer Rouge, reported that she likes the 7 January date because survivors like herself are then able to conduct religious ceremonies. She explained: 'We pray and wish for them [the spirits of the dead] for the next life that no one will hit them and to let them love each other.'[27] Furthermore, political leaders will sometimes also participate in religious ceremonies at the pagoda in the context of the broader programmes marking 7 January.

The SANE analysis: memory and the quality of peace

By the time all remaining Khmer Rouge leaders had surrendered or were militarily beaten the country had been wracked by conflict for almost three decades, including two periods of outright civil war and years of violence, repression and genocide in the late 1970s. The peace that prevailed in the late 1990s would prove to be a negative peace; hopes of democratisation and pluralism within the political system have – after positive developments after the turn of the century – been dashed, and human rights violations continued under Hun Sen's authoritarian rule. But the integration of surviving Khmer Rouge leaders and cadres, after they had been provided with amnesties, has allowed a positive, inclusive peace to develop. As alternative memories of the past are able to co-exist with the hegemonic narrative in those parts of the country that were strongholds of the Khmer Rouge during the second civil war (Manning, 2015), peace has become more entangled. A divisive issue that transcends various ways of remembering the past, and focuses on how it is dealt with today, can be found in the mnemonic formation of the dead. Having discussed the sites, agents, narratives and events that are particularly salient for the dead, both as bodies and spirits, we now interrogate the intersection of these four elements in order to augment our understanding of memory politics in general, and more specifically our appreciation of how this impacts on the quality of peace.

In studying the politics of memory surrounding spirits and bodies in Cambodia, we have seen that it is not sufficient to analyse sites from a material perspective, nor can understandings of social relations and agency be restricted purely to the living, given that the presence of spirits has an important impact on human relations too. This being so, sites and agents can be conceptualised beyond the official national level to incorporate both the living and dead, with their interactions occurring both in the context of official religious ceremonies and also in everyday life, particularly in the direct aftermath of the Democratic Kampuchea regime. By analytically incorporating this dimension, important realities for a large part of the population become visible, and it becomes easier to understand the lived politics of memory in Cambodia. Furthermore, people's interactions with key sites of memory, such as the Tuol Sleng Genocide Museum or the Choeung Ek Killing Fields, are pre-structured by these religious understandings, as well as by the fear of the bodily remains and the spiritual entities that may be encountered during visits to these sites.

More important for our understanding of entangled memory and its contribution to the quality of peace, a key question is who has control over the dead in Cambodia's politics of memory. On the one hand, the government's refusal to let bodies be cremated allows it to continue to exploit the bones as evidence that ultimately also supports its own legitimacy – which it traces to the toppling of the Khmer Rouge in 1979. The displays underline its claim to be providing security today and thus its continued legitimacy to govern. This appropriation of the physical remains for a political agenda has manifest consequences for family members, who cannot perform traditional funeral rites for their loved ones and fear that without this their family members will not be able to reincarnate. However, this conflict remains latent rather than explicitly voiced, not only because of the authoritarian nature of governance in Cambodia, which precludes too open a criticism of this policy, but above all because the identities of the vast majority of bodies are unclear due to population transfers during Democratic Kampuchea and the absence of any process of forensic identification. Given that the traditional practice is that each family should cremate its own dead, the absence of ties to specific bodies deflects this implicit conflict and facilitates an uneasy peace.

On the other hand, due to the Buddhist belief that without cremation rebirth becomes more difficult, the policy adopted by the government means that there are more spirits active in today's Cambodia. As the government does not have any control over these dead, the spirits exercise a form of non-human agency and one in which their interactions may run counter to government policy. Particularly in the 1980s, informal sites of memory such as mass graves and former detention centres (which were being brought back into use as schools and pagodas) haunted people due to the belief in the presence of malevolent spirits. The menace of these spaces has since somewhat reduced, however, as some spirits have been reborn or have faded away, particularly after the government allowed the revival of certain Buddhist practices that can placate the spirits.

This politics of memory in the 1980s led to a certain silencing of survivors' desires to placate spirits and support the deceased, which rendered the peace less inclusive than it could have been. Having said that, however, it was precisely the evidence-based approach and continued demonisation of the Khmer Rouge that supported a rallying around the flag effect during that decade. While this in itself did not lead to the end of the civil war, Hun Sen's much trumpeted credentials as the bringer of peace and stability have certainly supported his bid to stay in power. With a change in perspectives regarding the Khmer Rouge in the 1990s, from a demonisation rhetoric to universal victimhood for almost all cadres beyond the highest echelons of power, the peace has been structured more inclusively since, facilitating a more just peace for almost all Cambodians. In this sense, it is perhaps not surprising that what started as a hegemonic peace that silenced other memories of the past has gradually come to be accepted. Unlike other cases in this book, the absence of a truly entangled peace cannot be explained as the existence of parallel peace(s), but instead as an increased acceptance by larger parts of the population of the hegemonic understanding of the past and of the peace that this entails.

How victims' bones are treated after death is unquestionably important in any culture, and this is no different in Buddhist tradition. Framing the bones as evidence has important political or educational consequences, something which is regarded as beneficial by various interest groups. Nevertheless, this means that the bones become objectified as material remnants of Democratic Kampuchea and reduced to an anonymised by-product of violence; the memory of each individual is dehumanised and de-individualised. Further, the difficulty of offering appropriate funeral rites through cremation, due to the anonymity of the dead as discussed above, poses a significant challenge to the dignity of the deceased. Given the consequences that this has in terms of perpetuating the presence of malevolent spirits, this also decreases the dignity within which survivors live. They suffer in the knowledge that their loved ones could be among those unable to be reborn, and they also may have negative interactions with the spirits. As discussed, the presence of spirits was a much more significant issue in the 1980s, but even today the many uncremated remains of the deceased continue to instil fear among some survivors. With the reintroduction of Buddhist practice and the possibility of providing offerings to specific spirits, as well as the more general offerings made during the P'chum Ben festival, these tensions have eased somewhat, allowing the country's uneasy peace to mature.

Ultimately, the hegemonic structure of the memoryscape in Cambodia means that the treatment of the dead, whether as bones or as spirits, is not an issue of open political contention. It has surfaced in the political space only briefly and sporadically, most prominently in the letter sent by King Sihanouk regarding the skull map at the Tuol Sleng Genocide Memorial. As the dignity of the dead and of survivors is negatively impacted by these memory policies, it is, of course, a topic in private spaces, although even here some parts of the population continue to argue for the value of preserving bones as evidence. As the years go by and the spirits fade, and as younger generations grow up, it appears that the more inclusive peace that Hun Sen laid the groundwork for with the amnesties of the 1990s is bearing fruit. While the peace in Cambodia certainly cannot be seen as a pluralistic one, as the government's policy strongly dominates the scene, there is a growing acceptance that this way of dealing with the past facilitates peace in the country.

Conclusions

In this chapter we have studied the sites, agents, narratives and events in Cambodia's memoryscape that relate to the spirits and bodies of the dead. We have discussed how the meaning of the genocide may maintain a strong presence after the event, not only in terms of traumatic memories of the past carried by individuals as their private burdens, but also through the on-going presence of the dead and particularly the various political strategies adopted for dealing with these dead.

Taking the dead seriously in this analysis has been important not only for our understanding of post-genocide Cambodia and the manifestation of memory politics, but also in order to understand what kinds of interventions might be useful to individual survivors in their own recoveries. Classical Western responses to trauma are insufficient (Agger, 2015; Chhim, 2013), while other approaches to calming the mind can be achieved, including for example making 'merit' for the deceased and celebrating P'chum Ben (Agger, 2015) – practices that actively engage with the spirits of the deceased as agentive beings. While the gradual fading away of spirits means that the salience of this topic has considerably diminished today, the cremation of bones has still not been carried out, despite the country's return to Buddhist practices. The debate over what is the most expedient and appropriate handling of human remains therefore continues to be a meaningful one.

While the display of bones and skulls is not a common feature in post-conflict countries, with only Rwanda and Cambodia engaging in this to such a large degree, in this chapter we have demonstrated how the political response to these remains and the spirits seen to accompany them is important for the quality of peace. The hegemonic response supplied by the government precludes any adequate attribution of dignity both to the dead and to the living, even as shifts in memory politics have rendered society and memory more inclusive.

As the trials organised by the ECCC come to an end formally, it will be interesting to see whether the government will revisit the promise made in 2001 to hold a referendum on what to do with the bones of the deceased. It seems likely that in any referendum the government would be able to garner political capital from either outcome: a vote for the continued preservation of bones as evidence would support the government's on-going legitimation strategy; alternatively, mass cremations might be celebrated as a national act, reminding the nation who it was who saved them from the Khmer Rouge and brought peace to the country. How inclusive this process would be, and whether a plurality of voices would be admitted in the debates, remains an open question. However, a referendum would certainly have manifest consequences, and potentially positive ones, for the quality of peace in the country.

Notes

1 This book was written before Hun Sen left office and does not include Hun Manet's tenure in its analysis.
2 Interview, senior government advisor, Phnom Penh, February 2018.
3 Of course, there are other religious groups in Cambodia, most notably the Muslim Cham, but this chapter will focus on members of the religious majority, specifically their engagement with the spirits they encounter, who shape their perception of the politics of memory.
4 For the most in-depth study of Cambodian funeral rites see Davis (2016).
5 While in other places, such as in Srebrenica in Bosnia, the remains of people killed during the genocide are forensically examined to clarify their identities, no such attempts have been made in Cambodia. This is ostensibly due to the huge numbers of dead and a paucity of funds. There has also been a lack of interest by the Cambodian government and the international community (but see also Fleischman, 2016).
6 Audio guide stop 8 (English-language version of February 2018, obtained from Narrowcasters, the company that produces and rents out audio guides).
7 Interview, staff member of Tuol Sleng Genocide Museum, Phnom Penh, February 2018.
8 Audio guide stop 16 (English-language version of March 2013, obtained from Narrowcasters).
9 Interviews, various anonymous Tuol Sleng Genocide Museum staff members, Phnom Penh, February 2018.
10 Interview, anonymous male Tuol Sleng Genocide Museum staff member, Phnom Penh, February 2018.
11 Interview, senior government advisor, Phnom Penh, February 2018.
12 Interviews, various anonymous Tuol Sleng Genocide Museum staff members, Phnom Penh, February 2018.
13 Interviews, various anonymous Tuol Sleng Genocide Museum staff members, Phnom Penh, February 2018.
14 Interview, anonymous female Tuol Sleng Genocide Museum staff member, Phnom Penh, February 2018.
15 Interview, victim of the Khmer Rouge who had participated in NGO projects on dealing with the past, Kampong Cham province, May 2018. The interview was conducted by Julie Bernath in the context of a joint project with the fifth author, Timothy Williams.
16 Interview, anonymous female Tuol Sleng Genocide Museum staff member, Phnom Penh, February 2018.
17 Interview, anonymous Tuol Sleng Genocide Museum senior staff member involved in education programmes, Phnom Penh, February 2018.
18 Interview, anonymous Tuol Sleng Genocide Museum staff member, Phnom Penh, February 2018.
19 These are unpublished results of a survey, many other results of which were published in wider report on victims' perceptions of justice and reconciliation

in Cambodia (Williams et al., 2018). In this item, multiple answers could be selected.

20 Interview, victim of the Khmer Rouge who had participated in NGO projects on dealing with the past, Kampot province, May 2018. The interview was conducted by Julie Bernath in the context of a joint project with the fifth author.

21 Interview, victim of the Khmer Rouge who had participated in NGO projects on dealing with the past, Kampong Cham province, May 2018. The interview was conducted by Julie Bernath in the context of a joint project with the fifth author.

22 'Stop 16' of the English-language audio guide, version produced by Narrowcasters in March 2013.

23 Interview, anonymous Tuol Sleng Genocide Museum female staff member, Phnom Penh, February 2018.

24 The word often translated as 'anger' can also be translated as 'hatred'.

25 Interview, victim of the Khmer Rouge who was a civil party at the ECCC, Kampong Chhnang province, May 2018.

26 Interviews, various victims of the Khmer Rouge, various provinces, May to July 2018.

27 Interview, victim of the Khmer Rouge who had filed as a civil party in case 003 or 004 at the ECCC, Kampong Chhnang province, June 2018.

7

Memory and the quality of peace: plurality, dignity and inclusivity

Throughout this book we have engaged with legacies of violent and difficult pasts. Listening to stories of pain and spending time at sites of memory, we have been driven by a growing awareness that an analysis of memory politics enhances our understanding of the quality of peace. This process of analysis has allowed us to appreciate how the social fabric is moulded by competing and convergent understandings of the past, as well as what these memory dynamics tell about the social and political relations underpinning peace.

The investigation of five cases of mnemonic formations, considered as diagnostic sites, has demonstrated the strength with which memories of violence affect the quality of peace in the present. This has been in evidence with respect to the continuing division of Cyprus along nationalist lines, the lingering legacies of colonialism in South Africa, contestations around the use of human remains in Cambodia, the lasting mnemonic effects of the siege of Sarajevo as a key contestation in the Bosnian memoryscape and on-going controversies around the role of internationals in the Rwandan genocide. In this concluding chapter we draw comparatively on the insights gained from each of the preceding chapters and present our main findings regarding the impact of memory politics on the quality of peace. The findings lead us to suggest that the way memory entangles is key to the quality of peace. Across all five cases we find that three factors in how these memories are entangled are of particular importance in determining the quality of peace: plurality, the restoration of dignity to the victims of past violence and inclusivity. A just peace is possible if memory is entangled in a way that is plural, while also embracing dignity and inclusivity. The meaning of these three central factors will be further explicated later in the chapter. In contrast, if memory is entangled in a way that allows narratives to run parallel without interconnecting, a way that is divisive and leaves some victims' sufferings unacknowledged, the peace is most likely shallow.

The value of the analytical framework

Let us first note that the SANE framework has enabled us to carry out a systematic analysis through a focus on sites, agents, narratives, events and the interactions between them. It is through the emphasis on sites of memory such as memorials, monuments or museums that we have been able to capture the spatial and material dimensions of memory politics. Further, we have noted that it is crucial to acknowledge the role of agents who seek to exercise power and agency at various levels and settings. Given the centrality of language and discourse for constructing memory, we have also focused on narratives. Lastly, events have been analysed as a way of accessing the performativity of memory in its perhaps more temporal and shifting expressions. Importantly, it is the interaction of sites, agents, narratives and events that has constituted our analytical inroad.

Indeed, each empirical chapter brings out a richness and detail about these interactions in unique ways. In each mnemonic formation it is clear that sites such as memorials and museums are invested with particular meaning by being tied to social practices of place-making such as commemorative events, as memory agents make particular sites meaningful while others are ignored. The empirical chapters further demonstrate how any given mnemonic formation encompasses an array of memory agents, which may be formal or informal, local, national, international or transnational, collective or individual. Memory agency thus emerges as relational and reconstituted in social interactions, exercised through formal, public actions with political objectives, or sometimes through fleeting action in the margins of the mundane. Such events may be ritualistic or organic as people come together for political action; they may serve to maintain existing memories or on the contrary to assist in transformations of the post-war order. From these activities narratives emerge as meaning-making articulations that both shape and are shaped by sites, agents and events. As such they are constitutive of individual and collective identities.

The four conceptual entry points in the SANE framework have thus provided what Niewöhner and Scheffer (2010b: 3) refer to as 'analytical, cross-contextual framings that are meant to facilitate comparison'. As a next step, the analysis is taken one step further into a 'soft comparison' (Prus, 2010: 502), letting the richly contextual cases speak to each other. We synthesise the findings and return to our central puzzle: can the memory politics unpacked in these cases possibly tell us something beyond each case about how memory politics impacts on the quality of peace?

We find that that while the mnemonic formations that we have studied are each configured in unique and different ways, certain intriguing patterns emerge. Below, some key observations that hold true for all the cases will be synthesised. While we will not reiterate all the specific findings of each individual chapter, together they form the basis for the core conceptual developments regarding the quality of peace that we present here. Key to the analysis is the understanding of memory as entanglement – a concept that we define in the next section.

Key dimensions of entangled memories: plurality, dignity and inclusivity

In essence, we propose that the quality of peace can be assessed by the way memory is entangled in and through mnemonic formations. This entanglement is a result of the memory politics of various groups in society and reflects various interpretations of the violent past. As demonstrated in the empirical chapters, in societies emerging from violence – and societies more generally – there is not one hegemonic memory that dominates all interpretations of the past. It is of central importance how and whether competing views on the past and the present are accepted in a society, the extent to which they are integrated in the wider public sphere, and also the extent to which they manage to restore the dignity of victims, survivors and, broadly speaking, those who live with the long-term implications of systemic forms of violence. In each of the five cases that we have studied in this book, we can observe various entangled strands that sometimes conflict and collide, and at other times run parallel with no point of contact or mutually reinforce each other. Even in dictatorships or under totalitarianism, there are always groups who remember differently depending on their experience of the past, their situation in the present and their understanding of other groups in society. As Feindt et al. (2014: 31) suggest, 'acts of remembering are heterogeneous, dynamic, and therefore genuinely entangled'; they interact, interlace, connect, depart and break away, or develop together. Friction and fluidity are always elements of entanglement, too.

Entanglement is a concept that aids our understanding of different views of the past and their mutual interactions (Delanty, 2017; Heuman, 2014). The concept of entangled memories relates to the production of memories as a means to cast light on 'complex impulses in the present' (Conrad, 2003: 86). The notion of entanglement is very fruitful for understanding mnemonic formations since these complexities are highly significant for the constitution of peace in a conflict-affected society.

Collective identities are key to such entanglements. As Laanes (2020: 452) suggests, 'The view of cultural memory as intrinsically entangled cuts the ties between memory and group identity ... and introduces a new, comparative way of thinking about and studying the cultural memories of different groups, the interaction of those memories, and flows of influence'. In other words, identifying memory as entangled allows us to unpack it so that we can understand various groups and their interpretations of the past. This, in turn, offers insights into how these interpretations inform how groups see themselves, the other parties to the conflict and the prospects for peace in their society. In Cyprus, we see how the diverging versions of the island's past represented in the two museums refer back and inform the two different identities of Greek Cypriot and Turkish Cypriot, respectively. In Rwanda, ethnic identity is core to politics today, but is also shaped by, and in turn shapes, memory of the violent past, with Hutu and Tutsi interpretations of the past diverging.

From the five cases, we have been able to distil three primary facets of entanglement that we see as key for the quality of peace, namely: the extent to which memory-making is plural (in terms of encompassing diverse memories and commemoration practices); the extent to which it contributes to embracing dignity (in terms of acknowledging the injustices committed); and finally the extent to which it is inclusive (in terms of ethnicity, race, nationality, religion, age and gender, among other things). This definition incorporates the inherent fluidity and friction of memory politics and allows us to assess the impact that memory politics has on peace itself.

The focus on entangled memories allows us to conceptualise the relationship between the politics of memory and the quality of peace. If we investigate the entanglements and nodes of connection between competing views of the past within a mnemonic formation, we can grasp the quality of peace that emerges from such entanglements. Indeed, as our case studies highlight, where the respective mnemonic formation consists of multiple, intersectional entanglements and overlaps, there is more room for the negotiation of a plural and inclusive peace, and one that confers dignity on all victims. In contrast, where a mnemonic formation allows for very limited entanglements and cultivates views of the past as separate and isolated from one another, a variety of parallel peace(s) may emerge.

Plurality versus homogeneity

Plurality is a basic precondition of entangled memories. Often, where there is only one dominant way of remembering, there is a risk that it is obscuring more silent or marginalised voices in a society. This is the case in societies where commemoration is heavily dominated by a hegemonic actor, such as the state. Homogenised memories are mobilised to generate higher degrees of legitimacy for different forms of government and governance, with sometimes questionable ethics. We have, for instance, pointed to the control that the Rwandan and Cambodian governments exercise over the country's memory politics, and in Cyprus, as also in Bosnia and Herzegovina, we can see leadership structures dominated by the conflict's lines of division now driving the ways in which memory is mobilised and enacted. A lack of plurality of memory sites, agents, narratives and events in conflict-affected societies that are struggling with conflicting memories indicates a fairly closed political space, and one in which conflict lines are deeply entrenched and difficult to challenge. Efforts at promoting a just peace in such contexts will therefore struggle to make space for a plurality of voices and will find themselves confronted with a multitude of silences. In Rwanda, the state enforces the official narrative about the past with exceptional vigour, although there is a highly diverse memory of the 1994 genocide, and various social and political groups hold diverging understandings as to causes, consequences and responsibility for the violence. These frictions are, however, stifled by a highly hegemonic government narrative about the nature of the atrocity and its memory – to the point that dissenting accounts are forbidden by law on the grounds that they might promote divisions or genocide denial. As a consequence, there is much resentment on the part of groups who oppose the government narrative, as their position is not accepted. This leads to anger against the government and against ruling elites more generally, which stands in the way of a just peace being consolidated in the future.

It is the moment of conflict or contestation itself that generates the types of memorialisation that matter for the articulation of relevant conflict identities. The extent to which the memoryscape allows for a plurality of memories to co-exist (or not) tells us much about the quality of peace and the potential for a just peace. A just peace presupposes the existence of several threads that can be woven together, that is, a plurality of interpretations of the past. The diversity of practices of remembering and forgetting provides the raw material, so to speak, for this process through which competing sites, agents, narratives and events can be accommodated in any given society.

Our empirical analysis illustrates how the degree to which a mnemonic formation allows a plurality of sites, agents, narratives and events to co-exist has an important effect on the quality of peace. Where there is a strong degree of homogeneity, peace processes are at risk of excluding, silencing or marginalising divergent voices. In Cyprus, for instance, the high degree of bifurcation in the memory landscape has meant that largely separate versions of peace have been developed in the north and the south of the divided island. There is much internal homogeneity within those two separate spaces and little plurality in deviating from their dominant scripts. The bi-communal movement has to some extent challenged this rigidity and homogeneity, but – not unlike the frozen peace process on the island – has struggled to bring more pluralism to the very deep political fault lines that continue to divide the two communities. The highly scripted, nationalistic museums we have investigated operate on either side of these fault lines, which continue to undermine efforts towards cross-community engagement and the dismantling of enduring, engrained narratives about the past. At the same time there are other spaces that at times engage with and destabilise these mnemonic formations – in contemporary arts projects, for example. One such space is the Nicosia Municipal Arts Centre, which exhibits work from both sides of the Green Line. In this cultural space, memories emerge that reveal cracks in the hegemonic mnemonic formations of competing nationalisms.

In South Africa, we have identified somewhat similar tendencies of internally homogeneous, opposing memory camps, often (though not exclusively) defined by the colonial and apartheid legacies of racial divisions. Those opposing camps in turn are conditioned by their associated historical structures of inequality, which persist into the present day; they are often far apart from one another. The memories predominantly hosted by, for instance, Afrikaner communities nostalgic for colonial structures could barely be further from the calls for decolonisation voiced by recent student movements calling not only for the decolonisation of educational systems but also for reparative action (such as land return) and wider political transformation. At the same time, we can observe internal tensions within what seem like homogeneous camps, with solidarities and inclusive memory sites emerging (such as Freedom Park) – which are, as we have shown, not free from criticism due to the risk of their toning down calls for justice in the aftermath of colonial violence.

While Bosnia and Herzegovina is rigidly divided into three separate memory camps, our case study of the mnemonic formation of the siege of Sarajevo reveals a plurality of mnemonic agents that provide potentially transformative narratives. The hegemonic, top-down ethno-nationalist narrative, with its focus on military heroism is, in fact, repeatedly challenged by other narratives that highlight a shared urban identity as well as the everyday resilience and civic values upheld by ordinary citizens during the siege.

Feindt et al. (2014: 32) suggest that a more plural memoryscape allows for spaces of contestation, which take on significance at particularly crucial moments in time. Those moments can be moments of crisis and conflict, where certain memories are re-evoked while others are silenced. Changes in deeply embedded structures can be slow and gradual, as the bi-communal movement in Cyprus suggests; where it happens faster, such changes may be foregrounded against longer-term preparations that had been taking place under the radar. The #RhodesMustFall movement is illustrative of a situation where long-prepared battles have finally found a moment to emerge onto the surface to be met with stronger public sympathy and mobilisation.

In Cambodia, memory politics regarding how to deal with the dead has shifted over time, although two fundamentally different approaches remain pitted against each other. One narrative advocates for the cremation of bones allowing the spirits to be set free for rebirth and the other one argues for the bones to be kept on public display as evidence highlighting the horrors of the Khmer Rouge for generations to come.

Against this backdrop, a number of academic contributions have argued for the benefits of plural and entangled memories (see Delanty, 2017; Feindt et al., 2014). Our case studies highlight that attention also needs to be paid to the complexity of social interactions beyond a mere plurality. The fact that competing views of the past are present does not tell us enough about how they relate to each other, nor what this actually means for the ways in which a contested past is dealt with, especially in relation to how it engages with its victims, survivors and notions of reparation. For the plurality of memories to enhance the quality of peace, therefore, plurality needs to embrace inclusivity and dignity, as we shall see in the next sections.

Dignity versus lack of acknowledgement

The second factor for the quality of peace derived from our analysis of memory politics is the extent to which dignity is restored to the victims and survivors of violence, most frequently through their sufferings being acknowledged and the full extent of wrongdoings and violence they have undergone being openly recognised. We understand dignity as relational (Clark Miller, 2017; Ríos Oyola, 2019: 10), and entangled memories reflect the dignity of survivors of violence when coupled with an acknowledgement, by those responsible for it, of the harms this violence has done. Dignity is therefore an important factor in how memories are processed and eventually channelled into the ways in which a peace relationally deals with victims and perpetrators. In cases where no acknowledgement is given, the peace will remain brittle and vulnerable to breakdown.

The mnemonic formations analysed here vary significantly in this respect: some do indeed provide considerable space for telling narratives about the multiple ways in which violence has been experienced by its survivors, thus affording dignity to the victims. In Sarajevo, for example, several museums bring a close focus to bear on the everyday experiences of the city's residents during the siege. Their displays let the visitors create their own interactions and interpretations, promoted through the focus on ordinary objects as the carriers of meaning and emotions – a plastic water canister, a sign warning of snipers or a torn diary. The stories of the individual and social losses that war and violence entail, as well as of human resilience in the face of such challenges, are told through these things. For survivors, the focus on the fabric of everyday life is an acknowledgement of both the tangible and intangible losses they have experienced during the siege, and recognises their suffering on a local, national and international stage.

Commemorative events can have the power to demonstrate publicly the need for victims to be seen and heard. Across several of the cases, artistic interventions emerge as a practice that can address this need and speak to, and with, victims, beyond polarising narratives. The power of art in this context is aptly demonstrated by the artwork *Sarajevo Red Line* that consisted of more than 11,500 red chairs placed in rows that stretched for several hundred metres along the main street through the city centre. Each chair represented a killed person during the siege, shockingly communicating the ever-present loss from the urbanscape of neighbours, friends, relatives and familiar strangers. Such an art project brings back to centre-stage the impact of the siege on the citizens of Sarajevo and thus deems their grievances worthy of attention. This can be an integral part of their dignity, at the same time countering the dangers of denial and forgetting.

In contrast, other sites and events are predominantly perpetrator oriented and provide only limited room to commemorate the suffering of those who were at the receiving end of violence. Here, Cyprus stands as an important case in point, as the suffering of the victims of the other side is not acknowledged in either of the museums we studied, one from each community, and the resultant lack of dignity feeds into the parallel peace(s) that exist in both parts of the island. In Cambodia, meanwhile, the mnemonic formation of the contestations around human remains illustrates particularly well the importance of restoring dignity, in terms of how peace is experienced and negotiated in survivors' everyday lives: for many, treating the bones of the deceased with spiritual respect is an indispensable part of a just peace, despite the considerable political opposition to such demands.

One aspect of dignity that poses a challenge for many societies transitioning from violence to peace is that the victims who died, as well as those who survived, should recover from dehumanisation and violation (Rosoux and Anstey, 2017). It is this that King Sihanouk is referring to in Cambodia when he called for the cremation of bones of those killed under Khmer Rouge rule. Their lingering on as spirits unable to be reborn is seen as a form of further dehumanisation; setting them free would be the only way for them to regain dignity. At the same time, for survivors the quality of peace is eroded in the post-conflict context as survivors are haunted by spirits and are beset with worries over their lost loved ones' spiritual well-being.

Dignity as a result of productive memory entanglement has the potential to create links of solidarity between communities across time and space (Laanes, 2020: 452), as is exemplified in the bi-communal movement in Cyprus, where interaction between the two sides promotes an awareness of alternative perspectives and an acknowledgement of the suffering experienced in both communities. Dignity can strengthen ties between groups by highlighting a joint understanding of suffering in the past even if groups differ in many aspects other than the experience of violence, so that memory becomes multidirectional (Rothberg, 2009). Equally, an absence of acknowledgement will make cross-community relations more difficult.

Often, where acknowledgement and dignity are given, they come from inside one's own survivor group. This has been the case in all the mnemonic formations we have analysed, albeit to varying degrees. It is key to our understanding of the respective peace processes, though. In Sarajevo for instance, the difficulty of achieving a cross-ethnic acknowledgement of atrocities committed during the siege remains one of the main obstacles to meaningful peace. Those issues are partly addressed at the micro-level but struggle to translate into a national politics where members of each ethnic group might be able to recognise the different forms of suffering inflicted by their own group. Phenomena such as genocide denial regarding the genocide that took place in Srebrenica are part of this same problem.

When it is part of an entangled mnemonic process, on the other hand, dignity can resonate beyond the confines of one's own group and can contribute to the emergence of alliances, solidarities and expressions of justice (see Laanes, 2020: 452). This also means that on-going expressions of denial, through a refusal to commemorate and acknowledge, can undermine social connections and thus the emergence of a peace that would be just and sustainable, and indeed bearable, for the victims of violence. As such, acknowledgement and the restoration of dignity is often not something volunteered, but must be hard fought for. The South African case study aptly illustrates the long-term struggles that survivors of colonial violence have had to go through to obtain at least a degree of acknowledgement, not only of the sufferings of their ancestors, but also of the continuing impacts that colonial structures have on their lives. Community museums, political alliances and solidarity movements have been key in this respect, but it has taken a considerable investment of time, resources and energy on the part of many vulnerable groups in society. This is certainly not dissimilar to our Rwandan case study, where international states and organisations have only engaged in limited ways with the violence they contributed to, and primarily as a response to growing national and international pressure. Their engagement has been further inhibited by what the current government has considered acceptable, leaving little room for those primarily affected by the genocidal violence to have their voices heard and acknowledged.

The acknowledgement of memories of violence and suffering is an important tool in the restoration of dignity to victims and communities in post-conflict societies, particularly when they may otherwise be faced with manifestations of denial (Zubrzycki and Woźny, 2020: 185); in this context, we can also refer to this form of dignity as an element of 'memory-justice' (Booth, 2001). The Bosnian activist group 'Because it concerns me' makes interventions in the memoryscape by mounting temporary plaques that highlight war crimes and commemorate victims who otherwise are silenced and ignored. While their interventions do not make a lasting material mark, their demands for justice across ethnic boundaries resonate widely.

Dignity also functions as an umbrella term used by disenfranchised groups and communities who formulate their demands in mnemonic terms (Ríos Oyola, 2019: 10). Part of this formulation may also be references to how dignity is undermined as a result of material and non-material loss, stipulating that the restitution of dignity needs to push memory work beyond a simple acknowledgement of suffering, understanding it only as a first step towards compensation, reparation and apology. As such, it is a key element of memory politics, both immaterially and potentially with material implications. In South Africa, for instance, calls for reparations coming from the victims of colonialism and apartheid, and their descendants, are deeply connected to the quality of peace (see Walters, 2009). Groups, such as the Khulumani Support Group are dedicated to achieving compensation for survivors of violence from foreign companies that supported the apartheid regime and have taken legal action to that end. Certainly, such battles are long-winded and often have to face considerable political pressure and resistance, as the loss of the Khulumani court case in 2013 unfortunately demonstrates all too well.

Either way, the quest for dignity may take place in ways that are superficial and forced, or it can be accommodated in a dialogical, supportive way. This is why we propose that dignity needs to be inclusive to be meaningful (Clark Miller, 2017: 110) – inclusivity being the third dimension connecting memory politics and peace, as we shall now discuss.

Inclusivity versus exclusion

Memory politics can be either exclusive or inclusive in terms of how flexible it is in allowing for divergence among the various competing memories of the past; sometimes it can combine a mixture of exclusive and inclusive elements. Exclusion here means a lack of recognition that alternative interpretations of the past exist in parallel to each other and a choice not to engage with them, that is, to exclude them from one's own memory politics and to situate one's own group in opposition to it. By contrast, an entanglement that is inclusive sees actors entering into a dialogue with alternative memories that are based both on alternative experiences during the violence and alternative experiences in the present. Including them does not, however, suggest that they are being altered and homogenised; rather, it contributes to the formation of a wider, denser type of commemoration.

In Sarajevo, we see inclusivity happen at sites that are not primarily ethnically defined or oriented, such as in the urban spaces where members of the public mingle. It is also expressed at several museums and memorials, but those initiatives struggle to translate into the macro-politics of peace at state and international levels; there memory work is sharply divided between the two ethnically defined entities of Bosnia-Herzegovina and Republika Srpska. Urban areas seem to lend themselves more easily to such structures than do rural areas – which since the war have often remained ethnically homogenous.

As is evident in the case of Bosnia and Herzegovina as well as others in this book, the inclusivity or exclusivity of memories affect the collective identities of the parties to the conflict, that is, how they see and understand themselves, as well as how they see and understand the other parties to the conflict (Buckley-Zistel, 2006b; Strömbom, 2017; Wielenga, 2012). It is through narratives about the past that the parties to the conflict produce and reproduce their collective identities, either in antagonism to each other or in a more reconciliatory manner – or somewhere between these two poles. The necessary social transformation, which changes the way that the parties to the conflict relate to each other, depends on how the past is referred to in memory politics (Buckley-Zistel, 2006c: 3). In an extreme way, this dynamic is captured in Vakim Volkan's (1991: 5) concept of 'chosen trauma'. The memory of a traumatic event constructs the respective group's identity in opposition to the identity of the opponent who caused the trauma. It produces an us-feeling under the guise of victimhood. The same can of course be argued about victors, too, and indeed about many other actor groups in a post-conflict context.

In Rwanda, for example, the only publicly acceptable memory of the past is embedded in the official narrative advanced by the RPF government, which positions the Tutsi population as victims of Hutu violence. This suggests a very exclusive form of memory-making, one that not only fails to recognise, but also systematically marginalises, alternative perspectives. And yet, with regard to the mnemonic formation in focus here, that is, the role of internationals, there are moments in which the entanglement of memories can become somewhat more inclusive. The government's narratives regarding how the colonial past rendered the ethnic categories of Tutsi and Hutu politically salient, regarding the failure of the international community to intervene and stop the genocide, and also the allegations made against the French as having supported *génocidaires*, together produce a strong us-group of all Rwandans versus a them-group of the internationals – even if this is overall dwarfed by the otherwise exclusionary forms of memory-making.

Likewise, the bifurcated mnemonic formations of nationalism in Cyprus hide the fact that neither communities are ethnically homogenous. Acknowledging collective memories of the past held by minority communities such as the Armenian community in Cyprus would reveal cracks in the hegemonic mnemonic formations of nationalism. Yet these memories are rarely represented in official, public spaces, and they tend instead to be expressed in cultural spaces outside the curated official institutions of memory and history. Such spaces, although rare and often only momentarily available, may contribute to an opening up for voices and memories not currently acknowledged within the dominant mnemonic formations.

Somewhat differently, in Cambodia there are moments of friction and exclusivity in the mnemonic formation of the dead, with government dominance about the meaning of bones marginalising perspectives that are more preoccupied with the spiritual afterlife of the dead. And yet, for the most part, memories of the violent past rest on an inclusive form of entanglement that allows individuals to remember the Khmer Rouge period from a variety of perspectives, while at the same time all Cambodians can understand themselves as having been victims of that totalitarian regime.

As a consequence, an understanding of how identities are informed by memories of the past represents an important input into the constitution of peace in any given society. Inclusive memory will not lead to the creation of mutually exclusive identities in this context, but may encourage and foster a collaborative effort at identity-building, whether this be at community or state level. Memory is therefore an important building block in the formation of collective identities and feeds into the ways in which this process impacts on efforts at building a just peace. Densely entangled memories may thus provide multiple nodes of connection, which can be used to create bridges from one strand to another. In other words, where different memories engage with each other rather than drawing a sharp line, there is the potential for mutual acknowledgement and respect.

Our case studies are revealing in the degree to which mnemonic formations allow for the inclusion of a variety of perspectives expressed by multiple actors, through the sharing of narratives in mnemonic spaces and events. Tellingly, as the strict geographical separation of the island of Cyprus already suggests, the mainstream discourses held by the two sides there are largely separate and exclusive. The more inclusive sector represented by the bi-communal movement, which does try to integrate various views and perspectives, risks being sidelined from those powerful political currents that have high stakes in consolidating a bipolar status quo. In South Africa, too, the racial segregation established by colonial rule and further institutionalised by apartheid continues to shape the memory landscape and thus the quality of the peace that we (fail to) see emerging. There are smaller spaces in which different perspectives may meet – something that some of the government-funded projects seek to promote – but they are limited in terms of their popular appeal among a population that is hungry for a just peace rather than a form of reconciliation that is essentially an empty shell, without any deep engagement with the injustices committed in the past and the present. The increasing levels of critique of the notion of the rainbow nation – which celebrates diversity yet has failed to address persistent structural inequalities – is illustrative here.

Indeed, commemorative practices always suffer from such inequalities and marginalisations. Importantly, when it comes to the question of gender, all the case studies reveal a marginalisation of women's experiences, and gendered aspects of war are in general little noted or discussed at sites of commemoration. An exception is the museums in Sarajevo, which through their focus on objects of everyday experiences bring attention to gendered dimensions of the mundane aspects of life under siege. For example, they highlight cooking recipes shared among women who had to feed families on next to nothing. More typically, in Cyprus the narrative obliteration of certain women who were part of the historical struggles is evident on both sides of the conflict. The marginalisations of women's experiences of conflict tend to translate into gendered marginalisations in the post-conflict realm, so the lack of attention to women's memories, and memories of women, indicates a peace lacking in gender justice.

Inclusive memory politics is thus an important factor for the quality of peace. Through inclusivity (which, it should be noted, we do not understand as the value-free equalisation of different historical claims) various parts of a population can be reintegrated into society, providing them with a political voice, economic security and a stake in the collective identity. Inclusive peace entails a process that 'simultaneously addresses surface issues and changes underlying social structures and relationship patterns' (Lederach, 2003: 16). While such inclusion can entail frictions between former adversaries, a non-inclusive peace will not be sustainable in reforming inter-group relations and may even lay the groundwork for a resumption of hostilities.

Conclusions

To summarise, in this chapter we argued that in societies transitioning from violence there are diverse and conflicting interpretations of the past, and that these are reflected in mnemonic formations that can be studied through analysing sites, agents, narratives and events. The quality of peace can be determined by how memories are entangled. Our empirical analysis shows that a just peace is observed when memory is entangled in a plural, inclusive and dignified way. Conversely, a shallow peace persists when memory is entangled in a parallel or divisive way, or one that leaves the experiences of certain groups unrecognised. We will continue in the concluding chapter with reflections on what a just peace entails.

Conclusions

Drawing the arguments together, we propose that the potential held by entangled memory for plurality, dignity and inclusivity allows us to draw conclusions about the quality of peace. The mnemonic formations chosen for this study serve as diagnostic sites for peace. A just peace is, in our analysis, a function of entangled memory and stresses the key importance of plurality, dignity and inclusivity. This entangled memory is fluid and dynamic, and is constantly renegotiated, thus allowing for adaptations over time so that all parties to the conflict can shape their collective identity in relation to – rather than in opposition to – each other.

Viewing plurality, dignity and inclusivity as dimensions of entanglement prompts us to investigate both the mechanisms and contents through which a society's relationship to the past impacts on its current frictions, tensions and points of contestation. The analysis of how the three elements interplay allows for a nuanced conclusion as to the quality of peace, thus deviating from a linear understanding between the politics of memory and peace. Instead, a variety of configurations through which societies manage their pasts is thinkable, based on prevailing power relations and resource distribution as well as wider normative constraints. An understanding of a given mnemonic formation in light of its plurality, inclusivity and the degree of dignity it confers gives us the opportunity to advocate for peace as mnemonically grounded, intersubjective, relational and contextual.

This stands in contrast to mnemonic formations characterised by memory strands that have few mutual connections, reflect high degrees of homogeneity within each strand, and leave suffering unacknowledged and memory strands separate. While broad agreement about certain versions of the past does not have to be detrimental, in societies with high levels of contestations about the past it is more likely to produce a number of peace(s), each of which is turned inwards and is static in nature. Instead of an intersubjective understanding of a just peace they may lead to a form of co-existence which is susceptible to manipulation and division in the future. Parties to the conflict (in the widest sense) thus shape their collective identities in relation to each other. How they view the past will be an important factor in whether this relationship is predominantly cooperative or oppositional.

Importantly, a just peace is not a function of plurality alone, dignity alone or inclusivity alone. It is perfectly imaginable, for instance, that one might find a mnemonic manifestation shaped by a plurality of memories, with different interpretations of the past represented throughout society. As long as these interpretations fail to restore the dignity of the victims and survivors of violence, however, a just peace will not be possible. Similarly, inclusivity alone would not be sufficient for the emergence of a just form of peace, since there would always be a risk that the narratives of those suffering from violence and those who perpetrated it are put on an equal footing, empowering those who seek to erase past and present atrocities from public memory. Finally, dignity represented in such a mnemonic formation alone would also be limited, where such dignity is only extended to particular sectors of society and denied to others despite the plurality of memories permitted.

How memories of different actors, groups and collectives are entangled thus mirrors the very social relations that make up the quality of peace. How the social fabric of memory is woven together influences whether peace processes will flourish, or alternatively stall or regress. Memories emerge from the ways in which the past is dealt with in a given political and social context and have a considerable impact not only on how a society views its own story in the past but, importantly, on social relations within that society in the present and the future.

Where there is little mutual conversation about the past and hardly any attempts to acknowledge the suffering of all victim groups, a peaceful social order seems highly unlikely. It is imaginable as a negative, ceasefire-based peace at best, and is highly vulnerable to breakdown due to the grievances from the past that continue to simmer. In contrast, movements for peace will be better able to develop in a more pluralistic, dignified and inclusive memory landscape than in a homogeneous, stratified society where there is little acknowledgement of other groups' sufferings in the past and present. The former offers openings into new forms of collaboration, solidarity and conversation, while the latter makes such engagement risky for those challenging the status quo, or difficult at best. Where funding structures and political power alliances coincide to support a frozen status quo, even the best-intentioned peace efforts will struggle to gain sufficient momentum to be sustainable over a long period of time and to mobilise a sufficiently wide supporter base. Indeed, powerful gatekeepers may prevent more meaningful change from happening as it might threaten their power base.

So, while the memory processes that this book has looked at are collective in nature, they are not homogenous or flat. They are the product of multi-layered processes with a variety of interests involved, including the agendas of local organisations, peace organisations, ethnic entrepreneurs, civil society, governments, international organisations and tourists – all of whom may have different views on the peace process concerned. Some of these agents may be predominantly interested in notions of reconciliation, whereas others may prioritise justice as a precondition for the establishment of meaningful peace.

We therefore advocate for a contextually sensitive approach to memory-making and peace-making, that is, one that is highly specific to the society in which it unfolds. What plurality, dignity and inclusivity mean concretely varies from society to society and is subject to empirical analysis. There is always a need to take into account the historical and social particularities that affect the ways in which peace is emplaced, enacted, narrated and performed. One could, for instance, consider the given geographies in which peace unfolds: in divided societies a big challenge for peacebuilders is to locate spaces, agents, narratives and events that span across otherwise rigidly defined identity groups. This endeavour is particularly challenging where those groups are geographically separated or dispersed across a wider region in the form of large diasporas. In such cases, finding opportunities to create shared spaces requires an in-depth knowledge of society and its memory politics, and meaningful solutions are hardly ever applicable elsewhere, in a generalised way. Where such spaces have been successfully created, mobilised or activated, however, they have often served as microcosms for memory-engaged peace-building.

This does not mean, clearly, that such projects are done effortlessly in every political context. Moves towards more inclusive and dignified histories are often hard fought for rather than volunteered. These struggles are necessarily context-specific and each must be considered in its historical and social context if we are to comprehend the significance of each case for the emergence of just peace. In any of the contexts, mnemonic formations can be politically instrumentalised and exploited for the benefit of power holders and elites.

In all of these processes, it is crucial to think beyond linear temporalities, as peace is shaped by highly dynamic and complex uses of the past. The trauma and suffering that violence causes does not linearly fade from society. Instead, past injustices – even when they may have happened generations ago – translate into people's everyday lives in the present, sometimes in muted, sometimes in amplified, ways. Indeed, our case studies all demonstrate the lingering, fluctuating and often unpredictable effects that the legacies of colonial rule, spatial divisions, genocide denial or lack of respect for the deceased can have on survivors and descendants. In contemporary politics, fragments of the past can be selectively activated to bring particular grievances to light. Importantly, however, although these politics can sometimes be remarkably resilient, there may be moments of rupture and transformation where cracks in commemorative politics can open up for transformations towards a just peace.

Looking through the lens of memory politics thus enables a rethinking of peace. Peace can no longer be conceived of as an abstract, singular thing; something unobtainable, as noted by Dietrich and Sützl (1997). Instead, the findings of this book show that peace is grounded in particular times and in particular spaces; it is an entangled process rather than an outcome. By identifying the key factors of plurality, dignity and inclusivity in memory politics, it is possible to recognise the different ways in which a just peace may manifest itself in societies dealing with difficult memories of violence.

Hopes for the future: new avenues for Peace Studies and Memory Studies

Memory and peace are both value-laden concepts; they are contested, fluid and constantly under negotiation. It is not a small task to take on a more systematic reading of their interplay. Nevertheless, given their centrality for conflict-affected societies this has been our ambition. Building on and expanding insights and approaches from both Memory Studies and Peace Studies, this book has attempted to bridge the gap between those two fields.

As critical peace scholars, we have been inspired by the field of Memory Studies and its rich case studies of societies dealing with difficult heritages. The profound insights of Memory Studies have spoken to us and helped us criticise and bring nuance to research on peace-building, which at times has been overly instrumental, apolitical and technical, and constructed around a liberal peace agenda with little concern for the underlying, sometimes subtle tensions that play out in interrelational politics of memory. At the same time, from our viewpoint, the work of critical peace research regarding manifestations of agency in their spatial and temporal expressions can make important contributions to the study of memory, making visible how memory politics shape, legitimise and challenge peace across time and space, generating authority for particular versions of peace and social order. We thus hope that our work contributes to the literature of Memory Studies by highlighting the political and societal impacts of memory, as well as the contingency of memory within shifting political contexts of conflict-affected societies.

The comparison of five mnemonic formations in five very different conflict-affected societies has highlighted how deeply entwined memory-making and peace-making are. Inspired by the concept of the entanglement of memory, we have been able to identify systematically key facets of how memory work impacts the quality of peace. The findings are remarkable in their salience across all five cases. We also believe that the observations concerning the impact of the politics of memory on the quality of peace are generalisable, at least to a certain extent. Let us then, on this note, emphasise the wider meaning and applicability of the SANE analytical framework, which has formed the backbone of our studies across five cases. We hope that researchers may feel inspired to apply the framework to other case studies, thereby adding to an archive of cases varying in space and time that can be compared, generating further findings. Likewise, the methodology of using particular mnemonic formations as diagnostic sites means that other mnemonic formations in the case countries can be selected, to be compared and contrasted with the mnemonic formations that we chose to study.

The central contribution of this book generated through this ethnographic comparison is the theoretical conceptualisation of the ways in which memory entangles, identifying three factors that are of particular importance in determining the quality of peace: plurality, the restoration of dignity, and inclusivity. A just peace thus becomes possible when memory is entangled in a way that is pluralistic, inclusive and contributes to embracing dignity. As much as we hope that scholars of peace and of memory alike will find this synthesis of interest from a conceptual point of view, we also hope that policymakers and practitioners may be able to build on these insights, and may put them into practice in ways that contribute to the task of building a just peace by addressing inequalities, marginalisations and omissions in how the past is remembered.

References

Abrahams, Yvette. 1996. 'Disempowered to Consent: Sara Bartman and Khoisan Slavery in the Nineteenth-Century Cape Colony and Britain'. *South African Historical Journal* 35(1): 89–114.

Agger, Inger. 2015. 'Calming the Mind: Healing after Mass Atrocity in Cambodia'. *Transcultural Psychiatry* 52(4): 543–60.

Ahearn, Laura M. 2001. 'Language and Agency'. *Annual Review of Anthropology* 30(1): 109–37.

Aliefendioğlu, Hanife, and Pembe Behçetoğulları. 2019. 'Displacement, Memory and Home(Less) Identities: Turkish Cypriot Women's Narratives'. *Gender, Place & Culture* 26(10): 1472–92.

Allan, Pierre, and Alexis Keller, eds. 2006. *What Is a Just Peace?* Oxford; New York: Oxford University Press.

Altınay, Ayşe Gül, ed. 2019. *Women Mobilizing Memory*. New York: Columbia University Press.

Andreou, Evie. 2020. 'No Parades as Cyprus Marks Ochi Day'. https://web.archive.org/web/20221101012923/https://cyprus-mail.com/2020/10/28/no-parades-as-cyprus-marks-ochi-day/ (4 February 2024).

AP News. 'Milorad Dodik'. *Associated Press*. https://apnews.com/hub/milorad-dodik (10 June 2023).

Apeyitou, Eleni. 2003. 'Turkish-Cypriot Nationalism: Its History and Development (1571–1960)'. *The Cyprus Review* 15(1): 67–98.

Arendt, Hannah. 1985. *The Human Condition*. 1st ed. Chicago: University of Chicago Press.

Arensen, Lisa J. 2017. 'The Dead in the Land: Encounters with Bodies, Bones, and Ghosts in Northwestern Cambodia'. *The Journal of Asian Studies* 76(1): 69–86.

Armstrong, Jim, and Nigel Worden. 1989. 'The Slaves. 1652–1834'. In *The Shaping of South African Society 1652 – 1840*, eds. Richard Elphick and Hermann Giliomee. Cape Town: Maskew Miller Longman, 109–83.

Autry, Robyn Kimberley. 2012. 'The Monumental Reconstruction of Memory in South Africa: The Voortrekker Monument'. *Theory, Culture & Society* 29(6): 146–64.

Azaryahu, Maoz. 1996. 'The Power of Commemorative Street Names'. *Environment and Planning D: Society and Space* 14(3): 311–30.

Bădescu, Gruia. 2015. 'Dwelling in the Post-War City Urban Reconstruction and Home-Making in Sarajevo'. *Revue d'études comparatives Est-Ouest* 46(4): 35–60.

———. 2020. 'Post-War Reconstruction and Urban Imaginaries in Sarajevo and Beirut'. In *Controversial Heritage and Divided Memories from the Nineteenth Through the Twentieth Centuries: Multi-Ethnic Cities in the Mediterranean World*, ed. M Folin. New York: Routledge, 121–38.

Bădescu, Gruia, Britt Baillie and Francesco Mazzucchelli. 2021. *Transforming Heritage in the Former Yugoslavia*. Palgrave Studies in Cultural Heritage and Conflict. Cham: Palgrave Macmillan.

Baldwin, Gretchen. 2019. 'Constructing Identity through Commemoration: Kwibuka and the Rise of Survivor Nationalism in Post-Conflict Rwanda'. *The Journal of Modern African Studies* 57(3): 355–75.

Balthasar, Dominik. 2017. 'Peace-Building as State-Building? Rethinking Liberal Interventionism in Contexts of Emerging States'. *Conflict, Security & Development* 17(6): 473–91.

Barahona de Brito, Alexandra, Carmen Gonzalez Enriquez and Paloma Aguilar, eds. 2001. *The Politics of Memory and Democratization*. Oxford: Oxford University Press.

Barkan, Elazar, and Belma Bećirbašić. 2015. 'The Politics of Memory, Victimization and Activism in Post-Conflict Bosnia and Herzegovina'. In *Historical Justice and Memory*. Critical Human Rights, eds. Klaus Neumann and Janna Thompson. Madison, WI: Wisconsin University Press, 95–113.

Bassiouni, Cherif. 1994. 'Final Report of the United Nations Commission of Experts Established Pursuant to Security Council Resolution 780, Annex VI: Study of the Battle and Siege of Sarajevo'. https://web.archive.org/web/20010222115037/http:/www.ess.uwe.ac.uk/comexpert/ANX/VI-01.htm (10 June 2023).

Beban, Alice, and Courtney Work. 2014. 'The Spirits Are Crying: Dispossessing Land and Possessing Bodies in Rural Cambodia'. *Antipode* 46(3): 593–610.

Becker, Heike, and Carola Lentz. 2013. 'The Politics and Aesthetics of Commemoration: National Days in Southern Africa'. *Anthropology Southern Africa* 36(1–2): 1–10.

Beckstead, Zachary, Gabriel Twose, Emily Levesque-Gottlieb and Julia Rizzo. 2011. 'Collective Remembering through the Materiality and Organization of War Memorials'. *Journal of Material Culture* 16(2): 193–213.

Beinart, William, and Peter Delius. 2014. 'The Historical Context and Legacy of the Natives Land Act of 1913'. *Journal of Southern African Studies* 40(4): 667–88.

Bell, Duncan, ed. 2006. *Memory, Trauma and World Politics: Reflections on the Relationship between Past and Present*. Basingstoke; New York: Palgrave Macmillan.

Bennett, Caroline. 2015. 'To Live Amongst the Dead: An Ethnographic Exploration of Mass Graves in Cambodia'. PhD thesis. University of Kent.

———. 2018a. 'Karma after Democratic Kampuchea: Justice Outside the Khmer Rouge Tribunal'. *Genocide Studies and Prevention: An International Journal* 12(3): 68–82.

———. 2018b. 'Living with the Dead in the Killing Fields of Cambodia'. *Journal of Southeast Asian Studies* 49(2): 184–203.

Bentrovato, Denise. 2017. 'Accounting for Genocide: Transitional Justice, Mass (Re)Education and the Pedagogy of Truth in Present-Day Rwanda'. *Comparative Education* 53(3): 396–417.

Bernhard, Michael H., and Jan Kubik, eds. 2014. *Twenty Years after Communism: The Politics of Memory and Commemoration*. Oxford: Oxford University Press.

Bertrand, Didier. 2001. 'The Names and Identities of the "Boramey" Spirits Possessing Cambodian Mediums'. *Asian Folklore Studies* 60(1): 31–47.

Bickford, Louis. 2009. *Transforming a Legacy of Genocide: Pedagogy and Tourism at the Killing Fields of Choeung Ek*. New York: International Center of Transitional Justice.

———. 2014. 'MemoryWorks/Memory Works'. In *Transitional Justice, Culture, and Society: Beyond Outreach*, Advancing Transitional Justice, ed. Clara

Ramírez-Barat. New York: International Center for Transitional Justice and Social Science Research Council, 491–528.

Bijleveld, Catrien, Aafke Morssinkhof, and Alette Smeulers. 2009. 'Counting the Countless: Rape Victimization During the Rwandan Genocide'. *International Criminal Justice Review* 19(2): 208–24.

Billig, Michael. 1995. *Banal Nationalism*. London; Thousand Oaks, CA: SAGE.

Björkdahl, Annika, and Susanne Buckley-Zistel. 2016. *Spatialising Peace and Conflict: Mapping the Production of Places, Sites and Scales of Violence*. Basingstoke: Palgrave.

Björkdahl, Annika, and Stefanie Kappler. 2017. *Peacebuilding and Spatial Transformation: Peace, Space and Place*. London: Routledge.

———. 2019. 'The Creation of Transnational Memory Spaces: Professionalization and Commercialization'. *International Journal of Politics, Culture, and Society* 32(4): 383–401.

Björkdahl, Annika, and Johanna Mannergren Selimovic. 2015. 'Gendering Agency in Transitional Justice'. *Security Dialogue* 46(2): 165–82.

———. 2016a. 'A Tale of Three Bridges: Agency and Agonism in Peace Building'. *Third World Quarterly* 37(2): 321–35.

———. 2016b. 'Gender – the Missing Piece in the Peace Puzzle'. In *The Palgrave Handbook of Disciplinary and Regional Approaches to Peace*, eds. Oliver Richmond, Sandra Pogodda and Jasmin Ramovic. Basingstoke: Palgrave, 181–92.

Blackburn, Katarina. 2010. 'War Memory and Nation-Building in South East Asia'. *South East Asia Research* 18(1): 5–31.

Booth, James W. 2001. 'The Unforgotten: Memories of Justice'. *American Political Science Review* 95(4): 777–91.

Bose, Sumantra. 2002. *Bosnia after Dayton: Nationalist Partition and International Intervention*. New York; Oxford: Oxford University Press.

Bougarel, Xavier, Elissa Helms and Gerlachlus Duijzings. 2007. *The New Bosnian Mosaic Identities: Memories and Moral Claims in a Post-War Society*. London: Routledge.

Božić, Gordana. 2017. 'Diversity in Ethnicization: War Memory Landscape in Bosnia and Herzegovina'. *Memory Studies* 12(4): 412–32.

Bredekamp, Henry. 2006. 'Transforming Representations of Intangible Heritage at Iziko (National) Museums, South Africa'. *International Journal of Intangible Heritage* 1: 76–82.

Brehm, Hollie Nyseth, and Nicole Fox. 2017. 'Narrating Genocide: Time, Memory, and Blame'. *Sociological Forum* 32(1): 116–37.

Briel, Holger. 2008. 'The Will to Media'. In *Glocalisation. Electronic Media in South-Eastern Europe*, ed. Holger Briel. Skopje: Blesok, 13–28.

———. 2013. 'The Uses of Oral History in Cyprus: Ethics, Memory and Identity'. *Language and Intercultural Communication* 13(1): 27–43.

Bringa, Tone. 1995. *Being Muslim the Bosnian Way: Identity and Community in a Central Bosnian Village*. Princeton, NJ: Princeton University Press.

Brown, Caitlin, and Chris Millington. 2015. 'The Memory of the Cambodian Genocide: The Tuol Sleng Genocide Museum'. *History Compass* 13(2): 31–9.

Brown, Kris. 2013. '"High Resolution" Indicators in Peacebuilding: The Utility of Political Memory'. *Journal of Intervention and Statebuilding* 7(4): 492–513.

Brown, Sara E. 2017. *Gender and the Genocide in Rwanda: Women as Rescuers and Perpetrators*. Abingdon: Routledge.

Bruner, Jerome S. 2002. *Making Stories: Law, Literature, Life*. Cambridge, MA; London: Harvard University Press.

Bryant, Rebecca. 2010. *The Past in Pieces: Belonging in the New Cyprus*. Philadelphia, PA: University of Pennsylvania Press.

———. 2012. 'Partitions of Memory: Wounds and Witnessing in Cyprus'. *Comparative Studies in Society and History* 54(2): 332–60.

Bryant, Rebecca, and Mete Hatay. 2019. 'From Salvation to Struggle: Commemoration, Affect and Agency in Cyprus'. *History and Memory* 31(1): 25–58.

Bryant, Rebecca, and Yiannis Papadakis, eds. 2012. *Cyprus and the Politics of Memory: History, Community and Conflict*. London; New York: I.B. Tauris.

Buckley-Zistel, Susanne. 2006a. 'Dividing and Uniting: The Use of Citizenship Discourses in Conflict and Reconciliation in Rwanda'. *Global Society* 20(1): 101–13.

———. 2006b. 'Remembering to Forget: Chosen Amnesia as a Strategy for Local Coexistence in Post-Genocide Rwanda'. *Africa* 76(2): 131–50.

———. 2006c. 'In-Between War and Peace: Identities, Boundaries and Change after Violent Conflict'. *Millennium: Journal of International Studies* 35(1), 3–21.

———. 2007. 'Ethnographic Research after Violent Conflicts: Personal Reflections on Dilemmas and Challenges'. *Journal of Peace, Development and Security* 10(1): 1–9.

———. 2009. 'We Are Pretending Peace. Local Memory and the Absence of Social Transformation and Reconciliation in Rwanda'. In *After Genocide: Transitional Justice, Post-Conflict Reconstruction, and Reconciliation in Rwanda and Beyond*, eds. Philip Clark and Zachary D. Kaufman. New York: Columbia University Press, 153–71.

———. 2014. 'Narrative Truths: On the Construction of the Past in Truth Commissions'. In *Transitional Justice Theories*, eds. Susanne Buckley-Zistel, Teresa Koloma Beck, Christian Braun and Friederike Mieth. Abingdon: Routledge, 184–200.

———. 2020. 'Memorials and Transitional Justice'. In *The Palgrave Encyclopedia of Peace and Conflict Studies*, eds. Oliver Richmond and Gëzim Visoka. Basingstoke: Palgrave. https://link.springer.com/referenceworkentry/10.1007/978-3-030-11795-5_13-1 (4 February 2023).

———. 2021. 'Tracing the Politics of Aesthetics: From Imposing, via Counter to Affirmative Memorials to Violence'. *Memory Studies* 14(4): 781–96.

Buckley-Zistel, Susanne, and Stefanie Schäfer, eds. 2014a. *Memorials in Times of Transition*. Cambridge: Intersentia.

———. 2014b. 'Introduction: Memorials in Times of Transition'. In *Memorials in Times of Transition*, eds. Susanne Buckley-Zistel and Stefanie Schäfer. Cambridge: Intersentia, 1–26.

Buckley-Zistel, Susanne, and Timothy Williams. 2022. 'A 5* Destination. The Creation of New Transnational Moral Spaces of Remembrance on TripAdvisor'. *International Journal of Politics, Culture, and Society* 35: 221–38.

Bull, Anna Cento, Hans Lauge Hansen, Wulf Kansteiner and Nina Parish. 2019. 'War Museums as Agonistic Spaces: Possibilities, Opportunities and Constraints'. *International Journal of Heritage Studies* 25(6): 611–25.

Bultmann, Daniel. 2017. *Kambodscha unter den Roten Khmer. Die Erschaffung des Perfekten Sozialisten*. Paderborn: Ferdinand Schöningh.

Cameron, Hazel. 2015. 'The French Connection: Complicity in the 1994 Genocide in Rwanda'. *African Security* 8(2): 96–119.

Cawfood, Stephanie, and Jonathan Fisher. 2022. '"It Should be a Constant Reminder": Space, Meaning and Power in Post-liberation Africa'. *Political Geography* 99, 102782. ISSN 0962-6298. https://doi.org/10.1016/j.polgeo.2022.102782

CCHA Website. *Cyprus Critical History Archive: Reconsidering the Culture of Violence in Cyprus, 1955–64*. www.ccha-ahdr.info (4 February 2024).

Chanda, Nayan. 1986. *Brother Enemy*. New York: Collier Macmillan.

Chandler, David. 1999. *Brother Number One*. Boulder, CO: Westview.

———. 2008a. *A History of Cambodia*. 4th ed. Boulder, CO: Westview.

———. 2008b. 'Cambodia Deals with Its Past: Collective Memory, Demonisation and Induced Amnesia'. *Totalitarian Movements and Political Religions* 9(2–3): 355–69.

———. 2020. 'The S-21 Project'. *Encyclopédie des violences de masse*. www.sciencespo.fr/mass-violence-war-massacre-resistance/ (16 January 2020).

Chhim, Sotheara. 2013. 'Baksbat (Broken Courage): A Trauma-Based Cultural Syndrome in Cambodia'. *Medical Anthropology* 32(2): 160–73.

Clark Miller, Sarah. 2017. 'Reconsidering Dignity Relationally'. *Ethics and Social Welfare* 11(2): 108–21.

Conrad, Sebastian. 2003. 'Entangled Memories: Versions of the Past in Germany and Japan, 1945–2001'. *Journal of Contemporary History* 38(1): 85–99.

Conradie, Pieter. 1998. 'The Story of Eva (Krotoa): Translation Transgressed'. *Journal of Literary Studies* 14(1–2): 55–66.

Constantinou, Costas M., Olga Demetriou and Mete Hatay. 2012. 'Conflicts and Uses of Cultural Heritage in Cyprus'. *Journal of Balkan and Near Eastern Studies* 14(2): 177–98.

Constantinou, Costas M., and Oliver P. Richmond. 2005. 'The Long Mile of Empire: Power, Legitimation and the UK Bases in Cyprus'. *Mediterranean Politics* 10(1): 65–84.

Coombes, Annie E. 2003. *History after Apartheid: Visual Culture and Public Memory in a Democratic South Africa*. Durham, NC: Duke University Press.

Cougill, Wynne. 2007. 'Remains of the Dead: Buddhist Tradition, Evidence and Memory'. In *Night of the Khmer Rouge: Genocide and Justice in Cambodia. Exhibition Catalogue*, eds. Alexander Laban Hinton and Jorge Daniel Veneciano. New Brunswick, NJ: Rutgers, 32–47.

Coward, Martin. 2004. 'Urbicide in Bosnia'. In *Cities, War, and Terrorism*, ed. Stephen Graham. Oxford: John Wiley & Sons, Ltd, 154–71.

———. 2008. *Urbicide: The Politics of Urban Destruction*. Abingdon: Routledge.

Cruz, Manuel. 2016. *On the Difficulty of Living Together: Memory, Politics, and History*. New York: Columbia University Press.

Davis, Erik. 2016. *Deathpower: Buddhism's Ritual Imagination in Cambodia*. New York: Columbia University Press.

Delanty, Gerard. 2017. 'Entangled Memories: How to Study Europe's Cultural Heritage'. *The European Legacy* 22(2): 129–45.

Demetriou, Olga. 2012. *Life Stories: Greek Cypriot Community*. Oslo: Peace Research Institute Oslo.

Demirel, Cagla. 2023. 'Exploring Inclusive Victimhood Narratives: The Case of Bosnia-Herzegovina'. *Third World Quarterly* 44(8): 1770–89. https://doi.org/10.1080/01436597.2023.2205579

Department of Rural Development and Land Reform. 2017. *Phase II: Private Land Ownership by Race, Gender and Nationality*. South African Government.

Land Audit Report. www.gov.za/sites/default/files/gcis_document/201802/landauditreport13feb2018.pdf (1 June 2021).

Department of Sport, Arts and Culture. 2020. '10. What Are Legacy Projects'. https://web.archive.org/web/20230520141610/www.dac.gov.za/content/10-what-are-legacy-projects (16 March 2021).

Dietrich, Wolfgang, and Wolfgang Sützl. 1997. *A Call for Many Peaces.* Stadtschlaining, Austria: Peace Center Burg Schlaining.

Dominy, Graham, and Luli Callinicos. 1999. '"Is There Anything to Celebrate?" Paradoxes of Policy: An Examination of the State's Approach to Commemorating South Africa's Most Ambiguous Struggle'. *South African Historical Journal* 41(1): 388–403.

Donia, Robert J. 2006. *Sarajevo: A Biography.* Ann Arbor, MI: University of Michigan Press.

Doyle, Michael W. 1983. 'Kant, Liberal Legacies, and Foreign Affairs, Part 1'. *Philosophy & Public Affairs* 12(3): 205–35.

Drozdzewski, Danielle, Emma Waterton and Shanti Sumartojo. 2019. 'Cultural Memory and Identity in the Context of War: Experiential, Place-Based and Political Concerns'. *International Review of the Red Cross* 101(910): 251–72.

Duijzings, Gerlachlus. 2007. 'Commemorating Srebrenica: Histories of Violence and the Politics of Memory in Eastern Bosnia'. In *The New Bosnian Mosaic: Identities, Memories and Moral Claims in a Post-War Society*, eds. Gerlachlus Duijzings, Elissa Helms and Xavier Bougarel. London: Routledge, 141–66.

Dzaferagic, Nejra. 2021. 'Sarajevo Unveils Memorial to Victims of Kazani Pit Killings'. *Balkan Insight.* https://balkaninsight.com/2021/11/15/sarajevo-unveils-memorial-to-victims-of-kazani-pit-killings/ (31 March 2023).

Ea, Meng-Try. 2005. *The Chain of Terror. The Khmer Rouge Southwest Zone Security System.* Phnom Penh: Documentation Center of Cambodia.

Eastmond, Marita, and Johanna Mannergren Selimovic. 2012. 'Silence as Possibility in Postwar Everyday Life'. *International Journal of Transitional Justice* 6(3): 502–24.

East West Centre Sarajevo. n. d. 'Sarajevo Red Line – East West Center Sarajevo'. https://eastwest.ba/sarajevo-red-line/ (11 June 2023).

Eichelsheim, Veroni, Lidewyde Berckmoes, Theoneste Rutayisire, Annemiek Richtere and Barbora Hola. 2017. 'Intergenerational Legacies of the Genocide in Rwanda and Community Based Sociotherapy Identifying and Addressing Pathways of Transmission April'. Amsterdam; Kigali: NSCR/CBSP.

Elliott, Jane. 2005. *Using Narrative in Social Research.* London: SAGE Publications Ltd.

Eltringham, Nigel. 2004. *Accounting for Horror: Post-Genocide Debates in Rwanda.* London: Pluto Press.

Etcheson, Craig. 2005. *After the Killing Fields.* Westport, CT: Praeger.

Etzioni, Amitai. 2000. 'Toward a Theory of Public Ritual'. *Sociological Theory* 18(1): 44–59.

FAMA. 1993. *Sarajevo Survival Guide.* Sarajevo, Bosnia and Herzegovina: FAMA. http://famacollection.org/eng/fama-collection/fama-original-projects/04/index.html (31 March 2023).

Feindt, Gregor, Félix Krawatzek, Daniela Mehler, Friedemann Pestel and Rieke Trimçev. 2014. 'Entangled Memory: Toward a Third Wave in Memory Studies'. *History and Theory* 53(1): 24–44.

Feldman, Gregory. 2014. 'Understanding Others: Agency and Articulation in a Historical Perspective'. *Social Anthropology* 22(3): 288–92.

Fernandes, Sujatha. 2017. *Curated Stories: The Uses and Misuses of Storytelling*. New York: Oxford University Press.

Fleischman, Julie. 2016. 'Working with the Remains in Cambodia: Skeletal Analysis and Human Rights after Atrocity'. *Genocide Studies and Prevention: An International Journal* 10(2): 121–30.

Flint, Colin. 2011. 'Intertwined Spaces of Peace and War: The Perpetual Dynamism of Geopolitical Landscapes'. In *Reconstructing Conflict: Integrating War and Post-War Geographies*, eds. Scott Kirsch and Colin Flint. Farnham: Ashgate, 31–48.

Folin, Marcu, and Heleni Porfyriou, eds. 2020. *Multi-ethnic Cities in the Mediterranean World: Controversial Heritage and Divided Memories from the Nineteenth through the Twentieth Centuries*. Abingdon: Routledge.

Forde, Susan. 2019. *Movement as Conflict Transformation: Rescripting Mostar, Bosnia-Herzegovina*. Cham: Springer International Publishing.

Forde, Susan, Stefanie Kappler, and Annika Björkdahl. 2021. 'Peacebuilding, Structural Violence and Spatial Reparations in Post-Colonial South Africa'. *Journal of Intervention and Statebuilding* 15(3): 327–46.

Fox, Nicole. 2021. *After Genocide: Memory and Reconciliation in Rwanda*. Madison, WI: University of Wisconsin Press.

Fridman, Orli. 2022. *Memory Activism and Digital Practices after Conflict: Unwanted Memories*. Amsterdam: Amsterdam University Press.

Fujii, Lee Ann. 2009. *Killing Neighbors: Webs of Violence in Rwanda*. Ithaca, NY: Cornell University Press.

Gahongayire, Liberata. 2015. 'The Contribution of Memory in Healing and Preventing Genocide in Rwanda'. *International Journal of Innovation and Applied Studies* 10(1): 109–18.

Gahongayire, Liberata, and Anne Marie Nyiracumi. 2014. 'Breaking Silence: Documenting Individual Experiences Based on Visitors' 'Book of Kigali Genocide Memorial Centre, Rwanda'. *International Journal of Innovation and Applied Studies* 7(4): 1444–57.

Galtung, Johan. 1964. 'A Structural Theory of Aggression'. *Journal of Peace Research* 1(2): 95–119.

Geertz, Clifford. 1973. *The Interpretation of Cultures: Selected Essays*. New York: Basic Books.

Genocide Archive of Rwanda. n.d. 'Kigali Genocide Memorial'. https://genocidearchiverwanda.org.rw/index.php/Kigali_Genocide_Memorial (24 January 2024).

George, Alexander L., and Andrew Bennett. 2005. *Case Studies and Theory Development in the Social Sciences*. Cambridge, MA: MIT Press.

Giblin, John. 2017. 'The Performance of International Diplomacy at Kigali Memorial Centre, Rwanda'. *Journal of African Cultural Heritage Studies* 1(1): 49–67.

Giddens, Anthony. 1984. *The Constitution of Society: Outline of the Theory of Structuration*. Berkeley, CA: University of California Press.

Gidley, Rebecca. 2019. *Illiberal Transitional Justice and the Extraordinary Chambers in the Courts of Cambodia*. Cham: Palgrave.

Gray, Tallyn. 2012. *Justice and the Khmer Rouge: Concepts of a Just Response to the Crimes of the Democratic Kampuchean Regime in Buddhism at the Time of the Khmer Rouge Tribunal*. Lund: Center for East and South-East Asian Studies, Lund University. https://portal.research.lu.se/ws/files/3650221/3128820.pdf?gathStatIcon=true (24 June 2022).

Gregory, Derek. 2004. *The Colonial Present: Afghanistan, Palestine, and Iraq*. Malden, MA: Blackwell Publishing.

Grey, Rosemary, Yim Sotheary and Kum Somaly. 2019. 'The Khmer Rouge Tribunal's First Reparation for Gender-Based Crimes'. *Australian Journal of Human Rights* 25(3): 488–97.

Grundlingh, Albert. 2004. 'Reframing Remembrance: The Politics of the Centenary Commemoration of the South African War of 1899–1902'. *Journal of Southern African Studies* 30(2): 359–75.

Guichaoua, André. 2020. 'Counting the Rwandan Victims of War and Genocide: Concluding Reflections'. *Journal of Genocide Research* 22(1): 125–41.

Guillou, Anne Yvonne. 2012. 'An Alternative Memory of the Khmer Rouge Genocide: The Dead of the Mass Graves and the Land Guardian Spirits [Neak Ta]'. *South East Asia Research* 20(2): 207–26.

———. 2014. 'From Bones-as-Evidence to Tutelary Spirits: The Status of Bodies in the Aftermath of the Khmer Rouge Genocide'. In *Human Remains and Mass Violence: Methodological Approaches*, eds. Jean-Marc Dreyfuß and Élisabeth Anstett. Manchester: Manchester University Press, 146–60.

———. 2017. 'Khmer Potent Places: Pāramī and the Localisation of Buddhism and Monarchy in Cambodia'. *The Asia Pacific Journal of Anthropology* 18(5): 421–43.

Hadjipavlou, Maria. 2007. 'Multiple Stories'. *Innovation: The European Journal of Social Science Research* 20(1): 53–73.

———. 2010. *Women and Change in Cyprus: Feminisms and Gender in Conflict*. London: New York: Tauris Academic Studies; Distributed in the U.S. and Canada by Palgrave Macmillan.

Halbwachs, Maurice. 1992. *On Collective Memory*. Chicago: University of Chicago Press.

Hammack, Phillip L., and Andrew Pilecki. 2012. 'Narrative as a Root Metaphor for Political Psychology: Political Psychology and Narrative'. *Political Psychology* 33(1): 75–103.

Hansen, Lene. 2013. *Security as Practice: Discourse Analysis and the Bosnian War*. London: Routledge.

Harris, Ian. 2015. *Cambodian Buddhism: History and Practice*. Honolulu, HI: University of Hawai'i Press.

Henkin, Samuel. 2018. 'Postmemory and the Geographies of Violence at Kraing Ta Chan, Cambodia'. *GeoHumanities* 4(2): 462–80.

Heraclides, Alexis. 2004. 'The Cyprus Problem: An Open and Shut Case? Probing the Greek-Cypriot Rejection of the Annan Plan'. *The Cyprus Review* 16(2): 37–54.

Herwitz, Daniel. 2011. 'Monument, Ruin, and Redress in South African Heritage'. *The Germanic Review: Literature, Culture, Theory* 86(4): 232–48.

Heuman, Johannes. 2014. 'Entangled Memories: A Reassessment of 1950s French Holocaust Historiography'. *Holocaust and Genocide Studies* 28(3): 409–29.

Hintjens, Helen. 2022. 'Fluidity, Death, Denial: The Rwanda Genocide'. In *The Politics of Art, Death and Refuge: The Turning Tide*, ed. Helen Hintjens. Cham: Springer International Publishing, 109–42.

Hinton, Alexander Laban. 2016. *Man or Monster? The Trial of a Khmer Rouge Torturer*. Durham, NC: Duke University Press.

———. 2018. *The Justice Facade. Trials of Transition in Cambodia*. Oxford: Oxford University Press.

Holbrooke, Richard C. 1998. *To End a War*. 1st ed. New York: Random House.

Holmes, Carolyn E., and Melanie Loehwing. 2016. 'Icons of the Old Regime: Challenging South African Public Memory Strategies in #RhodesMustFall'. *Journal of Southern African Studies* 42(6): 1207–23.

Holt, John Clifford. 2012. 'Caring for the Dead Ritually in Cambodia'. *Southeast Asia Studies* 1(1): 3–75.
Hoskins, Janet. 2006. 'Agency, Biography and Objects'. In *Handbook of Material Culture*, eds. Christopher Tilley, Webb Keane, Susanne Küchler, Michael Rowlands and Patricia Spyer. London: SAGE, 74–84.
Hudson, Valerie M., Bonnie Ballif-Spanvill, Mary Caprioli and Chad F. Emmett, eds. 2012. *Sex and World Peace*. New York: Columbia University Press.
Hughes, Rachel. 2003. 'Nationalism and Memory at the Tuol Sleng Museum of Genocide Crimes, Cambodia'. In *Contested Pasts: The Politics of Memory*, eds. Katharine Hodgkin and Susannah Radstone. London: Routledge, 175–92.
———. 2006. 'Memory and Sovereignty in Post-1979 Cambodia: Choeung Ek and Local Genocide Memorials'. In *Genocide in Cambodia and Rwanda: New Perspectives*, ed. Susan Cook. London; New York: Routledge, 257–79.
———. 2008. 'Dutiful Tourism: Encountering the Cambodian Genocide'. *Asia Pacific Viewpoint* 49(3): 318–30.
———. 2015. 'Ordinary Theatre and Extraordinary Law at the Khmer Rouge Tribunal'. *Environment and Planning D: Society and Space* 33(4): 714–31.
Ibreck, Rachel. 2010. 'The Politics of Mourning: Survivor Contributions to Memorials in Post-Genocide Rwanda'. *Memory Studies* 3(4): 330–43.
———. 2013. 'International Constructions of National Memories: The Aims and Effects of Foreign Donors' Support for Genocide Remembrance in Rwanda'. *Journal of Intervention and Statebuilding* 7(2): 149–69.
Iziko. 2020a. 'Slave Lodge'. Iziko Museums of South Africa. www.iziko.org.za/museums/slave-lodge (16 March 2021).
———. 2020b. 'I Am What I Am'. Iziko Museums of South Africa. www.iziko.org.za/exhibitions/i-am-what-i-am/ (9 June 2023).
———. 2020c. 'Rethinking the William Fehr Collection'. Iziko Museums of South Africa. www.iziko.org.za/exhibitions/rethinking-william-fehr-collection (16 March 2021).
Jacobs, Janet. 2017. 'The Memorial at Srebrenica: Gender and the Social Meanings of Collective Memory in Bosnia-Herzegovina'. *Memory Studies* 10(4): 423–39.
Jäger, Siegfried, and Florentin Maier. 2009. 'Theoretical and Methodological Aspects of Foucauldian Critical Discourse Analysis and Dispositive Analysis'. In *Methods of Critical Discourse Analysis*, eds. Ruth Wodak and Michael Meyer. London: SAGE Publications Ltd, 34–61.
Jansen, Stef. 2013. 'People and Things in the Ethnography of Borders: Materialising the Division of Sarajevo'. *Social Anthropology/Anthropologie sociale* 21(1): 23–37.
Jerne, Christina. 2020. 'Event-Making the Past: Commemorations as Social Movement Catalysts'. *Memory Studies* 13(4): 486–501.
Jessee, Erin. 2017a. *Negotiating Genocide in Rwanda: The Politics of History*. Springer.
———. 2017b. 'The Danger of a Single Story: Iconic Stories in the Aftermath of the 1994 Rwandan Genocide'. *Memory Studies* 10(2): 144–63.
Jessee, Erin, and David Mwambari. 2022. 'Memory Law and the Duty to Remember the "1994 Genocide Against the Tutsi" in Rwanda'. In *Memory Laws and Historical Justice: The Politics of Criminalizing the Past*, eds. Elazar Barkan and Ariella Lang. Cham: Springer International Publishing, 291–319.
Jethro, Duane. 2016. '"Freedom Park, a Heritage Destination": Tour-Guiding and Visitor Experience at a Post-Apartheid Heritage Site'. *Tourist Studies* 16(4): 446–61.

———. 2017. 'Heritage Formation and Khoisan Indigenous Identity in Post-Apartheid South Africa'. In *Handbook of Indigenous Religion(s)*, eds. Greg Johnson and Siv Ellen Kraft. Leiden: Brill, 349–65.

Joshi, Madhav, and Peter Wallensteen, eds. 2018. *Understanding Quality Peace: Peacebuilding after Civil War*. Abingdon; New York: Routledge.

Kagame, Paul. 2009. 'Preface'. In *After Genocide: Transitional Justice, Post-Conflict Reconstruction and Reconciliation in Rwanda and Beyond*, eds Phil Clark and Zachary D. Kaufman. London: Hurst, i–xxiii.

Kantengwa, Odeth. 2013. 'The Role of the National Commission for the Fight Against Genocide in Combating Genocide Ideology and Denial'. In *Governance and Post-Conflict Reconstruction in Rwanda*. Addis Ababa: Organisation for Social Science Research in Eastern and Southern Africa, 100–21.

Kappler, Stefanie. 2015. 'The Dynamic Local: Delocalisation and (Re-)Localisation in the Search for Peacebuilding Identity'. *Third World Quarterly* 36(5): 875–89.

———. 2017. 'Sarajevo's Ambivalent Memoryscape: Spatial Stories of Peace and Conflict'. *Memory Studies* 10(2): 130–43. https://doi.org/10.1177/1750698016650484

———. 2020. 'Curating (Im)Mobility: Peri-Urban Agency in the Lwandle Migrant Labour Museum'. *Global Policy* 12(S2): 53–62.

Kappler, Stefanie, and Antoinette McKane. 2022. 'Negotiating Binaries in Curatorial Practice: Modality, Temporality, and Materiality in Cape Town's Community-Led Urban History Museums'. In *Contested Urban Spaces: Monuments, Traces, and Decentered Memories*, Palgrave Macmillan Memory Studies, eds. Ulrike Capdepón and Sarah Dornhof. Cham: Springer International Publishing, 65–82.

Karyos, Andreas. 2013. 'The Museum of National Struggle'. In *The Introduction to the History of Cyprus*, eds. Antonis Petrides, George Kazamias and Emmanouil Koumas. Nicosia: Open University of Cyprus, 434–6.

Katsourides, Yiannos. 2017. *The Greek Cypriot Nationalist Right in the Era of British Colonialism: Emergence, Mobilisation and Transformations of Right-Wing Party Politics*. 1st ed. 2017. Cham: Springer.

Kebede, Messay. 2001. 'The Rehabilitation of Violence and the Violence of Rehabilitation: Fanon and Colonialism'. *Journal of Black Studies* 31(5): 539–62.

Kiernan, Ben. 1985. *How Pol Pot Came to Power*. London: Verso.

———. 1996. *The Pol Pot Regime*. New Haven, CT: Yale University Press.

Kimonyo, Jean-Paul. 2019. *Transforming Rwanda*. Boulder, CO: Lynne Rienner Publishers.

King, Elisabeth. 2010. 'Memory Controversies in Post-Genocide Rwanda: Implications for Peacebuilding'. *Genocide Studies and Prevention* 5(3): 293–309.

Kizilyürek, Niyazi. 2002. 'Modernity, Nationalism and the Perspectives of a Cypriot Union'. *CEMOTI, Cahiers d'Études sur la Méditerranée Orientale et le monde Turco-Iranien* 34(1): 211–32.

Kondylis, Florence. 2010. 'Conflict Displacement and Labor Market Outcomes in Post-War Bosnia and Herzegovina'. *Journal of Development Economics* 93(2): 235–48.

Korman, Rémi. 2015. 'Mobilising the Dead? The Place of Bones and Corpses in the Commemoration of the Tutsi Genocide in Rwanda'. *Human Remains and Violence: An Interdisciplinary Journal* 1(2): 56–70.

Kuzio, Taras. 2002. 'History, Memory and Nation Building in the Post-Soviet Colonial Space'. *Nationalities Papers* 30(2): 241–64.

Laanes, Eneken. 2020. 'Entangled Memories of Human Rights in Kristina Norman's Video Art: Space, Visual Frames, Politics of Art'. *Journal of Baltic Studies* 51(3): 451–64.

Landgren, Karin. 1995. 'Safety Zones and International Protection: A Dark Grey Area'. *International Journal of Refugee Law* 7(3): 436–58.

Lederach, John Paul. 2003. *The Little Book of Conflict Transformation*. Intercourse, PA: Good Books.

Ledgerwood, Judy. 2012. 'Buddhist Ritual and the Reordering of Social Relations in Cambodia'. *South East Asia Research* 20(2): 191–205.

Lefebvre, Henri. 1996. *Writings on Cities*. Cambridge, MA: Blackwell Publishers.

Lindstrøm, Torill Christine. 2015. 'Agency 'in Itself'. A Discussion of Inanimate, Animal and Human Agency'. *Archaeological Dialogues* 22(2): 207–38.

———. 2017. 'Agency: A Response to Sørensen and Ribeiro'. *Archaeological Dialogues* 24(1): 109–16.

Longman, Timothy. 2017. *Memory and Justice in Post-Genocide Rwanda*. Cambridge: Cambridge University Press.

Longman, Timothy, and Théonèste Rutagengwa. 2004. 'Memory, Identity, and Community in Rwanda'. In *My Neighbor, My Enemy: Justice and Community in the Aftermath of Mass Atrocity*, eds. Eric Stover and Harvey M. Weinstein. New York: Cambridge University Press, 162–82.

Loyle, Cyanne, and Benjamin Appel. 2011. 'Justice and/or Peace: Post-Conflict Justice and Conflict Reoccurence'. Paper presented at the American Political Science Association Annual Meeting, Seattle, 1–4. www.researchgate.net/publication/228213615_Justice_andor_Peace_Post-Conflict_Justice_and_Conflict_Reoccurrence (15 February 2023).

Lukes, Steven. 1975. 'Political Ritual and Social Integration'. *Sociology* 9(2): 289–308.

Lwandle Migrant Labour Museum. 2020. 'Lwandle Migrant Labour Museum'. http://lwandle.com/ (17 March 2021).

Lyssiotis, Renos. 2016. *'My Marshall, I Surrender!': And 19 Other Stories*. Nicosia: Renos Lyssiotis.

Mac Ginty, Roger. 2006. *No War, No Peace: The Rejuvenation of Stalled Peace Processes and Peace Accords*. Basingstoke: Palgrave.

———. 2010. 'Hybrid Peace: The Interaction between Top-down and Bottom-up Peace'. *Security Dialogue* 41(4): 391–412.

———. 2021. *Everyday Peace: How So-Called Ordinary People Can Disrupt Violent Conflict*. Oxford; New York: Oxford University Press.

Mac Ginty, Roger, and Oliver P. Richmond. 2013. 'The Local Turn in Peace Building: A Critical Agenda for Peace'. *Third World Quarterly* 34(5): 763–83.

Maček, Ivana. 2009. *Sarajevo under Siege: Anthropology in Wartime*. Philadelphia: University of Pennsylvania Press.

MacLeod, Arlene Elowe. 1992. 'Hegemonic Relations and Gender Resistance: The New Veiling as Accommodating Protest in Cairo'. *Signs: Journal of Women in Culture and Society* 17(3): 533–57.

Maddison, Sarah. 2013. 'Indigenous Identity, "Authenticity" and the Structural Violence of Settler Colonialism'. *Identities* 20(3): 288–303.

Malcolm, Noel. 1996. *A Short History of Bosnia*. Basingstoke: Macmillan.

Mamdani, Mahmood. 2001. *When Victims Become Killers: Colonialism, Nativism, and the Genocide in Rwanda*. Princeton, NJ: Princeton University Press.

Mannergren Selimovic, Johanna. 2013. 'Making Peace, Making Memory: Peacebuilding and Politics of Remembrance at Memorials of Mass Atrocities'. *Peacebuilding* 1(3): 334–48.

———. 2020a. 'Gender, Narrative and Affect: Top-down Politics of Commemoration in Post-Genocide Rwanda'. *Memory Studies* 13(2): 131–45.

———. 2020b. 'Gendered Silences in Post-Conflict Societies: A Typology'. *Peacebuilding* 8(1): 1–15.

———. 2021. 'Articulating Presence of Absence: Everyday Memory and the Performance of Silence in Sarajevo'. In *Post-Conflict Memorialization*, eds. Olivette Otele, Luisa Gandolfo and Yoav Galai. Cham: Springer International Publishing, 15–34.

———. 2022a. 'Challenging the "Here" and "There" of Peace and Conflict Research: Migrants' Encounters with Streams of Violence and Streams of Peace'. *Journal of Intervention and Statebuilding* 16(5): 584–99.

———. 2022b. 'The Stuff from the Siege: Transitional Justice and the Power of Everyday Objects in Museums'. *International Journal of Transitional Justice* 16(2): 220–34.

Manning, Peter. 2015. 'Reconciliation and Perpetrator Memories in Cambodia'. *International Journal of Transitional Justice* 9(3): 386–406.

———. 2017. *Transitional Justice and Memory in Cambodia. Beyond the Extraordinary Chambers*. London; New York: Routledge.

Marschall, Sabine. 2006. 'Commemorating "Struggle Heroes": Constructing a Genealogy for the New South Africa'. *International Journal of Heritage Studies* 12(2): 176–93.

———. 2010. 'The Memory of Trauma and Resistance: Public Memorialization and Democracy in Post-Apartheid South Africa and Beyond'. *Safundi* 11(4): 361–81.

Maurantonio, Nicole. 2017. 'The Politics of Memory'. In *The Oxford Handbook of Political Communication*, eds. Kate Kenski and Kathleen Hall Jamieson. Oxford: Oxford University Press, 219–32.

McAteer, Christopher. 2006. 'In-Between War and Peace: Identities, Boundaries and Change after Violent Conflict'. *Millennium: Journal of International Studies* 35(1): 3–21.

McDoom, Omar Shahabudin. 2021. *The Path to Genocide in Rwanda: Security, Opportunity, and Authority in an Ethnocratic State*. Cambridge: Cambridge University Press.

———. 2022. 'Securocratic State-Building: The Rationales, Rebuttals, and Risks behind the Extraordinary Rise of Rwanda after the Genocide'. *African Affairs* 121(485): 535–67.

McDowell, Sara, and Máire Braniff. 2014. *Commemoration as Conflict: Space, Memory and Identity in Peace Processes*. Basingstoke: Palgrave.

McEwan, Cheryl. 2003. 'Building a Postcolonial Archive? Gender, Collective Memory and Citizenship in Post-Apartheid South Africa'. *Journal of Southern African Studies* 29(3): 739–57.

McKinney, Stephanie L. 2011. 'Narrating Genocide on the Streets of Kigali'. In *The Heritage of War*, eds. Martin Gegner and Bart Ziino. London: Routledge, 160–76.

McMillan, Nesam. 2016. 'Remembering "Rwanda"'. *Law, Culture and the Humanities* 12(2): 301–28.

McNay, Lois. 2000. *Gender and Agency: Reconfiguring the Subject in Feminist and Social Theory*. Cambridge: Malden, MA: Polity Press; Blackwell Publishers.

Meierhenrich, Jens. 2020. 'How Many Victims Were There in the Rwandan Genocide? A Statistical Debate'. *Journal of Genocide Research* 22(1): 72–82.

Meskell, Lynn, and Colette Scheermeyer. 2008. 'Heritage as Therapy: Set Pieces from the New South Africa'. *Journal of Material Culture* 13(2): 153–73.

Mgijima, Bongani, and Vusi Buthelezi. 2006. 'Mapping Museum–Community Relations in Lwandle'. *Journal of Southern African Studies* 32(4): 795–806.

Millar, Gearoid. 2020. 'Toward a Trans-Scalar Peace System: Challenging Complex Global Conflict Systems'. *Peacebuilding* 8(3): 261–78.

Miller, Kim, and Brenda Schmahmann, eds. 2017. *Public Art in South Africa: Bronze Warriors and Plastic Presidents*. Bloomington, IN: Indiana University Press.

Milliken, Jennifer. 1999. 'The Study of Discourse in International Relations: A Critique of Research and Methods'. *European Journal of International Relations* 5(2): 225–54.

Ministere de l'Administration Locale, du Developpement Communautaire et des Affaires Sociales. 2004. 'Dénombrement Des Victime Du Genocide: Rapport Final. Version Révisée. Rwanda'. Kigali.

Minkley, Gary, Ciraj Rassool and Leslie Witz. 2017. 'Oral History in South Africa. A Country Report'. In *Unsettled History: Making South African Public Pasts*, eds. Leslie Witz, Gary Minkley and Ciraj Rassool. Ann Arbor, MI: University of Michigan Press, 27–51.

Moll, Nicolas. 2015a. 'Cultures of History Forum: Division and Denial and Nothing Else? Culture of History and Memory Politics in Bosnia and Herzegovina'. *Cultures of History Forum*. www.cultures-of-history.uni-jena.de/debates/division-and-denial-and-nothing-else (2 April 2023).

———. 2015b. *'Sarajevska najpoznatija javna tajna': suočavanje sa Cacom, Kazanima i zločinima počinjenim nad Srbina u opkoljenom Sarajevu, od rata do 2015*. Sarajevo: Friedrich Ebert Stiftung.

Munro, Kathy. 2018. 'Rand Club – A Grand Past with an Uncertain Future'. *The Heritage Portal*. www.theheritageportal.co.za/article/rand-club-grand-past-uncertain-future (17 March 2021).

Murray, Noëleen, and Leslie Witz. 2014. *Hostels, Homes, Museum: Memorialising Migrant Labour Pasts in Lwandle, South Africa*. Claremont: UCT Press.

Museums of the World. 2023. 'Sarajevo Tunnel Museum'. http://museu.ms/museum/details/303 (11 June 2023).

Musi, Maja. 2014. 'The International Heritage Doctrine and the Management of Heritage in Sarajevo, Bosnia and Herzegovina: The Case of the Commission to Preserve National Monuments'. *International Journal of Heritage Studies* 20(1): 54–71.

———. 2021. 'Carving War onto the City: Monuments to the 1992–95 Conflict in Sarajevo'. In *Transforming Heritage in the Former Yugoslavia: Synchronous Pasts*, Palgrave Studies in Cultural Heritage and Conflict, eds. Gruia Bădescu, Britt Baillie and Francesco Mazzucchelli. Cham: Springer International Publishing, 55–82.

Mwambari, David. 2021. 'Agaciro, Vernacular Memory, and the Politics of Memory in Post-Genocide Rwanda'. *African Affairs* 120(481): 611–28.

Nadjarian, Nora. 2006. *Ledra Street: Stories*. Nicosia: Armida.

Navaro-Yashin, Yael. 2012. *The Make-Believe Space: Affective Geography in a Postwar Polity*. Durham, NC: Duke University Press.

Ndoro, Webber, and Gilbert Pwiti. 2001. 'Heritage Management in Southern Africa: Local, National and International Discourse'. *Public Archaeology* 2(1): 21–34.

Nettelfield, Lara J. 2010. *Courting Democracy in Bosnia and Herzegovina: The Hague Tribunal's Impact in a Postwar State*. New York: Cambridge University Press.

Nettelfield, Lara J., and Sarah E. Wagner. 2014. *Srebrenica in the Aftermath of Genocide*. 1st ed. Cambridge: Cambridge University Press.

New Statesman and Society. 1995. 'An Unjust Peace', 1 December.

Niewöhner, Jörg, and Jörg Scheffer. 2010a. 'Producing Comparability Ethnographically. Reply to Robert Prus. Ethnographic Comparisons, Complexities and Conceptualities: Generic Social Processes and the Pragmatic Accomplishment of Group Life'. *Comparative Sociology* 9(4): 528–36.

———. 2010b. 'Thickening Comparison. On the Multiple Facets of Comparability'. In *Thick Comparison: Reviving the Ethnographic Aspiration*, eds. Jörg Niewöhner and Jörg Scheffer. Leiden: Brill, 1–15.

Nora, Pierre. 1996. 'General Introduction: Between Memory and History'. In *Realms of Memory: Rethinking the French Past*, eds. Pierre Nora and Lawrence D. Kritzman. New York: Columbia University Press, 1–20.

Nyseth Brehm, Hollie, Christopher Uggen, and Jean-Damascène Gasanabo. 2014. 'Genocide, Justice, and Rwanda's Gacaca Courts'. *Journal of Contemporary Criminal Justice* 30(3): 333–52.

Office of the High Representative. 'Annex 10'. n.d. *Office of the High Representative*. www.ohr.int/dayton-peace-agreement/annex-10/ (11 June 2023).

———. 'Mandate'. *Office of the High Representative*. www.ohr.int/about-ohr/mandate/ (11 June 2023).

Office of the President. 1999. 'The Unity of Rwandans. Before the Colonial Period and under the Colonial Rule and under the First Republic'. Kigali: Office of the President.

Orentlicher, Diane. 2018. *Some Kind of Justice: The ICTY's Impact in Bosnia and Serbia*. Oxford: Oxford University Press.

———. 2020. "Worth the Effort'? Assessing the Khmer Rouge Tribunal'. *Journal of International Criminal Justice* 18(3): 615–40.

Paffenholz, Thania. 2015. 'Unpacking the Local Turn in Peacebuilding: A Critical Assessment towards an Agenda for Future Research'. *Third World Quarterly* 36(5): 857–74.

Pain, Rachel. 2015. 'Intimate War'. *Political Geography* 44: 64–73.

Palmberger, Monika. 2016. *How Generations Remember: Conflicting Histories and Shared Memories in Post-War Bosnia and Herzegovina*. Berlin: Springer Nature.

Papadakis, Yiannis. 1993. 'The Politics of Memory and Forgetting in Cyprus'. *Journal of Mediterranean Studies* 3(1): 139–54.

———. 1994. 'The National Struggle Museums of a Divided City'. *Ethnic and Racial Studies* 17(3): 400–419.

———. 1998. 'Greek Cypriot Narratives of History and Collective Identity: Nationalism as a Contested Process'. *American Ethnologist* 25(2): 149–65.

———. 2003. 'Nation, Narrative and Commemoration: Political Ritual in Divided Cyprus'. *History and Anthropology* 14(3): 253–70.

———. 2005. *Echoes from the Dead Zone: Across the Cyprus Divide*. London; New York: I.B. Tauris; Distributed in the U.S.A. by Palgrave Macmillan.

Papadakis, Yiannis, Nicos Peristianis and Gisela Welz, eds. 2006. *Divided Cyprus: Modernity, History, and an Island in Conflict*. Bloomington, IN: Indiana University Press.

Paris, Roland. 2004. *At War's End: Building Peace After Civil Conflict*. Cambridge: Cambridge University Press.

Parnell, Susan. 2002. 'Winning the Battles but Losing the War: The Racial Segregation of Johannesburg under the Natives (Urban Areas) Act of 1923'. *Journal of Historical Geography* 28(2): 258–81.
Pickering, Michael, and Emily Keightley. 2006. 'The Modalities of Nostalgia'. *Current Sociology* 54(6): 919–41.
Pierce, Joseph, Deborah G. Martin and James T. Murphy. 2011. 'Relational Place-making: The Networked Politics of Place'. *Transactions of the Institute of British Geographers* 36(1): 54–70.
'Posit'. *Posit.* www.posit.co/ (16 June 2023).
Pottier, Johan. 2002. *Re-Imagining Rwanda: Conflict, Survival and Disinformation in the Late Twentieth Century.* Cambridge: Cambridge University Press.
Pozzi, C. 2013. 'Museums as Agonistic Spaces'. In *European Museums in the 21st Century: Setting the Framework*, eds. Luca Basso Peressut, Francesca Lanz and Gennaro Postiglione. Milan: MeLa Books, 7–15.
Prus, Robert. 2010. 'Ethnographic Comparisons, Complexities and Conceptualities: Generic Social Processes and the Pragmatic Accomplishment of Group Life'. *Comparative Sociology* 9(4): 496–527.
Purdeková, Andrea, and David Mwambari. 2022. 'Post-Genocide Identity Politics and Colonial Durabilities in Rwanda'. *Critical African Studies* 14(1): 19–37.
Ramutsindela, Maano F. 2001. 'Down the Post-Colonial Road: Reconstructing the Post-Apartheid State in South Africa'. *Political Geography* 20(1): 57–84.
Rand Club. n.d. 'Events – Rand Club'. www.randclub.co.za/events/ (9 June 2023).
Rassool, Ciraj. 2000. 'The Rise of Heritage and the Reconstitution of History in South Africa'. *Kronos* (26): 1–21.
Reggers, Wouter, Valérie Rosoux and David Mwambari. 2022. 'In Memory of Peacekeepers: Belgian Blue Helmets and Belgian Politics'. *International Peacekeeping* 29(2): 258–81.
Reinermann, Jan. 2020. *'They Should Cremate It': Youth Perceptions towards Skeletal Remains in Cambodia's Genocide Memorials.* Stockholm: The Swedish Institute of International Affairs.
Renan, Ernest. 2018. *What Is a Nation? And Other Political Writings.* New York: Columbia University Press.
Reyntjens, Filip. 2011. 'Constructing the Truth, Dealing with Dissent, Domesticating the World: Governance in Post-Genocide Rwanda'. *African Affairs* 110(438): 1–34.
Ribeiro, Artur. 2016. 'Against Object Agency. A Counterreaction to Sørensen's "Hammers and Nails"'. *Archaeological Dialogues* 23(2): 229–35.
Richmond, Oliver P. 2008. 'Reclaiming Peace in International Relations'. *Millennium: Journal of International Studies* 36(3): 439–70.
———. 2010. 'Resistance and the Post-Liberal Peace'. *Millennium: Journal of International Studies* 38: 665–92.
———. 2016. *Peace Formation and Political Order in Conflict Affected Societies.* Oxford; New York: Oxford University Press.
———. 2022. *The Grand Design: The Evolution of the International Peace Architecture.* New York: Oxford University Press.
Richmond, Oliver P., and Audra Mitchell, eds. 2011. *Hybrid Forms of Peace: From Everyday Agency to Post-Liberalism.* Basingstoke: Palgrave.
Rieder, Heide, and Thomas Elbert. 2013. 'Rwanda – Lasting Imprints of a Genocide: Trauma, Mental Health and Psychosocial Conditions in Survivors, Former Prisoners and Their Children'. *Conflict and Health* 7(1): 6.

Ríos Oyola, Sandra Milena. 2019. 'Human Dignity, Memory and Reparations: Towards a New Understanding of Transitional Justice', Working Paper No. 3. Stockholm: Research Cluster on Peace, Memory and Cultural Heritage.

Ristic, Mirjana. 2018. *Architecture, Urban Space and War*. New York: Springer Science+Business Media.

Rosoux, Valerie, and Mark Anstey, eds. 2017. *Negotiating Reconciliation in Peacemaking*. Cham: Springer International Publishing.

Rothberg, Michael. 2009. *Multidirectional Memory: Remembering the Holocaust in the Age of Decolonization. Cultural Memory in the Present*. Stanford, CA: Stanford University Press.

Rufer, Mario. 2012. *Politics of Memory*. InterAmerican Wiki: Terms – Concepts – Critical Perspectives. www.uni-bielefeld.de/einrichtungen/cias/publikationen/wiki/p/politics-of-memory.xml (18 December 2020).

Russell, S. Garnett. 2019. *Becoming Rwandan: Education, Reconciliation, and the Making of a Post-Genocide Citizen*. New Brunswick, NJ: Rutgers University Press.

Rutikanga, Bernard Noel. 2013. 'The 1994 Failure of Peace-Keeping in Rwanda'. In *Governance and Post-Conflict Reconstruction in Rwanda*. Addis Ababa: Organisation for Social Science Research in Eastern and Southern Africa, 1–15. www.ossrea.net/rwanda/images/rwanda-chapter-monograph-2.pdf#page=13 (1 June 2023).

Ryan, Heather, and Laura McGrew. 2016. 'Performance and Perception. The Impact of the Extraordinary Chambers in the Courts of Cambodia'. New York: Open Society Foundations.

Salehi, Mariam, and Timothy Williams. 2016. 'Beyond Peace vs. Justice: Assessing Transitional Justice's Impact on Enduring Peace Using Qualitative Comparative Analysis'. *Transitional Justice Review* 1(4). http://ir.lib.uwo.ca/tjreview/vol1/iss4/4 (8 April 2022).

Samuelson, Meg. 2007. *Remembering the Nation, Dismembering Women? Stories of the South African Transition*. Scottsville, South Africa: University of KwaZulu-Natal Press.

Sarajevo Roses. A Cinematic Essay. 2016. Igniter Loop.

Sartori, Giovanni. 1970. 'Concept Misformation in Comparative Politics'. *American Political Science Review* 64(4): 1033–53.

Sather-Wagstaff, Joy. 2017. 'Making Polysense of the World: Affect, Memory and Emotion'. In *Heritage, Affect and Emotion: Politics, Practices and Infrastructures*, eds. Divya P. Tolia-Kelly, Emma Waterton and Steve Watson. London; New York: Routledge, 14–31.

Scott, Julie. 2002. 'Mapping the Past: Turkish Cypriot Narratives of Time and Place in the Canbulat Museum, Northern Cyprus'. *History and Anthropology* 13(3): 217–30.

Selimović, Jasenko. 2020. *Sarajevo – Minnen från en belägring (Sarajevo – Memories from a Siege)*. Stockholm: Albert Bonniers förlag.

Shapiro-Phim, Toni. 2020. 'Embodying the Pain and Cruelty of Others'. *International Journal of Transitional Justice* 14(1): 209–19.

Sheftel, Anna. 2012. '"Monument to the International Community, from the Grateful Citizens of Sarajevo": Dark Humour as Counter-Memory in Post-Conflict Bosnia-Herzegovina'. *Memory Studies* 5(2): 145–64.

Shinko, Rosemary E. 2008. 'Agonistic Peace: A Postmodern Reading'. *Millennium: Journal of International Studies* 36(3): 473–91.

Shyaka, Anastase. 2003. 'Refondation de la Rwandité': Stratégie de Résolution des Conflits, de Démocratisation et de Développement durable du Rwanda'. In *Rwanda. Identité et Citoyennete*, eds. Faustin Rutembesa, Anastase Shyaka and Josias Semujanga. Butare: Université Nationale du Rwanda, 18–43.

Simmons, Erica S., and Nicholas Rush Smith. 2019. 'The Case for Comparative Ethnography'. *Comparative Politics* 51(3): 341–59.

Sion, Brigitte. 2011. 'Conflicting Sites of Memory in Post-Genocide Cambodia'. *Humanity: An International Journal of Human Rights, Humanitarianism, and Development* 2(1): 1–21.

———. 2014. 'Conflicting Sites of Memory in Post-Genocide Cambodia'. In *Death Tourism: Disaster Sites as Recreational Landscape*, ed. Brigitte Sion. London: Seagull Books, 97–120.

Sitze, Adam. 2013. *The Impossible Machine: A Genealogy of South Africa's Truth and Reconciliation Commission*. Ann Arbor, MI: University of Michigan Press.

Snowball, Jeanette D., and Sinead Courtney. 2010. 'Cultural Heritage Routes in South Africa: Effective Tools for Heritage Conservation and Local Economic Development?' *Development Southern Africa* 27(4): 563–76.

Sodaro, Amy. 2018. *Exhibiting Atrocity: Memorial Museums and the Politics of Past Violence*. New Brunswick, NJ: Rutgers University Press.

Sørensen, Tim Flohr. 2016. 'Hammers and Nails. A Response to Lindstrøm and to Olsen and Witmore'. *Archaeological Dialogues* 23(1): 115–27.

———. 2018. 'Agency (Again). A Response to Lindstrøm and Ribeiro'. *Archaeological Dialogues* 25(1): 95–101.

Sperfeldt, Christoph. 2012. 'Cambodian Civil Society and the Khmer Rouge Tribunal'. *International Journal of Transitional Justice* 6(1): 149–60.

———. 2020. 'Reparations at the Extraordinary Chambers in the Courts of Cambodia'. In *Reparations for Victims of Genocide, War Crimes and Crimes Against Humanity: Systems in Place and Systems in the Making*, eds. Carla Ferstman and Mariana Goetz. Leiden: Brill, 479–504.

Stanley, Liz, and Helen Dampier. 2005. 'Aftermaths: Post/Memory, Commemoration and the Concentration Camps of the South African War 1899–1902'. *European Review of History: Revue européenne d'histoire* 12(1): 91–119.

Stefansson, Anders. 2007. 'Urban Exile: Locals, Newcomers and the Cultural Transformation of Sarajevo'. In *The New Bosnian Mosaic*, eds. Elissa Helms, Xavier Bougarel and Gerlachlus Duijzings. Abingdon: Routledge.

Stevens, Quentin, and Mirjana Ristic. 2015. 'Memories Come to the Surface: Pavement Memorials in Urban Public Spaces'. *Journal of Urban Design* 20(2): 273–90.

Stiglmayer, Alexandra, ed. 1994. *Mass Rape: The War against Women in Bosnia-Herzegovina*. Lincoln, NE: Bison Books.

Straus, Scott. 2006. *The Order of Genocide: Race, Power, and War in Rwanda*. Ithaca, NY: Cornell University Press.

———. 2019. 'The Limits of a Genocide Lens: Violence Against Rwandans in the 1990s'. *Journal of Genocide Research* 21(4): 504–24.

Straus, Scott and Lars Waldorf. 2011. 'Introduction: Seeing Like a Post-Conflict State'. In Remaking Rwanda. State Building and Human Rights after Mass Violence, eds. Lars Waldorf and Scott Straus. Madison, WI: University of Wisconsin Press, 3–23

Strömbom, Lisa. 2017. *Memory and Agency in Intractable Conflicts: Revisited Pasts*. Historical Dialogues, Justice, and Memory Network Working Paper Series. New York: Historical Dialogues, Justice, and Memory Network.

Subotic, Jelena. 2019. *Yellow Star, Red Star: Holocaust Remembrance after Communism*. Ithaca, NY: Cornell University Press.

Tabeau, Ewa, and They Kheam. 2009. *Demographic Expert Report: The Khmer Rouge Victims in Cambodia, April 1975 – January 1979. A Critical Assessment of Major Estimates*. Phnom Penh: ECCC.

Temin, David Myer, and Adam Dahl. 2017. 'Narrating Historical Injustice: Political Responsibility and the Politics of Memory'. *Political Research Quarterly* 70(4): 905–17.

The Historical Museum. 2018. 'Historical Museum Website'. https://muzej.ba/ (31 March 2023).

The United Nations International Criminal Tribunal for former Yugoslavia. 'Radovan Karadžić Case – Key Information & Timeline'. www.icty.org/en/cases/radovan-karadzic-trial-key-information (11 June 2023).

Thomson, Susan. 2018. *Rwanda: From Genocide to Precarious Peace*. New Haven, CT: Yale University Press.

Till, Karen. 2003. 'Places of Memory'. In Companion to Political Geography', eds. John Agnew, Katharyne Mitchell and Gerard Toal. Malden, MA: Blackwell Publishing, 289–301.

Tirrell, Lynne. 2013. 'Apologizing for Atrocity: Rwanda and Recognition'. In *Justice, Responsibility and Reconciliation in the Wake of Conflict*, Boston Studies in Philosophy, Religion and Public Life, eds. Alice MacLachlan and Allen Speight. Dordrecht: Springer Netherlands, 159–82.

Tokača, Mirsad. 2012. *The Bosnian Book of the Dead: Human Losses in Bosnia and Herzegovina 1991–1995*. Sarajevo: Research and Documentation Center.

Tolia-Kelly, Divya P., Emma Waterton and Steve Watson. 2018. *Heritage, Affect and Emotion: Politics, Practices and Infrastructures*. London: Routledge.

Toumazis, Yiannis. 2014. 'Pride and Prejudice: Photography and Memory in Cyprus'. In *Photography and Cyprus. Time, Place and Identity*, eds. Liz Wells, Theopisti Stylianou-Lambert and Nicos Philippou. New York: I.B. Tauris & Co. Ltd., 79–97.

———. 2017. 'Saints, Martyrs and Heroes: "Sacred Displays" or the Iconography of Death in Cypriot Museums'. In *Museums and Photography, Displaying Death*, eds. Elena Stylianou and Theopisti Stylianou-Lambert. London; New York: Routledge, 84–110.

Tuol Sleng Genocide Museum. 2019. 'Exhibition Catalogue of "Tuol Sleng Genocide Museum. 40 Years: Remembering the Victims of S-21" '.

TV1 BiH. 2016. 'Izetbegović Na Kazanima Odao Počast Srpskim Žrtvama i Najavio Izgradnju Spomen Obilježja'. www.youtube.com/watch?v=ig15aKWJF88 (11 June 2023).

Tyner, James A., Savina Sirik and Samuel Henkin. 2014. 'Violence and the Dialectics of Landscape: Memorialization in Cambodia'. *Geographical Review* 104(3): 277–93.

Un, Kheang. 2019. *Cambodia: Return to Authoritarianism*. Cambridge: Cambridge University Press.

United Nations Commission of Experts. 1994. 'Annex VI Part 1 (Study of the Battle and Siege of Sarajevo) to the Final Report of the United Nations Commission of Experts Established Pursuant to Security Council Resolution 780 (1992)'. www.legal-tools.org/doc/17f8df/ (2 April 2023).

Vassiliou, George. 2003. 'Cypriot Accession to the EU and the Solution to the Cyprus Problem'. *The Brown Journal of World Affairs* 10(1): 213–21.

Viebach, Julia. 2014. 'Alétheia and the Making of the World: Inner and Outer Dimensions of Memorials in Rwanda'. In *Memorials in Times of Transition*, eds. Susanne Buckley-Zistel and Stefanie Schäfer. Cambridge: Intersentia, 69–94.

———. 2020. 'Mediating "Absence-Presence" at Rwanda's Genocide Memorials: Of Care-Taking, Memory and Proximity to the Dead'. *Critical African Studies* 12(2): 237–69.

Volkan, Vamik D. 1991. 'On Chosen Trauma'. *Mind and Human Interaction* 4: 3–19.

Vora, Jay A., and Erika Vora. 2004. 'The Effectiveness of South Africa's Truth and Reconciliation Commission: Perceptions of Xhosa, Afrikaner, and English South Africans'. *Journal of Black Studies* 34(3): 301–22.

Wagner-Pacifici, Robin. 2015. 'Reconceptualizing Memory as Event: From "Difficult Pasts" to "Restless Events"'. In *Routledge International Handbook of Memory Studies*, eds. Anna Lisa Tota and Trever Hagen. London: Routledge, 22–27.

Walters, Ronald. 2009. *The Price of Racial Reconciliation*. Ann Arbor, MI: University of Michigan Press.

War Childhood Museum. n.d. 'Partners and Supporters'. *War Childhood Museum*. https://warchildhood.org/partners/ (11 June 2023).

———. 'War Childhood Museum'. *War Childhood Museum*. https://warchildhood.org/ (11 June 2023).

Waterton, Emma. 2014. 'A More-Than-Representational Understanding of Heritage? The "Past" and the Politics of Affect'. *Geography Compass* 8(11): 823–33.

Wertsch, James V. 2002. *Voices of Collective Remembering*. Cambridge; New York: Cambridge University Press.

Whitebrook, Maureen. 2001. *Identity, Narrative, and Politics*. London; New York: Routledge.

Wielenga, Cori. 2012. 'Remembering Together in Rwanda and South Africa'. Paper presented at the *Conflict, Memory, and Reconciliation: Bridging Past, Present, and Future*, Kigali, 10–13 January. https://digitalcollections.sit.edu/cgi/viewcontent.cgi?article=1098&context=conflict_reconcilation_symposium (5 May 2023).

Williams, Philippa. 2015. *Everyday Peace? Politics, Citizenship and Muslim Lives in India*. Chichester, UK; Malden, MA: John Wiley and Sons.

Williams, Timothy. 2019. 'NGO Interventions in the Post-Conflict Memoryscape. The Effect of Competing "Mnemonic Role Attributions" on Reconciliation in Cambodia'. *Journal of Intervention and Statebuilding* 13(2): 158–79.

———. 2021. 'Resilience in Post-Khmer Rouge Cambodia: Systemic Dimensions and the Limited Contributions of Transitional Justice'. In *Resilience, Adaptive Peacebuilding and Transitional Justice: How Societies Recover after Collective Violence*, eds. Janine Natalya Clark and Michael Terence Ungar. Cambridge: Cambridge University Press, 164–86.

———. 2022. 'Remembering and Silencing Complexity in Post-Genocide Memorialisation: Cambodia's Tuol Sleng Genocide Museum'. *Memory Studies* 15(1): 3–19.

———. forthcoming. *Memory Politics after Mass Violence. Attributing Roles in the Memoryscape*. Bristol: Bristol University Press.

Williams, Timothy, Julie Bernath, Boravin Tann and Somaly Kum. 2018. *Justice and Reconciliation for the Victims of the Khmer Rouge? Victim Participation in Cambodia's Transitional Justice Process*. Marburg: Centre for Conflict Studies; Phnom Penh: Centre for the Study of Humanitarian Law; Bern: swisspeace.

Winter, Jay. 2006. 'Notes on the Memory Boom: War Remembrance and the Uses of the Past'. In *Memory, Trauma and World Politics: Reflections on the Relationship between the Past and the Present*, ed. Duncan Bell. Basingstoke: Palgrave, 54–73.

———. 2010. 'Introduction'. In *Performing the Past: Memory, History, and Identity in Modern Europe*, eds. Karin Tilmans and Frank van Vree. Amsterdam: Amsterdam University Press.

Witz, Leslie, Gary Minkley and Ciraj Rassool. 2017. *Unsettled History: Making South African Public Pasts*. Ann Arbor, MI: University of Michigan Press.

Wolfe, Stephanie. 2020. 'Memorialization in Rwanda: The Legal, Social, and Digital Constructions of the Memorial Narrative'. In *Mass Violence and Memory in the Digital Age: Memorialization Unmoored*, eds. Eve Monique Zucker and David J. Simon. Cham: Springer International Publishing, 19–44.

Worden, Nigel. 2009. 'The Changing Politics of Slave Heritage in the Western Cape, South Africa'. *The Journal of African History* 50(1): 23–40.

Work, Courtney. 2017. 'The Persistent Presence of Cambodian Spirits: Contemporary Knowledge Production in Cambodia'. In *The Handbook of Contemporary Cambodia*, eds. Katherine Brickell and Simon Springer. Abingdon: Routledge, 389–98.

Yakinthou, Christalla. 2009. *Political Settlements in Divided Societies: Consocialism and Cyprus*. New York: Palgrave Macmillan.

———. 2012. 'A Never-Ending Story: Cyprus'. In *Conflict Management in Divided Societies*, London; New York: Routledge, 233–48.

Zubrzycki, Geneviève, and Anna Woźny. 2020. 'The Comparative Politics of Collective Memory'. *Annual Review of Sociology* 46(1): 175–94.

Zucker, Eve Monique. 2009. 'Matters of Morality: The Case of a Former Khmer Rouge Village Chief'. *Anthropology and Humanism* 34(1): 31–40.

———. 2013. 'Trauma and Its Aftermath: Local Configurations of Reconciliation in Cambodia and the Khmer Rouge Tribunal'. *The Journal of Asian Studies* 72(4): 793–800.

Index